Forever
Numerology
Includes Master Numbers 11–99

Lynn Buess

86

Forever Numerology

Includes Master Numbers 11–99

Lynn Buess

Light Technology Publishing

ISBN 1-891824-65-1

Cover Art:
Stardust
by Angela "Wizzle' Wilczynski
www.wizzleworld.com

Published by

3-LIGHT
Technology
PUBLISHING
800-450-0985
www.lighttechnology.com

Printed by

GraphTech
DIGITAL & PRINTING
PO Box 3540
Flagstaff, AZ 86003

Table of Contents

Preface

In 1977 I started writing my first numerology book, which was to become *Numerology for the New Age*. As indicated in the preface of that edition, I felt that no attention had been given to the deeper issues of psychology, spirituality and cosmology in the numerological literature of that time, and I wrote the book to fill this void. Judging from the global response, many readers felt it did a pretty good job of accomplishing that intent, and for years *Numerology for the New Age* was one of the best-selling numerology books. It was negotiated for translation into several languages.

As the author, I was very pleased with the volume, even though many questions regarding numbers still exerted strain upon my inquiring mind and soul, as was indicated in the Epilogue of that volume: "Even at the moment of completion I can look back at parts [of the book] that I would not write the same way today. To give in to the temptation to revise would trap me into a project ever cyclical, no end possible.'

From the vantage point of time passed and age, it has become more understandable to me what was happening. Much of that volume was written by intuition and inspiration. I believed it was valid and insightful material, yet I had not really experienced much of the information in real life. Over the past twenty-four years, however, I have been rewarded with extraordinary events in both the outer and the inner world. I have conducted tens of thousands of sessions, including several thousand in cultures other than my own, and my skills as a psychotherapist and consultant have gained added depth and perspective from this introduction to myriad traditions and lifestyles. During this time, I also opened the door to the issues of alcoholism, gambling, sexual dysfunction and victimhood in my own family background. I invested hundreds of hours in professional therapy and healing sessions to face the conflict with the dark side of my own shadow self and move toward resolution.

These past years have also been enriched by mystical, tantric and spiritual moments of extraordinary dimension, and perhaps one of the most profound moments came out of cosmological inquiry and research. On that sojourn, I went through the center of the Earth and out, on a cosmic journey through time, space and wormholes of light. The excursion took me back into the center of creation and light. It felt as if I was in the womb of creation, infinitely blessed with universal love and bliss. Suddenly the push of life sent me spiraling out into creation. I traveled through galaxies and evolutions untold. Finally I sensed that I had entered this solar system and journeyed through the lessons on several of the planetary schools of life in this system. Then came the realization of entry into planet Earth, attended by an awareness of certain lessons I brought from other realms, to be integrated in this realm of physical and material planet. From the first moment of birth from the cosmic womb, the feeling of being separated from Source was accompanied by anger. My anger and rebellious nature created a struggle within my being, and on occasion I aligned with the forces of rebellion around the universe.

The interpretations and experiences presented in this book are given through the symbolic wisdom of numbers. Obviously, the interpretations are partially biased by my personal perception. It is pretty much impossible for humans to separate themselves from their own experiences. I am pleased once again with this new book you now hold. I feel it brings much closer to completeness the story of numbers I wish to convey.

In 1998 blood clots developed in my small intestine, and I required emergency surgery. Within a period of ten days, I had a double near-death experience, twice approaching the precipice of physical transition. It is common for a person coming out of such an event to believe he or she has some special purpose to do before life ends. I felt that one thing I wanted to get done for certain was the completion of a book on the cosmology and psychology of numerology.

The reader who is familiar with my previous writing will note that I have made many fundamental changes in the art of chart construction as well as in numerical interpretation. These changes, which are indicated where appropriate, were based upon results from tens of thousands of charts and upon intuition and experience where lesser data was available. Truly, no complete volume can be written on any subject. However, I am content that this edition you hold comes closer than ever to portraying the evolution of consciousness through the symbology of numbers. I hope that it will be of help in your journey through life and in your search for the meaning of numbers.

" Lynn Buess, July 2005

Introduction:
Suggested Strategy for Reading This Book

It may seem a little presumptuous for an author to tell you how to read his or her book. If you feel that way, however, you have probably not gotten this far anyway! The text is diverse, and you may be uncertain about where to begin, which is particularly true if you are just starting to study numbers.

For Beginners

You are possibly a little overwhelmed by cosmological theory and karmic accumulation. You may not know what a progressed chart is and have never really considered letters to have symbolic importance. You are, however, interested in yourself and your immediate life. If so, I would suggest that you go to chapter six, "The Wisdom in Your Name.' Very carefully follow the guidelines for giving each letter a numerical value. After calculating the numbers, read about your own personality number, then your soul number and finally about the integrated self.

By that time, hopefully you will have become intrigued enough to go further into the subject. A good second step would be to go to chapter seven and compute your life number and your personal year. By then you will have a little feeling for the subject matter and are encouraged to follow your intuition as to what becomes your next priority. Best wishes for discovery and added growth.

For the Experienced Numerology Reader

If you already have your own terminology and technique, it is easy to just rush to the interpretations without looking at the manner in which the numbers were calculated. Almost every category of numerical calculation herein is a departure from the previous standards, written in the 1930s, 1970s, 1990s and so on. I have, on several occasions, altered my own previous methods because new information coming in seems timely and appropriate for the moment and age in which we live.

You might choose to adapt the ideas presented herein. Regardless of whether you choose to implement them or not, be very careful to see how the numbers have been calculated so as not to confuse them with previous methodologies. These interpretations have been aligned cosmologically, systematically and humanly as best I understand them at this time. They are, of course, influenced by my human limitations and are subject to change upon enlightenment!

For All Readers

At times you may feel that the information for your chart does not seem accurate. All authors have a personal perspective and style of presentation, and perhaps my style simply does not resonate with your way of receiving. It is possible that you may not have thought about some of the information presented, making it entirely new to you, and it is possible that you have worked through the issues described. However, if you find yourself strongly rejecting the information that deals with negative issues and dysfunction, it is very likely that you are in denial.

Although I have tried not to use formal psychological and diagnostic jargon, there are many occasions where I have presented specific toxic and dysfunctional descriptive phrases. You may want to discuss such issues with a trusted insightful friend or second party. Another suggestion would be to read the same information at a later date, since time tends to bring truth into light.

Having practiced for decades as a psychotherapist, I have naturally uncovered deeply repressed blocks and negative unconscious complexes. I have worked some of the insights for recognizing dysfunction into the interpretation of numerology in the hopes of awakening new seekers to the dark side of the self. Once you recognize this, you have the possibility of working it out of your life. Until then you remain the victim of your own hidden nature. There are suggested strategies, particularly in chapter fourteen, that give you guidelines for getting out of negative patterns.

Every family has dysfunction. Every human has some hidden issues to work through. I trust that with time, you will appreciate the truth you find herein" the good, the bad and the ugly.

Condensed History

T he exact origin of numerology"the study of symbol, cycle and vibration"is discretely buried in the mists of time. The study began with
humans÷ earliest attempts to understand the relationship between self and the
cosmos. In recorded history, it is known that numbers were significant in the
Sanskrit of the ancient Hindu culture. The evolution of modern numerology
was also influenced by the Arabic system of numbers. Yet another important
branch is in the tradition and symbolism of the Kabbalah. Within the writ-
ings of these cultures is a wealth of yet undiscovered wisdom based upon the
esoteric teachings of their numerical traditions. The Bible is also richly laden
with symbolism based upon numbers.

The individual most responsible for influencing the method of numerology
in use today is Pythagoras, a Greek philosopher born between approximately
600 and 590 B.C. Pythagoras founded a school where the instruction of mathematics, music, astronomy and philosophy was conducted in conjunction with
esoteric wisdom. He taught the relationship between humans and the divine
laws as reflected in the mathematics of numbers. Upon his philosophical
strength, the study of numerology as it is today has been established.

Today÷s scientists and technologists are paying ever-increasing attention to
the use of vibrations and frequencies. The advent of electricity introduced
whole new applications of working with natural cycles. Radio, television,
x-ray and subatomic cycles are some facets of modern technology that have
opened the door to greater study and application of the principles of cyclical
oscillations. Physicists have learned that materials previously defined as inert

also have their own identity, which is established by their rate of vibration, or frequency. New findings on the biorhythm cycles have made the public more knowledgeable about just how important it is to be aware of the cyclical patterns in their daily lives.

Numerology provides a means of understanding cyclical patterns or qualities related specifically to an individuals personal life. By understanding ones own particular rhythm, it becomes easier to flow with life, and one can become the master of fate rather than a victim of destinys circumstances. Numerology is just as significant today as it was for the ancient seeker. In fact, its application may be more meaningful in todays age of rampant materialism and existential crisis.

The historical portrait provided herein is admittedly succinct, because the emphasis of this volume is upon the application of numerical knowledge in the here and now. Other writers on the subject have provided more details for the historically minded.

Cosmology and Consciousness

Numerology is the study of cycle, symbol and vibration. Its origins are rooted in the very beginning of consciousness, and one can even speculate that numerology predates consciousness. This is especially true if we acknowledge consciousness as part of the manifested creation or include it in the realm of preexistence. Sound complicated? It can be helpful to realize that the discussion of esoteric cosmology is best conceived of as a metaphor. By contemplating the metaphor, it is possible to release the mind and soul from the bondage of mundane intellectual considerations, which allows awareness to soar into the expanded realms of higher cosmic consciousness. From that vantage point, we can dance with the cosmic choreography and directly experience the imprint of expanded cosmic vibrations in our daily lives.

Let us begin our journey into the meaning of numbers by contemplating what might be considered as the divine unconscious. We start before the dawn of creation. Because we are members of the created (manifest) world, it is difficult for us to comprehend the unmanifest" that which predates existence. Perhaps the safest thing to say about the unmanifest is that it is.

The unmanifest is pure being; it is unity. It is the source of infinite potential from which everything will come. One might consider it as interstellar space resting in complete homeostasis, and sages speak of the void or inner silence in an attempt to describe this state. Because we are of the manifest, it is impossible to fathom or experience it. With movement comes the beginning of manifestation, and manifestation brings the beginning of duality.

Ring Cosmos, Ring Chaos and Ring Pass-Not

We might think of manifestation as arising from desire. As the desire for manifestation becomes stronger than the force of homeostatic stability, it creates a movement in space. At this point, nothing occurs in space to cause friction, so the movement flows ceaselessly. Simultaneously occurring is a desire to return to the stability and balance of the unmanifest. This secondary desire acts as resistance upon the primary desire (movement), thus causing the primary desire (motion) to curve as it progresses. As a result of this resistance, over eons of time, the movement forms a great circle, and the completion of the first cycle results in a vast, spinning ring.

One term given to this initial spinning ring is "ring cosmos.‘ The nature of the ring cosmos is evolutionary, and its movement lies toward the center. One might say that it seeks to embrace and integrate new experience. As it spins its way through space, it conveys this motion into the space around it, which draws more of the space into its influence. This spinning on one plane continues until the combined stresses of the spinning action evoke a secondary reaction, setting off a new movement at a right angle and in opposition to the first. One term given to this second spinning movement is "ring chaos.‘

The tendency of the ring chaos is to move outward from the center, and its desire is to return to the unmanifest. It is the presence of this force that creates the prime duality within manifestation, or creation. It is the contrasting reaction upon which consciousness is built. It provides the basis for awareness. Without this opposition, the original motion would go on unchecked, with nothing to provide it with the sensation of movement. It is this dualistic pressure that underlies all later dualities of matter and spirit, good and evil, masculine and feminine, day and night, life and death and so forth.

These two forces, ring cosmos and ring chaos, now begin in earnest a vast cosmic dance as grandfather and grandmother flirt with each other in a come-hither, back-away dance of attraction and repulsion that arises out of the polarity of this duality. Another analogy that describes this rhythm is to think of this cycle of expansion and contraction as the breath of cosmic life, or the cosmic day and night. These are two spinning rings acting out on a plane. At the same time, they are moving rapidly through interstellar space, forming threadlike streams of motion like the intertwining threads of a double helix. The ongoing tug and push of these two forces eventually gives rise to a third spinning motion emanating from the first, primal ring.

The term given to this third movement is "ring pass-not.‘ The ring pass-not brings stability to the evolutionary forces at work and sets the boundaries of manifestation. Anything outside of the ring pass-not would revert back to the unmanifest. A term used to describe the nature of creation at this point is "prime trinity‘ or "the absolute.‘ It is a metaphorical attempt to imagine the threefold nature of our Creator. In more contemporary terms, the dynam-

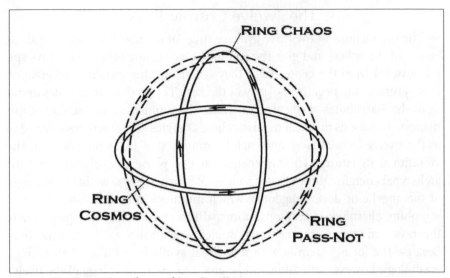

Figure 1: Ring Cosmos, Ring Chaos and Ring Pass-Not.

ics of the rings might be thought of as the original black hole, first expanding forth as if in a big bang, then extending itself until reaching the extremity of creation as defined by the balancing action of the ring pass-not, and finally returning to the center, bringing everything in creation with it.

Numerologically speaking, until this point in creation, you might think of 1 as being the unmanifest, which contains all there is to be. The first duality, 2, is manifestation. From the vantage point of the manifested realm, 1 is the ring cosmos and 2 is the ring chaos. Combined, they compose the basis of duality. With the ring pass-not comes 3, which completes the formation of the prime trinity. Figure 1 may help to provide a visual and mental clue to the nature of these forces.

Imagine that each of these rings spins in its orbit while at the same time revolving in a gyroscopic motion. An analogy that might help is to think of a phonograph record turning on its turntable. The needle moves toward the center (an action similar to that of the ring cosmos). Now visualize picking the record up and turning it over and over and over again; this gives you a sense of the gyroscope effect. Each ring spins and each one turns in its gyroscopic motion. As an end result of this interaction, a spherical body is formed.

The active dynamics of creation are revealed in recurring cycles of expansion, contraction and balance. When the forces of the ring chaos predominate, there is an inflationary expansion of awareness and the creative flow. As the tide turns to the ring cosmos, all that has been experienced is attracted back toward the center and becomes integrated and at rest. The stabilizing influence of the ring pass-not has its way until, once again, the desire for movement becomes stronger than the desire for balance, and a renewed cycle of expansion begins.

The Twelve Cosmic Rays

The interactions of the three primary rings of the absolute converge at the center of the sphere and give rise to the twelve cosmic rays. These rays spiral outward from the center until they reach the ring pass-not, whereupon they return as the negative polarity of the ray. The twelve ray energies derive from the 3 attributes of the absolute times the number 4, the number of formation. In various mystical treatises, these energies are sometimes referred to as the twelve faces of God, and each is composed of its own color, tone and vibrational signature. The ray energies at this phase of evolution form the archetypal energies of the greater zodiac. With these rays, we have the origin of the angelic or devic kingdoms, which might include the cosmic hosts of seraphim, cherubim, dominions, principalities and virtues. The point where the rays converge at the center is sometimes known as the Central Sun. Because the focus herein is with numerical symbolism rather than esoteric cosmology, however, attention will be given to the numerology of the twelve ray energies.

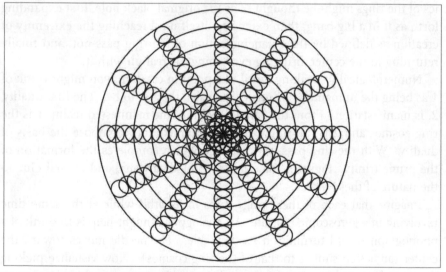

Figure 2: The Twelve Rays and the Seven Cosmic Planes.

As the ray energies return from their cosmic sojourn, they converge at the center of the spheroid mass, which gives rise to another series of swirling energy patterns that emanate outward from the center. These seven emanating circles (the three primary creative forces plus the four components of formation) eventually stabilize to become the seven cosmic planes. Figure 2 below provides a visual stimulus that hopefully will assist you in conceptualizing this process. It is a two-dimensional display that attempts to portray the third-dimensional interaction of the twelve rays and the seven cosmic planes.

The term given to the development of creation up until this point is "cosmos.' This includes the activities of the rings, twelve rays and seven cosmic planes. The cosmos breathes in recurring cycles of expansion and contraction. During the influence of the ring chaos, the rays move outward in spiraling fashion until they reach the ring pass-not. Then, as the tide swings to the influence of the ring cosmos, the ray energy returns along the negative polarity, or the opposite ray" the first returns along the twelfth, the second along the eleventh, the third along the tenth and so forth.

If we were to stretch the spiral motion of the rays for visual insight, it would look like the waves in Figure 3, the signature of the sine wave. As the strands of the rays work their way through the cosmic planes, they break those planes up into lesser segments of space (see Figures 3 and 4).

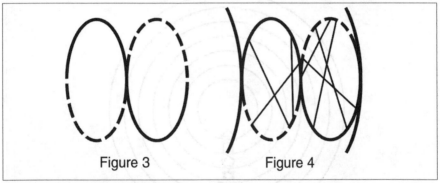

Figure 3   Figure 4

Figures 3 and 4: Spiral Motion of a Ray.

Primal Atom and Composite Atoms

The attraction and tension created between the two ray paths causes the formation of lines of stress within these segments. These lines of attraction are known as tangentials. As the paths of divergent tangentials cross, a vortex is set up by the opposing influences that modify the action of each. Therefore, a relatively stable composite unit is set up that is influenced by the two factors of itself and, to a lesser extent, the greater forces of the cosmos. This new unit is called a "primal atom,' a vortex of forces gyrating in tight units rather than circling the grand limits of the cosmos.

The same laws that started the ring cosmos and ring chaos on their evolutionary journey are at work in the primal atom. The axiom "as above, so below, but in another manner' certainly is most true here. The two opposing movements that gyrate around each other give rise to a secondary movement known as the angular path. Other primal atoms moving along the angular paths become attracted and form composite atoms. These composite atoms gain in weight and mass, eventually responding to the primal forces working upon the cosmic planes. The number of facets, or angular paths, is related to the nature of primal rhythms upon the cosmic plane where they are formed.

Upon the first cosmic plane, primary forces reflect the subconscious nature of the absolute; therefore, the composite atoms are three faceted. The number of facets upon the second cosmic plane is four; on the third cosmic plane, it is five; on the fourth, it is six; on the fifth, it is seven; on the sixth, it is eight; and on the seventh cosmic plane, the number of facets is nine (see Figure 5). Herein lies a clue that will follow throughout the study of numbers: The numbers 1 through 9 reveal the spiral of life toward perfection; 10 is the number of evolution.

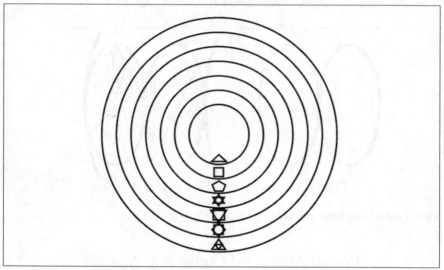

Figure 5: Facets on the Cosmic Planes.

With the advent of the composite atoms, activity increases rapidly within the confines of creation. The composite atoms, because of their growing mass, respond to the cosmic cycles: As the ring chaos predominates, they begin to move outward in space, following the lines of least resistance" the rays. Such composite atoms are on each of the cosmic planes, and they now become traveling atoms. These atoms spiral through the cosmic planes, eventually experiencing each cosmic plane from every possible angle (a clue for the astrologer). Once the influence of the ring cosmos again predominates, the atom spirals toward the central stillness, taking with it the experiences of that cycle, which are absorbed and integrated into the absolute. The atom then rides the next impulse of the ring chaos, moving outward along the complementary ray path. This progressive journey continues until the atom has experienced all of the ray energies from every angle upon all of the cosmic planes.

In the course of its journey, the composite atom is stimulated by the tides of the cosmos and imprinted with experiences from interaction with the different cosmic planes and nuances from traveling each of the ray energies. As a result of these experiences, the traveling atom develops the beginning of self-consciousness. Once the traveling atoms of a given tide have all completed their journey through the rays and planes, the entire experience is drawn back to the Central Sun, which goes into a vast cosmic night of integration and stillness.

Eventually though, the desire for movement becomes stronger than the desire for stillness, and the dawning of a new cosmic day begins. There is now a collection of traveling atoms that have gone through the entire circuit of experiences and no longer need to repeat the journey. These atoms seek the appropriate plane, according to their facets, and begin to orbit around the Central Sun. Having become awakened and aware of self from the previous journey, the atoms now have the potential to become cocreators. The common term given to these newly awakened beings is "Great Entity' or "Solar Logos.'

We have traced, in laymens terms, the origin of a sun. There are suns on each of the seven planes. We will be speaking now of our Sun, which manifests on the seventh cosmic, or material, plane.

The Three Waves of Lords

Having become aware of Itself, the Solar Logos extends Its aura or, if you will, a thought form of Itself, into a portion of the cosmos and organizes the region like unto Itself. In simple terms, the Solar Logos forms a solar system, giving rise to the birth of planets in a manner much like Its own process of development in the cosmos.

Traveling atoms form into composite atoms in a manner similar to the cosmic process. Eventually, these atoms begin to orbit the Sun, becoming the children of the Solar Logos, or planets. Yet another series of cycles then evolves, and out of the heart of the Solar Logos radiate waves of divine sparks that will bring the entire spectrum of life into manifestation.

The first wave is known as the lords of flame. They establish an archetypal outline for the new planet. Those of the second wave, the lords of form, have a little more time, because they must wait for their predecessors. These entities work to give the planet its bodies of manifestation, from spiritual to increasingly more dense, on the following return cycles. During the final cycles of passing, they bring the systemic ingredients for the material, or physical, body of the planet.

Those of the third wave, known as the lords of mind, have excess time on each of their runs, because they must wait for the preceding waves to complete their intent. We might say that metaphorically, they have a little time to use their imagination while waiting for their predecessors to complete their mission. The lords of mind use this time, along with a little imagination, to develop some unique characteristics of evolution for each planet rather than repeating the evolutionary process of the Solar Logos. This process is sometimes called epigenesis.

Once the first three waves of lords have gone through their rounds of manifestation, the planet is formed and develops life. Those of the next wave are often known as the lords of humanity, and they implant the individual spark of life, bringing the awakening of self-consciousness in the life form and distinguishing it from the group consciousness experienced in the other kingdoms.

At this point in the story of consciousness, we are describing the beginning of the divine sparks journey into human experience. It is a story of our collective journey and of your individual journey. Before continuing that journey, let us examine some of the numerical metaphors further.

The 1 is all. From unmanifest comes manifestation, the first duality and the first appearance of 2. The interplay of the 2 gives rise to the third stabilizing force and consequent manifestation of the absolute, or prime trinity (having three attributes). In the progressive stages of cosmic evolution, 1 is the absolute, 2 is the manifest, 3 pertains to evolution (creation), 4 pertains to formation, and 5 becomes the number for life. The number 3 (creation) plus 4 (formation) results in the cosmic planes. The number 3 (creation) multiplied by 4 (formation) results in the cosmic rays. The reader is reminded here once more that this should not just become an intellectual conclusion from reading a cosmological theory. Ones own meditation and dedicated contemplation are encouraged to make this a living realization rather than a reached conclusion.

For the reader who is further interested in cosmology, I highly recommend *The Cosmic Doctrine* by Dion Fortune. It is this extraordinary text that has inspired me with the wonderment of creation.

3

Numerology of Cosmology

Having provided a cosmological foundation in the previous chapter, the intent now will be to introduce the human equation and experience into the story of numerology. The story of creation up to the point where the lords of humanity started their sojourn into the ongoing cosmic panorama has been told. It is the descent of this divine spark" manifesting the attributes of its logos" into the bodies of mind, emotion and finally matter that initiates the dawn of the individual human being in the meaning most familiar to us. To set the stage for better understanding of this human evolution, let us return to the cosmos from a more human perspective.

First, in order to hopefully provide the reader with other possibly familiar symbolic points of reference, let us consider for a moment the story of cosmology in regard to various symbolic systems. Perhaps a very pivotal point of reference is in the tree-of-life glyph of the ancient Kabbalah. Illustrated here is the simple glyph.

These ten spheres, or sephirot, depict the three attributes of deity

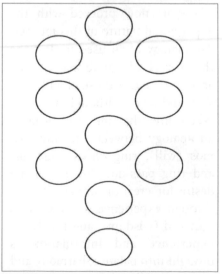

Figure 6: The Tree of Life Glyph.

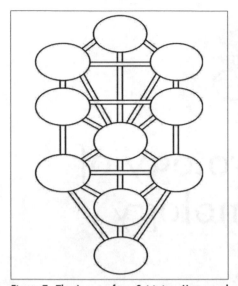

Figure 7: The Journey from Spirit into Matter and Back into Spirit.

plus the seven planes of consciousness. The top three, sometimes called the supernal triad, are symbolic of the attributes of deity, or the prime trinity. The remaining seven spheres are symbolic of the seven planes of consciousness. By connecting these paths as shown in Figure 7, we are given a very powerful symbolic metaphor depicting the journey of consciousness from spirit into matter and the return to spirit.

As you will note, there are a total of thirty-two paths when including the spheres as part of the journey. The twenty-two paths" counted without the spheres" are related to the twenty-two major arcana cards of the tarot. These can also be related to the twelve Houses, or signs of the zodiac, plus the ten calculated orbs (the planets plus the Sun and Moon). The thirty-two paths of involution plus the same of evolution are related to the sixty-four hexagrams of the *I Ching*. When considering the sixty-four plus fourteen (the journey down and back up the seven planes), we have seventy-eight, the number of cards in the tarot deck. The reader can easily grasp the significance contained in the glyph and is left with much to contemplate and integrate into awareness.

Let us now proceed with the experiential nature of this journey. An analogy often used to describe the threefold attributes of the absolute include those of will, wisdom and love. Although not to be taken literally, one can imagine an analogy between the ring cosmos (will), ring chaos (wisdom) and ring pass-not (love): Divine desire for creation initiates (will); through experience, knowledge is acquired (wisdom); and finally, all experience and information is brought into balance, harmony and integration (love).

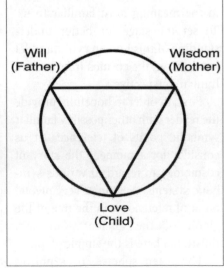

Figure 8: The Attributes of the Absolute.

The initial journey of the individualized divine spark is intimately related to its creator. Perhaps the initial step is like leaving a blissful state of being immersed in a bath of infinite white light. Within that womb of creation is a sense of complete security, trust and love. One can imagine the overwhelming impact upon the spark as it leaves this awesome sanctity for the first time, and herein is a most important point for contemplation: At this moment of departure, the sparks reaction to separation shapes its cosmic behavior for eons to come" although perhaps it is more appropriate to say that the sparks reaction to the *illusion* of separation will impact its journey for eons to come! That is, as the spark leaves the cosmic womb, there is a potentially devastating sense of losing direct contact with ones creator (Mother/Father God). Although there truly is never any loss of being with and within our Source, the impact of that moment of illusion is so strong that the divine spark can be overcome with fear, rejection, anger, loss, betrayal, abandonment or any number of what becomes the foundation of negative thoughts and emotions. At that moment of illusion, the spark develops the ego and attaches to the ego for survival in its now perceived to be hostile journey into creation. This is a most important concept and invites one to give it the utmost attention in the process of returning to *at-one-ment* (atonement).

The sparks reaction to and identification with a particular negative energy shape its personality through time and space. At the moment of illusion of separation, self-identity shifts away from oneness with Source and the state of harmony with the threefold atomic dance within self. Identity now transfers to the ego and the need for survival. The ego cleverly manipulates self-pity, guilt and anger. This attachment to ego is a very strong bond that later in evolution can become difficult to relinquish. The struggle to give up the egos control often becomes monumental during the exploration of reintegration back with Source, so much so that in many cases, the ego will turn on the personality in an attempt to destroy the personality rather than face its own fear of dissolution.

Before developing the numerological aspects of cosmology, attention will be directed at this time to further exploring the psychological foundations of negative consciousness in its earliest phases. At the point of illusion of separation from Source, the spark undergoes its premier experience with abandonment. The initial feeling is a loss of connection with the parent(s): Mother/Father God. Depending upon the cosmic tides and conditions, this sense of loss may be more strongly attached either to the mother (feminine) polarity or the father (masculine) polarity.

The experience of abandonment can lead to many reactions within the developing consciousness. Some of the primary ones can be betrayal, confusion, fear, distrust and anger. Of course, there can also be numerous combinations of these. Whatever form each individual spark takes, the basis of negative reaction can essentially be reduced to fear and anger. The fear is derived from loss of certainty associated with being at one with our self (Source). Once out of synchronization with the rhythms of life (the cosmic dance), negative reaction takes control.

Possibly the most prominent negative reaction is anger, the egos first defiant act as it takes over control. As a therapist, I have come to see a clients anger as a negative loop of passion (the zeal for life) that turns back on the individual to become self-destructive. Cosmologically, it is similar to" that is, one might metaphorically think of it as" contempt toward the parents (Mother/Father God) for taking away the good life. Homilies aside, displaced passion can be an overriding force throughout evolution until it is understood and brought to rest.

Perhaps the greatest fear is the fear of failure (mistakes). Once the spark experiences disassociation from Source, insecurity takes over. No longer feeling guided by Source, the desperate spark gives reign to negative imagination. Confusion is a form of fear; distrust comes out of fear; betrayal is rooted in fear of abandonment. In the end, even fear can basically be reduced to fear of our own anger with its massive destructive force.

From the experience of fear and anger comes the formation of the numerous dysfunctional patterns exhibited by humans. Some of the primary forms of dysfunction in human behavior include abandonment, abuse, incest (sexual abuse), addiction (particularly to alcohol and drugs) and codependency (addiction to relationships). Every family has dysfunction, some more so than others. By knowing the patterns in your life, you can recognize them and take responsibility for resolving their negative effects.

Let us continue with yet another dimension of how the study of numbers can help us solve the puzzle of our own humanity and accelerate the trip back home to our Source. Numerologically, the initial attributes of divine will are represented by the number 1, wisdom is represented by the number 2 and love by the number 3. Here are some basic ego qualities attached to these numbers as a result of the illusion of separation: 1" rebellion, defiance and competition; 2" conceit, arrogance and doubt; 3" betrayal, abandonment and rejection. Expressions of self-pity, guilt and anger can result from any of the numbers.

A further examination of this theme adds another insight to the ongoing search for the meaning in numbers. Figure 9 sheds light on this. The numbers 1, 4 and 8 are numbers of action; 2, 5 and 7 are numbers of thought; 3, 6 and 9 are numbers of reaction (emotion/feeling). Those who are 1s are actively pursuing their personal self-interests, 4s put action into their work, 8s put action into organization and accomplishment, 2s would like to understand how to get along, 5s want to understand life, 7s want to understand themselves in relation to life, 3s want to feel loved, 6s want love from

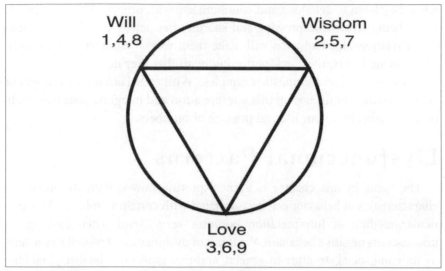

Figure 9: The Attributes of the Absolute in Terms of Numerology.

another, 9s seek to create love for all. A further insight into the dynamics of numbers is contained in the table below.

	Will	Wisdom	Love
Will	1	8	4
Wisdom	2	7	5
Love	3	6	9

The subtle dynamics of numbers take on more meaning as one explores the ramifications of the above illustration in its application to a better under-standing of human behavior. Revealed here are archetypal, underlying energy matrices that shed further light upon the dynamics of numerical expression.

Each of the numbers is shaded in meaning by the overtone of the three attributes of creation. For example, each of the three numbers of will (1, 4, 8) resonates to the three elements of its source" will, wisdom and love. The same interpretive nuance applies to the numbers of wisdom and love. The horizontal lines indicate the primary qualities, whereas the vertical columns indicate secondary aspects of this delineation.

Here are some examples of how these combinations manifest in behavior. Number 1s are centered within themselves and are singularly driven to accomplish whatever it is that is important to them; they give little attention to the impact this might have upon others. The 8s think things through and want to see a tangible result from their effort; they give thought to others and to the outcome. Number 4s love what they are doing and put complete effort into the work at hand, and 5s are driven to experience whatever they can and are learning to love life. The 7s love knowledge for knowledges sake; 2s use what they learn to get along and communicate with others. The 3s intensely enjoy being creative, expressing and sharing themselves, and 6s are curious about relationships and what will make them work. Number 9s seek to be the ultimate lovers; they seek perfection in all that they do.

These are brief and simplistic examples. With added attention, you will be able to see the significance of this interpretation and integrate your own additional insights into your life and practice of numbers.

Dysfunctional Patterns

The focus in this chapter is upon exploring how certain dysfunctional characteristics of behavior can be associated with certain numbers. This particular method of interpretation becomes very useful when looking for unconscious negative behavior. We think of dysfunction as rooted in the family unit and social structure in general, and that aspect will be discussed later in this volume. It is also readily seen that to some extent dysfunction started with that first moment of illusion of separation at origin" as the ego formed, the roots of negative reality became implanted.

The cosmological components for dysfunction were exploited and exaggerated by Lucifer and the dark forces. Lucifer served to reveal to evolving life forms the struggle through dichotomy along the path of unification. By living through the various choices of duality, evolving souls learn to make choices and become appreciative of Source. This reconciliation comes from having lived through the struggle of darkness and evil until finally making a conscious choice to reconcile with Source and live in harmony with the atom of light within, the higher self. Historically, Lucifer is associated with Satan and the devil. However, all Luciferian angels do is reflect back to us our struggle with illusion. It is exoteric religion that made these angels into evil forces and created further fear and conflict associated with the path of reconciliation. Even in present human behavior, these primordial patterns can be seen along with the human components.

Thousands of volumes have been written teaching the positive behaviors of spiritually connected individuals, and all religious denominations have been teaching these principles for thousands of years. Yet the majority of Earths population still lives in the illusion and darkness of the unconscious or subconscious forces. Therefore, I have chosen to recognize and emphasize these unconscious negative forces and bring them into light. An exploration through those dysfunctional patterns can be most helpful to the individual seeking personal growth. Working with a professional practitioner or one qualified to resolve such issues is strongly encouraged. It is very difficult to recognize and resolve the hidden agendas alone, which is why we need others to help reflect and reveal unconscious issues back to us. Once negative patterns are recognized and addressed, we can release their hold upon our life and reconnect naturally to our divine heritage and resources. With that in mind, let us continue our exposé of these negative unconscious patterns.

On Gambling

Gambling is rooted in the misuse of will (defiance of divine will) paired with distorted intellect. The rebellious spark will not concede that divine law is impeccable and uniform. The gambler is always trying to beat the odds, to disprove the probabilities, to find flaws in the orderliness of universal law by hitting the long shot (a proof of deviation from perfection and inevitability). The gambler feeds on repeating adrenaline highs, trying to prove God (mother-father) wrong by finding a flaw in the orderliness of events, and this series of negative peak experiences gives a distorted impression of being alive. The repetition and pursuit of these negative realities distracts from the opportunity to have wholesome life experiences.

The compulsive gambler resents God's will, believing that he or she has no free will or real choice of fate. The compulsive gambler pursues unrealistic odds and inevitably loses because of a negative belief system, which includes the expectation, "If all is orderly and regulated, I will receive nothing because I have been so bad." The gambler wants a demonstration of the Source's generosity. However, the negative ego sabotages the possibility of positive results and reinforces the negative expectation of being rejected again! Gambling is not just limited to excessive speculation on racing, sports, card games, the stock market or other obvious venues. A person taking compulsive, excessive risks in everyday life (job, relationships, driving, health, eating and more) can be a victim of the gambling syndrome just as well.

Number 1s are rebellious about following the rules of acquisition and, because of self-importance, nurture grandiose fantasies about hitting "the big one." The 4s will gamble with work and career, expecting unearned advancement or favors for services rendered. They are prone to exaggerate their accomplishments or abilities. They will sacrifice a steady and secure situation and put themselves and their families in jeopardy in pursuit of an unrealistic dream. Number 8s tend to gamble with power and authority. They distrust authority and use this distrust to justify making their own rules. They can misuse funds of their own or others' with ruthless abandon and can throw away an esteemed position of wealth and authority, risking it all for what appears to be a more glamorous opportunity.

On Alcoholism

Alcoholism (drug addiction) is rooted in the human search for the intoxication that comes from direct access to God's infinite supply of wisdom and life. The need to deny responsibility for one's actions results in numerous rationales for distorted behavior. Troubled deeply by their deeds of darkness and missing the intoxication and joy that come from direct contact with Source, many humans have sought chemical spirits of Earth to anesthetize their sorrow and pain. The separation from Source leads to Godlike power being given to the ego. Cut off from infinite wisdom, the struggling human becomes a know-it-all with grandiose illusions of false omnipotence. The all-knowing addict is unable to alter a failing course of action, because that would be admitting fallibility within self, which is the very thing these addicts are trying to prove about their God.

Number 2s seek to manipulate and convert others into their world of negative living; they seek partnership in crime, so to speak. The 5s crave life and believe that their world of experience is enhanced by the added potency of chemical assistance. They indulge and flood the senses seeking the fullness of life that has been lost in the separation from Source. Number 7s retreat into distorted, self-proclaimed doctrines of living that justify their erratic and unsuccessful behavior.

On Sexual and Emotional Abuse

Sexual and emotional abuse is rooted in the desire for love. Victims of such abuse are almost always seeking love, and the perpetrators will often insist that they are just giving love. But sexual abuse is not a loving act; other motives enter into the act of abuse. The sexual relationship is the closest that two mortals can come in approximating the sense of union with God; it is seeking for a merging of the two dual polarities of humanity. The negative ego develops roadblocks to love, such as jealousy, possessiveness, envy, lust, dominance and violence, to mention a few. When sexual abuse (incest, molestation, rape, harassment and so on) occurs, there is always an element of emotional abuse connected with the act.

The form of emotional abuse most overlooked by society and many professional practitioners is passive abuse. Usually, passive abuse is rooted in anger and takes on the form of withholding the healthy expression of love and emotion. The inner child and negative ego of the passive manipulator are very angry at not having received their share of love. This anger becomes overwhelming and the victim is frightened of the rage, which becomes internalized and is frozen into unconsciousness. The inner child and negative ego are saying, "You didn't give me a thing, and I'm not going to give you anything either."

A young boy who feels he did not get love from his mother will grow up to punish the women in his life (his wife, his daughters, his own inner woman) by withholding love, intimacy, encouragement, warmth and communication. Similarly, a young girl with those feelings about her father grows up to manipulate the men in her life (her husband, her sons, her own inner male). Passive abuse is difficult to recognize, because the perpetrator does nothing that is obvious. After a while, the partner will react to passive manipulation by acting out, which makes the active one appear to be the villain and scapegoat, whereas the passive one "looks good." Neighbors will remark, "He's such a nice man and she's such a bitch." Or, "She's such an angel and he's a real bastard." Where there is a crazy, there is a crazy maker. Passive abuse is subtle, clever and cruel. It is just as damaging as active abuse, if not more so—more damaging perhaps because it is unseen and unrecognized.

When 3s appear in the chart prominently, there is often an indication of sexual abuse; 3s reflect the will-love combination. For a male, child incest can take on the form of emotional incest as a result of the mother not having had a healthy relationship with the father and having transferred her needs to the child rather than nurturing that child in a healthy manner. Frozen 3s suggest the deeply repressed anger associated with some form of abuse. The number 6 is the archetype of codependency—addiction to a relationship—so 6s are often compulsive helpers and healers. They see others' suffering without realizing their own, and they become enmeshed in the most complicated relationships. Many excellent texts are available detailing the myriad facets of this dysfunction where the abused victim often identifies with the abuser. The 9s are very idealistic by nature and tend to see things romantically and dreamily. Excessive euphemism, idealization and exaggeration about someone's character are often indicators of past abuse by that person. For example, a child who heaps inordinately lavish praise upon a father, grandparent or uncle has very likely been abused by that person. An insistence that someone is so good is usually a clue as to how severe a negative experience in earlier years has been.

On Anger

Because anger is at the heart of virtually every dysfunction, emphasis is directed to the numerology of anger. Cloaked within each number is an archetypal human behavioral tendency for expression of anger, and the trained observer knows that much of our behavior is disguised to appear as something different. The following descriptions often do not become immediately evident to casual observation and go unnoticed in daily social interaction, which is one reason why anger is not readily recognized and accounted for in daily life. The patterns of suppressed anger described below are often expressed unconsciously, and it might take extra effort for them to be fully realized.

Patterns of Repressed Anger

1 Domination and intimidation are forces that 1s use to stay in charge of their environment. In conversation they may constantly ask questions or use will to determine the topic of conversation so as not to be threatened or caught off-guard. In daily matters, they are also dominating and forceful in virtually every situation. They impose ideas and opinions upon everyone in their world in order to maintain control and prevent being seen in their negative reality.

You have attracted much anger from many experiences where you found yourself not in control over your world. These experiences occurred because a domineering person in your life, usually a parent, never gave you the chance to control the situation.

2 Compulsive and excessive kindness are 2s' most effective and clever disguises for anger. They are constantly helpful, smiling and going out of their way to do something for others. Their manner is syrupy, sweet, sticky and gooey. It is easy to feel uncomfortable and agitated in their presence, but there is a sense of guilt about confronting someone who is so "nice." They desperately want others' approval, and when this approval is not received, they tend to become even angrier—and nicer; people who are always nice are always "pissed." However, this does not mean that when someone is doing a good deed, that person is doing it out of anger. The key here is compulsive behavior.

This 2 pattern comes from using giving as a means to manipulate. What you cannot admit to yourself is how desperately you want others to do something for you just as you see yourself doing for them. When they take your goodness and do not give you what you manipulatively expected, you become angrier and angrier—and hence "nicer" and "nicer."

3 The 3s' archetypal anger pattern is rooted in affected emotional behavior and frozen feelings. They can fluctuate back and forth from passive to active forms of anger. Over time the angry 3 personality will usually settle into a repetitive form of expression favoring one of these forms. The active form is the chatty 3, who is constantly talking and says nothing. These 3s demonstrate a publicly cheerful and constantly bouncy, nervous disposition; they appear jovial and festive to a fault.

When they are not verbally abusive, they are frequently passive abusers. Their repressed anger takes the form of cold, sullen, depressed moods. They manipulate and control by withholding what would be normal or healthy input to the partner or the person with whom they are interacting. In desperate need of attention, they extend their victimhood into the world, where they can be like a big, black emotional hole traveling through and sucking in any type of emotional energy they can get.

You have been abused in the past and are afraid of clean, direct, healthy expression of true feelings. As you work through this repressed memory and forgive and release the injuries and pain, you will start restoring the manifestation of your inner gifts of expression.

4 Number 4s manifest anger in extremely rigid behavior and excessive discipline. Overbearing military-type personalities come to mind—every aspect of their behavior is repeated at the same time every day, and they follow the same belief, habit and thought. This repetitious behavior, 4s think, will prevent unwanted and out-of-control emotions or thoughts from creep-

ing into their life experience. The insistence upon routine prevents any change or improvement in their circumstances. By involving everyone around them in the same behavior, these angry individuals hope to keep issues in check and their dark sides at bay.

You have become so angry in another time and place that your anger got out of control at the expense of considerable harm and possibly death to another. Therefore, you are so frightened of your inner rage that you must keep everything in control for fear of a tiny slip-up.

5 The 5s' strategy for avoiding anger is constant activity—it is very difficult to hit a moving target. They don't have to face real issues if there never is enough time to do so. Escapism can include destructive behavior such as drugs, alcohol or sexual misadventure as well as a host of other overindulgences. Perhaps they keep relocating from one place to another to another. Americans are particularly effective at creating numerous new activities and diversions to avoid existential responsibility.

You have been hurt deeply in the past and do not trust anyone or yourself. The traveling nomad feels no commitment to anyone and forms no allegiances, and you do not see that it is yourself who has the problem, not everyone else.

6 Becoming compulsively immersed in other people's problems to the denial of their own is the 6s' path of anger avoidance. This can include rescuers, enablers and do-gooders. Compulsive counselors give advice and force help upon those who do not ask for help and who may not need help. The 6 vibration includes, among other things, the archetypal pattern of codependency.

You experience deep guilt for having caused severe injury to another in a previous time and place. Rather than acknowledge how badly you feel, you see suffering in others and feel compelled to help them. If you give as much time and energy to helping yourself, the issue will be solved.

7 The 7s' route of avoidance is that of intellectual detachment. Their way out of dealing with feeling is to become obsessed with analysis, evaluation, rationalization and discussion. This is not to discount the valid path of research and reason; rather, it is to point out how easily 7s can escape into the mind and haven of thought. The escapist behavior is usually energized by cynical, judgmental and caustic remarks, which are a tip-off to underlying anger.

You have previously been totally out of control and responsible for tragic suffering and pain to others. You think that by living in your head, you do not have to deal with the grief in your heart. As you participate fully and naturally in life's experiences, you will find your way through this.

8 Number 8s take over whatever situation they enter, demanding authority and control, using their power and position to regulate and dictate. Angry 8s have to take over whatever situation they enter using overbearing authority and control. They use their power and position to regulate every-

thing around them, and they dictate how anyone near them should behave, following their unconscious belief of, "If I can control everyone and everything in my life, I will not have to face my own uncontrolled anger." As part of their arsenal in their efforts to control who and what is around them, they use the threat of loss of privilege, possible disgrace and heavy punishment. Misuse of power and authority are common practices of repressed 8s.

Your very fear of power lets you control the very thing—that is, power—that you could use to most effectively serve humanity. Once you see the magnitude of your true strength with an open heart and a pure soul, you will be able to move mountains and empower many.

9 Superidealism is a frequent disguise used by 9s to avoid their inner anger. The constant use of euphemism, exaggeration and hyperbole is a sure indicator of covered up and repressed anger. The current trendy phrase "I just surround them in unconditional love" is frequently used when they cannot admit to their anger. Recognizing only positive qualities about themselves and others is typically a reminder that they have not dealt with their dark side and hidden anger.

Often the amount of excessive idealism is proportionate to the amount of hidden, dark secrets in the negative shadow self. Be willing to face all of your past and all of your experience, and you will find your ideal self.

In the remaining chapters, we will explore numerous procedures for using numbers as an interpretive tool for uncovering more information about human behavior. You are strongly encouraged to review these early chapters again and again so that the archetypal patterns of numbers become deeply ingrained into memory. Having established this inner connection with the deeper aspects, you will then be able to know why you are saying what you say. You will also open the door for intuition to bring in your own personal modifiers and special insight into the components of behavior you best recognize.

The Vibrational
Aspects of 1 to 9 (with 0)

T he glyph of each number is a static form symbolizing vibration and motion. Each number has its own particular signature or set of characteristics. There can be too much of the vibration or too little, or there can be the balanced, harmonious purity of expression.

To better understand a specific number and the lessons it imparts, refer to both the number that comes before and the one that comes after. Here are examples:

1 From the inspiration of attainment in the previous evolution (9), you initiate a search for identity and purpose (1) in the new experience. To find your own self and purpose, you start to interact and cooperate (2) with other sojourners on the same path.

2 In order to find true balance in the cooperative process of number 2, you must first have a defined sense of your own individuality (1) and be in touch with your own true feelings (3).

3 In order to balance out the 3, you must have become disciplined and steady (4) in the realization of your own true feelings so you can avoid getting caught in the vacillations and opinions of society and those around you (2)

4 Discipline (4) comes from having established behavior consistent with your true feelings (3), thus allowing you to chart a steady course through all of life's changes and opportunities (5).

5 Integration of life experiences (5) occurs when you have become disciplined (4) in your actions and learn to take responsibility (6) for what you do.

6 Having followed your experiences (5) in a healthy and consistent manner, you reflect upon yourself (7). And having established a healthy relationship (6) with self, you can enter into a healthy relationship with another.

7 Having met outer responsibilities well (6), there is time to nurture an inner relationship with your divine self (7). Thus you can become more directly connected to your true source of power (8).

8 By becoming focused on your inner wisdom and light (7), you take control over your destiny (8) and begin to see the possibility of fulfilling your life dream (9).

9 As you take charge of self, the desire to empower others grows (8). The realization occurs that fulfilling your own true dream benefits all humankind (9). By serving the collective good, you discover your own unique individuality (1).

❋   ❋   ❋

Following are fundamental descriptions for each of the single-digit numbers 1 to 9.

1—Individuality (Will)

Assertive: Willful, domineering, selfish, arrogant, boastful, impulsive, aggressive, intimidating.

Passive: Dependent, submissive, indecisive, stubborn, procrastinating.

Harmonious: Strong-willed, ambitious, considerate of others, courageous; organizer, leader, pioneer, individual, original thinker.

When a 1 occurs in numerology, you frequently find Aries or Leo prominent in the astrology chart. The number 1 is related to the head, spine and lungs.

2—Cooperation (Peace)

Assertive: Meddling, arbitrary, careless, strident, tactless, extremist, dishonest; overlooks detail, creates divisiveness.

Passive: Vacillating, sullen, devious, faultfinding, overly meticulous, unable to take a stand.

Harmonious: Diplomatic, adaptable, able to fuse divergent opinions or groups, rhythmic, gentle, gathers information about both sides of a position before taking a stand.

When the 2 occurs in numerology, you frequently find Virgo or Libra prominent in the natal horoscope. The number 2 corresponds to the brain, nerves, the right shoulder and arm.

3—Self-Expression (Creativity)

Assertive: Superficial, extravagant; likes to gossip, has false vanity and wasteful ego attachment to creative gifts; gaudy taste; whiny; dislikes the practical.

Over the years, some authors have given the 10 a status similar to that of the master numbers. When calculating the addition of numbers, some practitioners do not even break the 10 down into a 1. You may want to keep this in mind, and eventually you will want to establish your own preference.

I do recognize that the 0 has an added quality and take this into consideration when it appears in the chart, although I usually do not give it quite the same status as a master number. Thus, when any number with a 0 appears, it has the qualities of the single-digit number along with that additional indicator of evolving into something on a higher level; the presence of the 0 suggests emphasis upon the qualities of invention and creative innovation.

A 20 might be particularly good at negotiating or might be able to change roles easily to accommodate new demands. A 30 might be an effective public speaker or produce exceptionally creative contributions to humanity. Take into consideration the 40—it suggests finding a new manner of doing your work. Depending upon its placement in the chart, it can also suggest teaching others new ways of performing a task or getting the job done. Or perhaps this 40 could be a very disciplined athlete or performer.

The 50 manifests added charisma and a person who knows people and finds new avenues to improve life and growth. This could be someone who mimics life, like an actor or comedian. The 60 might be a dramatic actor, religious leader or leading spokesperson on human behavior. A 70 can step back from a situation to analyze it like an actor, military leader or executive. The 80 can be innovative with ways to make money or new methods of management, and the 90 might be an inspired artist or public reformer. You will begin to see many other expansive ways of looking at numbers that contain 0s.

The presence of a 0 often indicates added charismatic, magnetic, colorful and influential qualities attributed to the individual. It suggests a person with heightened sensitivity and a more universal grasp of events. The negative side of 0 is resistance to change or fear of the unknown. Other manifestations might be skepticism, doubt and attempts to block the discovery of new things for fear of losing status or upsetting the status quo.

5

Master Numbers

I n earlier numerology texts and teachings, the numbers 11, 22 and some- times 33 were called master numbers, and they seemed to suggest an added potential and power, beyond single-digit and other double-digit num- bers. This work includes the entire range of double-digit master numbers, from 11 to 99—numbers that represent steps of initiation along the path of planetary and systemic evolution.

The number 9 is the number of perfection or completion, and 10 is the number of evolution. Evolution on this planet is represented by ten journeys through the ten spheres of the Tree of Life (see the cosmology chapters for the Tree of Life metaphor). Ten multiplied by ten (10) is one hundred (100), which is the evolutionary number opening the door to the next level of our journey in consciousness. The master numbers represent initiatory steps along the way for those desiring transformation.

There are schools of metaphysical thought that teach of ascended masters who sometimes do incarnate upon the planet, and there are some numerolo- gists who teach that a person with a master number in his or her name is an ascended master. Although it is possible that an incarnated ascended master could have a name that contains a master number, the appearance of a mas- ter number in a person's chart does not necessarily indicate that individual as such. Rather, the master number indicates an opportunity to master a partic- ular moment or talent during this lifetime.

In most cases, the presence of master numbers suggests an older soul com- ing into this lifetime to make an important contribution to humanity in a field that is spiritual, scientific, medical, religious, educational, governmental or technological in nature. Often master numbers indicate an older soul trained in the ancient esoteric schools during many previous lifetimes who now returns to manifest or teach particular higher-level methods of healing, psychic development or invention. The presence of master numbers may indicate a dynamic soul who is incarnating at this time from another planet or solar system to fulfill some specific destiny or mission. Yet many old, important, masterful souls have names and birth dates with no master numbers, so we must be careful to keep this whole matter in perspective.

My studies have brought me to the tentative conclusion that no matter where the master number may appear, the higher vibration does not fully unfold until the soul has awakened and the individual takes conscious steps to develop the attributes of the master number. In some instances, certain gifts manifest through grace. In fact, the individual possessing a gift may not even have initiated conscious discipline and study of spiritual law in this lifetime.

Those who have master numbers appearing in the name or birth date generally are endowed with special tendencies toward leadership and inspiration that set them apart from mass consciousness. Because the numbers are of intensified vibration and potency, those who possess them have a heightened obligation in life, such as greater requirements of self-discipline and purification of consciousness.

Following are fundamental descriptions for each of the master numbers 11 to 99.

11—Revelation

Assertive: Fanatical; joins cults or fanatical religious sects; overzealous; lacks practical realities, attacks dissimilar viewpoints, uses psychic or divine gift for self-purpose, loves ideals over humanity.

Passive: Fails to apply inspiration, overreacts to criticism; apathetic; fears higher energies and gifts; oversensitive to public reaction, cynical toward society.

Harmonious: Gifted channel or clairvoyant; seeks to express higher consciousness, unites spiritual truth to material plane; inventive, visionary leader.

22—Sacred Structuralization

Assertive: Tendency to overevaluate self-importance; exaggerates information and personal credentials, promotes hasty causes, resents lack of recognition, misuses wisdom or power.

Passive: Apathetic toward human needs; at the extreme uses heightened awareness for criminal goals or black magic; unable to adapt self to group needs, envious of others' successes.

Harmonious: Integrates higher wisdom into organizational administration, is in control of self and environment, puts universal goal ahead of self-pride; a practical mystic.

33—Universal Service

Assertive: Forceful in attempts to serve others, intolerant of differing mores and opinions, overemotional; won't adjust to needs of others, sees another person's problems but not his or her own.

Passive: Overprotective, rebellious; hides from positions of responsibility, seeks praise; inactive martyr; cannot establish clear boundaries, resists making changes in self; worried.

Harmonious: Sympathetic; is a good counselor (often psychic or spiritual), has concern for the welfare of the masses; a kind of cosmic parent or guardian; creates harmony at home and at work; a leader in institutions of positive welfare and human service.

44—Structured Power

Assertive: Rigid in administrating ideas and beliefs, emotionally insensitive to others' shortcomings; can attach to appearance rather than real achievement; outspoken critic of authority; forces social changes, abuses industrial power, uses money to control.

Passive: Possesses good ideas but expects others to carry them out; distaste of personal discipline, silently critical and envious of successful people; expects people to respond to his or her ideas; unconscious resistance to real responsibility and use of power.

Harmonious: Keystone in the building of a group consciousness, well-trained mental abilities; trusts the wisdom of own inner authority; practical visionary; has the potential to create new modes of income and prosperity; combines artistry with practicality, helps manifest empowerment.

55—Divine Will

Assertive: Confuses rebellion and freedom to escape responsibility and commitment; pessimistic and defeatist; indulges habits while criticizing others; egocentric to a fault; believes own opinion to be universal truth, justifies own faultfinding (toward others) as revelation; impatient.

Passive: Indulges in long bouts of animus projection with few results, blames fate or other people for setbacks, passively resists higher will; repressed anger creates overly aggressive actions.

Harmonious: Seeks to blend individual will with higher will; innovative and inventive while inspiring the originality in others, pioneer of movements in new thinking and reform; encourages others from tribal dependency to individualized awareness; dynamic leader.

66—Universal Joy

Assertive: Forces emotional confrontation before others are ready; confused emotions create aura of discouragement and despair; critical of others' emotional phobias and insecurities; falsely oversentimental; sees self as messiah-like figure, preys upon the emotional weakness in others.

Passive: Inability to recognize and admit own emotional blocks; good silent victim; expects others to "read" his or her moods of suffering and pain, blames lack of happiness on external people and events, wallows in negative anima.

Harmonious: Involved in causes (institutions) helping to alleviate human (animal, planetary) suffering; excellent counselor and healer, inspired artist who works on the archetypal level; helps bring the joy of nature and angels to humankind; positive ray in gloomy environs.

77—Creative Thought

Assertive: Intellectual elitist, has prolonged fantasy spells with no practical benefit; a martyr; uses self-created realities as escapist justification; negative criticism of social change; lives in an idealized state; extremist in thought and action; overtaxing of emotions.

Passive: Unsociable and detached, pessimistic about change in human nature; feels caught in a noncreative environment, explains inability to communicate his or her ideas as being "ahead of the times," wants recognition, fears the pleasure of the body, denies emotions.

Harmonious: Possesses the originality of thought to innovate and invent new systems for benefiting humankind, uses intuition with scientific and technological support, explores new theologies and philosophies of living, seeks to release others from self-limiting barriers.

88—Divine Knowing

Assertive: Has a power complex; maintains a slightly haughty arrogance, separating self from others; likes to challenge people in positions of authority; in the extreme, can be very destructive; intellectual arrogance; devious in attempting to get to the "top"; is a know-it-all; destructive attacks against religious and ideological institutions.

Passive: Passive resistance to authority; distrusts promptings of intuition and higher consciousness, blames life's setbacks on those in control; caught up in parent's unconscious head games; ungracious in defeat; can be fraudulent and exaggerate credentials; oblivious to others' inner convictions and feelings.

Harmonious: Teaches universal laws that improve management skills, delegates authority in a way that gives each person his or her own sense of power, works to find cooperation with the higher laws of mathematics; leader in metaphysical philosophies; respects integrity and clarity; develops new ideas and theories of thermodynamics, hydraulics and engineering.

99—Universal Love

Assertive: Gets trapped in modicum of syrupy idealism, wants to be seen as "ideal lover" while denying obvious selfish motives, uses group dynamics to avoid self-responsibility, struggles to recognize and express true feelings; impractical strategies for interpersonal relationships.

Passive: Becomes easily mired in pain, hurt, rejection and denial; unable to take responsibility as the creator of his or her own negative existence; smiles politely while being secretly resentful of others' happiness and joy; gloomy, accomplished martyr; benefits from seeking outside professional help.

Harmonious: Catches a glimpse of the greater plan for the planet and works to bring the higher light to humankind; learns to release and let go of all personality illusions; master teacher of self-awareness education; must learn to open heart center in practical ways; works with pulse of Mother Earth; visionary artist, poet and musician.

The Wisdom in Your Name

W hen interpreting the meaning of a name, all authors of numerology work with the vowels separately, the consonants separately and the two combined. However, this is where the similarities end. They all have their own terminologies and procedures for interpretation, and new students sometimes become confused by the differences. Try to remember that each system has its place and works within itself, and eventually you can take the best of each for your own edification.

For the interpretation of a name, I use the personality number (derived from the consonants), the soul number (derived from the vowels) and the number of the integrated self (derived from the total name). When I mention the term "personality" in this volume, I am referring to the little self that each of us uses for manifesting in this life sojourn. The personality is composed of the synthesis of activity expressed through the vehicles of the lower self—the physical, etheric, astral (emotional) and mental (intellectual) bodies.

The soul represents our inner consciousness of the ageless wisdom that is the repository of all our past-life sojourns. It is the soul who seeks further evolution through the vehicle of the personality. The soul strives for balance in and completion of the Earth experience so that it might be free to continue into other realms, planets or systems of evolution. The soul is not the higher self or the spark of our divinity; rather, the soul is the accumulation of experience and is learning just as the personality is learning.

Personality Number, Soul Number and Number of the Integrated Self

Each of these separate numbers is present and influences the total. It works in a manner similar to your astrology chart, where your Sun sign might be different than your Moon sign. Although these signs are quite important, all the energies of the solar system—both planetary and zodiacal—are present while the energy flows through focal points such as the Sun sign, Moon sign or the planets, according to their placement and angle of relationship.

P The personality number is the focal point through which you express yourself in the daily world of events. It indicates the primary lessons an individual is focusing upon during this life. It is the part of our behavior most readily seen in the external exchanges of everyday life. It gives us insight into our potential, our shortcomings, our strengths and our abilities. It does not attempt to describe the entire personality; rather, it indicates the primary lessons and attributes of self that we have chosen to concentrate on in this lifetime.

S The soul number reveals the particular vibration that the soul will stress— through the personality—in this lifetime. It is the energy pattern that the soul, in conjunction with higher self, foresees as most appropriate for accomplishing the predetermined growth lessons during this lifetime. The soul possesses knowledge of all the vibrations, yet it chooses a specific vibration for each lifetime in order to accelerate the process of learning the lessons related to a specific number.

The soul is not the higher self or divine spark. Rather, it is the accumulation of experience through numerous personalities over eons of evolution, and it is learning and adding to its pool of experience. The soul number gives a clue as to the primary lessons and energies the soul has chosen to accomplish. It tells us what is going on inside the deeper dimensions of an individual.

IS The number for the integrated self indicates what the person aspires to attain in terms of growth as a result of this lifetime. Because of the karmic challenges and multiple distractions upon this planet, it is not an easy task to reach the desired goal that has been set by the soul and higher self. Demands of the personality and the ego get in the way of the aspiring child of light. The individualized expression of self happens when the soul and personality function in complete harmony. Once these two are in harmony, an opening is expanded that lets in the guidance and light of the higher self. The personality can then experience increased moments of enlightenment.

The influence of the integrated-self number is somewhat dormant until the experience of integration takes place. Prior to integration with the higher self, its expression is distorted as it passes through the troubled personality. Prior to the manifestation of healthy integration, the integrated-self behavior pattern is similar to the personality behavior pattern.

Deriving the Numbers of a Name

When interpreting a chart, always remember that there is much more to interpretation than just reading the different sections of this book for each numerical description. The full chart should be intuitively linked after an examination of the parts. Then you can look at the parts again with a better grasp on and appreciation of everything contained therein. In working with this chapter particularly, remember that the soul number comes through the personality, as does the integrated-self number.

As human beings, we all have certain problems, neuroses, blocks and dysfunctional patterns. Most people who are attracted into the self-awareness movement are consciously working on recognizing and releasing negative dysfunctional behavior. As the personality becomes relatively clear and healthy, the soul can manifest through it more cleanly. Then the individual reaches toward a state of integration and consistent wellbeing.

The procedure for deriving each of the numerical values of a name starts with knowing which number corresponds to which letter. Here is a reference chart for these correspondences:

1	2	3	4	5	6	7	8	9
A	B	C	D	E	F	G	H	I
J	K	L	M	N	O	P	Q	R
S	T	U	V	W	X	Y	Z	

To start, write down the full name at birth—first, middle (one or more) and last. If there is a Jr., III or IV, write it out as *Junior, the Third* or *the Fourth.* Robert Jones Jr. would be written out as *Robert Jones Junior*; Robert Jones III would be written out as *Robert Jones the Third.*

The usual rule of thumb is to use the name on the person's birth certificate. There can be some exceptions: If a mistake was made on the birth certificate and corrected immediately, I usually go with the corrected name. In cases of adoption, I usually go with the original name; however, if this birth name was changed shortly thereafter, I may go with the adoptive name. There is no exact rule for how much time is too much. Even just a few days or weeks can be enough time for a name to get established. The name you receive at birth is similar to the natal chart in astrology. It is, in effect, your entire life. As you later change names (for marriage, career, nicknames, stage names and so on), these new names can be given consideration for the vibrational change they create. However, they do not replace the name given at birth. See the later section on changes in the name for further clarification.

Once you have written the name down, place the appropriate number under each letter using the above chart as a guideline. Then add across the line, getting a total number for the full name. This is called the pure number. Once you have a total, reduce it to a single digit by simple addition and you have the integrated-self number (IS).

Next, on another line, place a number under the vowels only (A, E, I, O, U and Y). Then add across and get a total for the vowels of the full name. This is the pure number. Now reduce it to a single digit by simple addition, and you have the soul number (S). Here is an important note: There is debate among some numerologists regarding the use of Y as a vowel or consonant. I struggled with the issue during my early years in practice, and after many years and tens of thousands of charts and consultation with other intuitive professional practitioners, I have come to consider the letter Y always as a vowel.

Finally, on a third line, write the numbers under each of the consonants only. Then add them across until you get a total. This is the pure number. Reduce it to a single digit by simple addition and you have the personality number (P).

Here is an example:

	G	E	O	R	G	E	W	A	L	K	E	R	B	U	S	H
IS	7	5	6	9	7	5	5	1	3	2	5	9	2	3	1	8
	$7 + 5 + 6 + 9 + 7 + 5 + 5 + 1 + 3 + 2 + 5 + 9 + 2 + 3 + 1 + 8 = 78 =$ $15 = 1 + 5 = 6$															
S		5	6			5		1			5			3		
	$5 + 6 + 5 + 1 + 5 + 3 = 25 = 2 + 5 = 7$															
P	7			9	7		5		3	2		9	2		1	8
	$7 + 9 + 7 + 5 + 3 + 2 + 9 + 2 + 1 + 8 = 53 = 5 + 3 = 8$															

Here is another example, with master numbers:

	R	O	B	E	R	T	S	T	O	R	E
IS	9	6	2	5	9	2	1	2	6	9	5
	$9 + 6 + 2 + 5 + 9 + 2 + 1 + 2 + 6 + 8 + 5 = 55 = 10 = 1$										
S		6		5					6		5
	$6 + 5 + 6 + 5 = 22 = 22 (4)$										
P	9		2		9	2	1	2		9	
	$9 + 2 + 9 + 2 + 1 + 2 + 9 = 34 = 3 + 4 = 7$										

The general rule of thumb when adding is not to reduce master numbers. For example, in the above name, some practitioners might indicate that Robert Store's IS number is 2 (11), because an IS number is not the pure number. I, on the other hand, have given it as an 11 (2), because it is an 11 before it is reduced to a 2. This is a picky procedural point for experienced practitioners. Just know for now that it is an 11. For the soul number, we have 22 (4), which indicates it is first a pure 22 and then it is reduced to a 4. When dealing with master numbers, we say, per our Robert Store example, that this is a 22 (4) or an 11 (2). When a number is in parentheses, it can also denote a potential master number.

Here is a little helpful hint to the beginner: Make a quick examination to be sure that the pure numbers add up—that is, that the sum of the vowels and the sum of the consonants add up to the sum of the whole name. It is just a quick check to catch possible errors in your additions.

Personality Numbers

In the following pages, you will find complete descriptions for the meaning of the numbers in your name. For each number, see also the appropriate life number description for additional insight, since the life number and personality numbers are very similar to each other.

Personality Number 1

Yours is the number of individuality, self-reliance and originality. You add to whatever interests you become involved in. You are driven by strong willpower, and when you have a definite goal in mind, you are enormously productive. Your magnetism and radiant personality help you to achieve desired results. Without such determined intent, you are less than enthusiastic and settle for adequate accomplishment. A 1 is prone to self-centeredness and wants to be first in all things, so you can become selfish and contrary if things do not roll your way.

You will likely have to deal with a domineering parent (or parents) in childhood. Read the 1 life number for added insight; the experiential components of behavior are very similar to those found in the personality number. In the rebellious stage, your separateness and belligerence can be very annoying. You find it difficult to accept orders from others and might choose to go against the wishes of the group just to assert self-identity. You hide your insecurity behind brash and assertive outer expression. You love to give directions; you listen to others but seldom take their advice, instead smugly relying upon your own intense convictions. Once you are convinced of a better way of doing something, however, you are ardent in your praise and can quickly stir up enthusiasm in those around you. Your natural drive to the top has you seeking positions of supervision and leadership.

When confidence has been undermined in early years, the 1 personality lacks initiative and confidence, bemoaning lost chances as bad luck or unjust circumstances. Number 1s will brag about their abilities rather than produce. When a very passive orientation to life develops in the personality, 1s no longer trust self-initiative, preferring to let their spouses, parents, society or government take care of their needs. It is easy for them to take the course of gambling to make up for lost time and energy. Although the number 8 is usually associated with money, any number can attract money, and when they are in harmony with self, 1s tend to be lucky with finances. They seem to attract money when needed. This expectation of receiving can be overused or abused. When under pressure, 1s are inclined toward gambling and quick-fix schemes.

You are rather blunt, often witty, dignified and to the point in communication with others. You prefer having one close friendship rather than many that are superficial. You are demanding, seek change from routine and enjoy being around other go-getters. At the extreme, your self-centered value system can find a way to justify exploiting others or taking what you desire without respect for the value of self-creativity.

It is best for you to maintain a close companion or spouse who is also strong-willed, supportive and patient. Despite all the bravado about individuality, you need the security of a steady relationship to get the most out of life. Loyalty and attraction are key elements to a satisfactory relationship with you. You tend toward directness in romance and approach it with a straightforward intensity. Because 1s are typically highly charged sexual partners, you might choose sex primarily for release. Once committed to a partner, though, you can be loyal and ardent.

When a relationship goes awry, you are prone to quick fits of temper, caustic bluntness and isolated silence. If insecure, you become a stickler over cleanliness, regulations and petty whims. You need affection and can give totally to your mate. There is little time for small talk and subtlety. When balance is upset, you can become tyrannical, domineering and even brutal with those who are close to you. When out of control, you can be attracted to gambling and unrealistic speculation.

You are at your best in a profession or employment where you have the freedom to be original and independent. It is difficult for you to take orders, so you could be most comfortable in your own business. Explorers, inventors, managers, designers, entertainers, owners of small businesses and athletes are frequently people with the 1 prominent in their charts.

Typically, 1s are robust and healthy even though they are prone to headaches and arthritis; however, this can be jeopardized by overwork without time for rest and relaxation. They are inclined to overestimate the limits of their abundant energy. The 1 is an intense male energy and, in a woman's chart, suggests strong animus.

Personality Number 2

This is the number of cooperation, diplomacy and tact. You work subtly behind the scenes to accomplish desired objectives and attain success through diplomacy, not by the coercive forcing of issues. You are able to adapt comfortably to varied circumstances and to people from diverse social, political, religious and ethnic backgrounds. You are in the process of realizing that by facilitating another's learning, you define your own strength as you give that person empowerment and both of you accomplish more in life. You are at your best when you are with agreeable and sincere associates.

In your early childhood, you might have encountered considerable criticism and pettiness around you, which might have left you unusually sensitive and with a nervous system that overreacts to tension and disagreement. You have a subconscious desire to avoid friction, which manifests in outward attempts to establish harmony wherever you are. Although subconscious karmic pressure is not the only reason why you seek harmony, it is one of the strongest. You seek a balance for transgressions in a previous life where you lashed out at others with an abrasive tongue. You might wonder why you became the center of someone else's unexpected criticism.

You are naturally gregarious and prefer to be in the company of others, so it hurts you deeply when you are misunderstood or rejected because of a disagreement. When things go badly, it is easy for you to blame yourself and make everything your fault. Fear of others' reaction is a negative attitude worth confronting and releasing. You can benefit from taking an attitude of detachment and noncritical acceptance of others' actions.

As an adjunct to your persuasive manner, you accumulate and quote facts readily. At times this recitation of information cloaks doubts about your own intellectual capacity. You can use facts accurately and profusely to enhance your bargaining position. At worst, you can manipulate data to support your opinion.

Although 2s often appear easygoing and indecisive when compared to the more aggressive personality numbers, underneath that easygoing nature is a grim determination to meet opposition convincingly. Your exterior can be gentle and calm, but underneath the sweetness and smile is a touch of strength and tenacity. You are sometimes thought to be stubborn, but those who know you realize that you are paralyzed by fear of being powerless and overwhelmed by others. When thwarted, you can become very cunning and scheming to get your way. People might have the impression that you are contrived and hypocritical. When you notice this, be wary of slogging through a mire of self-pity and becoming withdrawn and secretive.

Your charm and manner attract people who want to be of assistance to you. You know you will succeed because of an innate belief that good triumphs over evil. You have the ability to attract the type of people who get things done. Whereas 1s are aggressive and want to rise to the top, you are more often found in second-echelon positions, finding your strength in a role supportive to leadership. This does not prevent you from being at the top, but it does mean that your drive will articulate itself in a less obvious manner.

In personal matters, 2s tend toward an easygoing style. If pushed too far, they can become vindictive and contemptuous. An innate ability to see both sides of an issue clearly enhances a 2's qualities as negotiator and peacemaker. As mediators 2s come alive and work constantly to establish an accord between opposing elements.

You enjoy social activities with the necessary games and rules. You are most comfortable in marriage, for you need understanding and are uncomfortable alone. You are likely to choose a quiet, reserved and supportive spouse who is immaculate and orderly around the home. In romance you are very susceptible to details pertaining to your partner and milieu. You enjoy the delicate touch and intrigue of tender interplay. Little things like small physical flaws in your partner's body or a dripping faucet can break the spell of the moment, disrupting your pleasure. In love and sex, be careful to honor your own boundaries. It is easy to put your lover's needs before your own, and this can lead to inner resentment toward sex and romantic shutdown.

As parents 2s are patient and considerate. However, if disharmony prevails, they become critical and nagging about petty circumstances. When out of control, 2s are vulnerable to alcoholism and abuse of drugs. They are typically found in careers or professions such as politics, public relations, statistics, psychics, technical fields and religions. They work best in groups. The 2 is a very feminine energy symbolically, and when appearing in a man's chart, it suggests strong anima.

The negative 2s' penchant for critical speech makes them prone to sore throats and tonsil and thyroid conditions. The 2 also relates to the brain and nervous system, so people under the 2 vibration react emotionally to strident or raucous conditions, which can activate nervous disorders.

Personality Number 3

This is the number of joy, beauty and self-expression through words or creativity. Your natural demeanor is cheerful, entertaining and sociable. You enjoy having friends around you and are a natural host or hostess. As a 3, you work in the realm of imagination and creativity; you will elaborate and exaggerate in conversation, preferring to overlook the drab and mundane. Your disposition is optimistic and hopeful about the future, and you can cheer up a lifeless party and dissipate gloom. But be careful—it is easy to spread your many potential gifts thin, making you superficial and contrived.

You enjoy the good life and naturally desire lavish surroundings. You might have gaudy tastes. When harmony prevails, your innate sense of artistry creates a tasteful environment. If you put luxury, ease and self-indulgence ahead of productive creativity, you can become immersed in shallow, egocentric and worrisome thinking.

You are a natural with words, and at your best you can be fluid, funny and fascinating. On the other side of the coin, you are very capable of talking too much but saying little. Words are a natural part of expressing your creative self. There are often circumstances in your childhood environment that inhibit your self-expression and natural-born talents. The likelihood is very high that there has been a pattern of sexual abuse within your family history and possibly within your own life.

Insecure 3s are superficial and restless in their search for knowledge. They need to discipline themselves in order to locate the essence of wisdom that runs below the surface. When restless, they can get caught up in fads and crazes. Avoid these negative experiences. If unable to feel productive, 3s can lose their sense of value to others. They then become detached and distant in relationships and are perhaps even unable to maintain warm interpersonal contact.

Below the cheerful, good-natured exterior, you have a dramatic feeling of self-importance. When this is out of proportion, you are capable of great melodramatic episodes, elaborating upon your disappointments and hurts. When properly channeled, this self-esteem can propel you to great heights of attainment and prestige.

You are a good friend and friends are important to you—3s are mixers and need company around them. You are trustworthy, although you might forget what you have previously stated. You are particularly comfortable with and attractive to the opposite sex. A perpetual romantic, you often find yourself entangled in adventurous affairs. Your life is full of incredible and intriguing experiences; if you teach, write or counsel others, this will provide a rich potpourri of anecdotes for you to draw from for examples. You are quick to pick things up but need to balance practicality with imagination. With other steadying influences in the chart (8s and/or 4s, for instance), you can become quite successful in expansive, imaginative business pursuits. You are attracted to careers in areas such as the arts, the clergy, media, sales, law, education, social work, beauty, jewelry, entertainment, travel and many other, similar careers.

In romance 3s enjoy colorful surroundings and cheerful verbal interplay. You innately want pleasure for both parties and can adjust to little whims. You are sexually curious and enjoy many forms of union. Lighting, music and considerate manners help set a mood that glamorizes the overall experience. It is easy for you to slip into toxic relations and addictive sex. If you wake up and wonder why you are feeling used and exploited, you could have been the recipient of early childhood abuse.

Emotional harmony is a must for sustaining any relationship or marriage. You are deeply affectionate and self-sacrificing in love and marriage but become quite stubborn if not shown appreciation. The home is usually artistically decorated, radiating warmth and making guests feel welcome. You seek peace and balance in the home and usually prefer a mate who is strong and responsible.

A 3 in health relates to the voice, throat, eyes and ears. When creativity is blocked, there can be disturbances with the sexual anatomy. Subconscious conflicts disturb the yin-yang (anima-animus) integration.

Personality Number 4

The 4 vibration is one of loyalty, dedication, dignity, honesty and hard work. You desire a solid foundation in your home, community and business. Your natural drive causes you to perform the work at hand steadily and methodically, and you gather respect in return.

You do not take much time for fun and pleasure but prefer to be left alone to perform the task at hand. This can become a fault because it is very easy to slip into a narrow rut, and you are one of the personalities for whom it is most difficult to change habits. Often an early childhood environment places exaggerated emphasis on working. You are a bit tight with finances and personal belongings and read hardship into situations that might not justify your stringent evaluation.

The symbol of the 4 is the square, and you can be just that. If anyone has boxed you in, it is you. If you feel harshly restricted by circumstance, you can be quite vocal. Your temper builds over a long period of time and then— boom! If you do not like your work, everyone around you will feel it and suffer. If you do not receive compensation or praise for your labors, your self-image suffers and you can become quite jealous and envious of others who seem to get more than they deserve.

Your general attitude is conservative, and the 4 is often intolerant or even hostile toward people who seem unwilling to earn their way in life. Thrift, orderliness and prudence are given top ratings on your list of priorities. Much of your self-image is based upon your accomplishments and the achievements of your family. Property, proper social standing and success are very much related to your personal security. When your subconscious instincts are active, you are unlikely to take risks if your security might be jeopardized. However, when pushed too far, you are prone to gambling and shortcuts.

You take pride in your work. Unfortunately, you are not above censuring another's work while ignoring the fact that yours might be no better. You are not one to waste time. Often you can be found tinkering around the home, with the car or wherever there is a need. You like routine. Imagination is not your forte. Your practicality, organizational poise, technical adroitness and industrious manners help you get ahead in life.

You are most comfortable when working for an industry or cause in which you can put your trust and esteem. You will gladly work hard to help others, and this can cause others to take advantage of your labor. Because your natural tendency is to hold in your emotions, when they do come out, it can be in hysterical bursts of worry and concern. You might enjoy acting them out on the stage or in a dramatic fashion. You are steadfast, honest and generally dependable.

It is not easy for you to mingle with others and trade small talk. Your fixed attitudes draw very opinionated definitions of right and wrong without much tolerance for people you place in the latter category. If your firm baseline is shaken, you can become scattered and defenseless, and under those conditions you react defensively, argumentatively and stubbornly. Although 4s are noted for their control and rigidity, you are strangely prone to sudden hysterical outbursts that catch those close to you off guard.

If 4s are approached logically and patiently, an amiable solution can be reached, especially if it is practical. You are not one to rush into anything brashly, which will normally give you security, but many times you might find that you want to kick yourself in the rear end for missing out on a big opportunity. When out of control, you can get hooked on gambling as a quick fix to catch up for lost moments.

It is not easy for you to spontaneously enjoy the fun in life; you have to work at it! In romance you are ardent but control your passion. You can manifest sexual vitality and power but might have difficulty with the soft talk and sentimental exchanges more natural to other numbers. You are loyal and consistent in companionship and technique. You are uncomfortable playing the field, as you have little patience learning the variety of games and guises often associated with pursuing a potential mate.

You find solace and security in marriage. A productive husband or wife and children help to build your ego. Loyalty and sacrifice come easily if you are proud of those you protect. At times you give no quarter and rule with military discipline. A comfortable home life is a good tonic for relaxing you and giving you relief from the tension and strain of your labors.

Professions and careers harmonious to the 4 include electricians, craftsmen, builders, chemists, scientists, farmers, naturalists, bankers, military people, accountants, office workers and police.

Health problems associated with the 4 include neuralgia, hardening of the arteries, tendonitis, bone disorders and baldness (men).

Personality Number 5

The 5 carries an atmosphere of change, restlessness, curiosity, sensuality and freedom. You are witty, carefree and enjoy travel and meeting new acquaintances. You deplore monotony and are a spring of nervous tension looking for an outlet. You enjoy crowds and events of speed, competition and excitement.

You crave change innately, and this is an excellent impetus for growth. However, you need to take time to learn and absorb from the lesson at hand. Your abandon can sometimes lead to trouble and disregard for legal and moral codes. It is easy for you to run from your problems by overindulgence in sensual stimulation (drugs, alcohol, food or sexuality). When out of control, you can be very prone toward addictions, and you might mistake overindulgence for freedom. An important lesson for the 5 is to learn that true freedom comes after building a stable foundation and disciplined lifestyle.

When insecure, a 5 will repeat the same experiences over and over in an almost infantile manner, failing to learn from the experience itself. The insecure 5 wants life to stay as it is and is fearful of moving on to the next phase of learning. Fives like to roam constantly and find it difficult to stay attached to people or places for a long time. They see life as a gamble, and taking chances is their game. They dabble in philosophy and religion but usually not very deeply; they are more inclined to be unorthodox in their beliefs. They are adroit with words and ideas that allow them to blend in with all sorts of characters. They can fit into any crowd and seem like one of its members.

The 5 is fascinated by events around him or her and prefers to participate in jubilation rather than be left out of it. Your attitude is generally progressive and independent, with a willingness to adapt. If anything holds you back, it's the fact that you are capable of so many diverse aptitudes that you have difficulty concentrating on one in particular. You can become impatient and critical with slow-moving situations or delays. You'll find yourself most uneasy around the 4 vibration and to some extent the 7.

You enjoy the company of the opposite sex and are usually surrounded by friends of both sexes. You are not one to probe very deeply below the surface, and you become uneasy when someone attempts to delve into your psyche. This is not so much because you are frightened that they might find some deeply hidden secret; more likely it is because you are afraid they will discover that you have not looked very deeply into the subjects you present. You do not want to be exposed for your lack of depth, and consequently, you are apt to use quick wit and unusual repartee to avoid threatening issues. This escapist attitude can lead to role playing and a con-artist personality.

In romance you are flirtatious, fickle and fun, and you prefer sexual variety in mates and methods. You are easily addicted to sex and vulnerable to promiscuity. Sometimes your curiosity leads you into the far-out and possibly kinky. It is difficult to tie you down, but you have a lot to give when you are around.

In marriage you need a lot of latitude for your varied interests. You will want your own space. Your romantic and sexual interests are varied and curious. You like activity and a mate who is versatile. Athletic and outdoor activities are important to your physical well-being and fitness. It is not easy for you to adjust to the demands of family and home, but if content, you can be an entertaining and colorful companion.

Vocations compatible with the 5 include entertainers, civil servants, speakers, salespersons and travel consultants, to mention a few. If you work in an office, you will need excuses for leaving your desk and circulating with coworkers. Tour guides, clerks, owners or workers in stores handling many goods, athletes and circus people are a few more positions in which a 5 would find interest. A wide range of possibilities exists for this busy number.

Health matters related to the 5 include disabilities of the senses (eyes, ears, skin and so on). Nervous ailments can arise if you remain overactive. Problems with the liver and gall bladder are also associated with the 5.

Personality Number 6

The 6 is the vibration of responsibility, service, domesticity and attainment of emotional harmony. Your thoughts turn naturally to others and the needs of those close to you. Whenever someone is in need, you desire to serve and be of assistance. You are considerate and sympathetic; you are sensitive to anguish and disharmony in the world around you. Your idealistic nature and hope for the improvement of humanity lead you in the direction of helping others. Although you enjoy comfort and harmonious surroundings, you do not need luxury to be content.

As a 6, you are reserved but can become alternately suspicious and gullible in the company of new acquaintances. You try hard to live within the conventions of society but will alter your patterns if it suits immediate needs. When threatened emotionally, you can become most illogical, defending your actions almost to the point of irrationality. You have an excellent knack for mentally and emotionally placing yourself in another person's state of mind and emotion. Empathy, used positively, can allow you to help many associates get through troubled times. On the dark side, this empathy can also be used very subtly to manipulate others by aggravating their insecurities. You are something of a martyr and tend to fight lost causes with a quixotic zest.

You can become overly sensitive to negative feelings around you, which can cause you to slip into moody and discouraged states. You are capable of deep affection and sacrifice, but attachment to another sometimes hides your own deep insecurity. This inner anxiety can be seen in angry outbursts of righteous indignation when a loved one does not respond with the loyalty, affection and concern you believe to be your due. You place high standards upon relationships and can be quite contrary when your mate does not meet those standards. When out of control, you are highly prone to toxic and/or codependent relationships, so you particularly want to take the time to learn about the patterns of codependent behavior.

Sixes are naturals as counselors once they have resolved their own problems or have learned to set aside their own conflicts sufficiently to empathize with a troubled friend. You find it difficult to stand idly by when you see someone suffering. Be careful, or those you try to help might become dependent and could easily create a drain on your energy. A feeling of duty to others seems to be an intrinsic part of your nature. If you learn to serve selflessly and without regret, you have a chance to deeply etch the slate of the karmic record.

When involved in business, the 6 can compensate for emotional needs by wanting to supply products, goods or services. You can become driven to provide a better product or way of life to the masses. When this occurs, you can be very successful in business ventures. You might turn to other ways of acting out emotional needs that cannot be expressed openly and naturally, perhaps acting for the theater or television.

Sixes live from the heart and feel very intently what is right or wrong. You are adamant when injustice occurs and demand fair treatment for all of life's citizens. Some might mistake your need to serve as weakness. You take offense when misunderstood and can readily dismay others because of your seeming hurt and pettiness over trivial matters.

Friends are very important to you, and a refreshing evening with congenial friends can be a real lift to your spirits. You are easily influenced by the approval and praise others lavish upon you. You are faithful to tradition and to those who share a similar respect. You often think that you know what is best for others. When this tendency grows out of hand, you can become an overbearing nuisance by interfering when uninvited.

In romance 6s are sentimental, considerate and protective. You are idealistic and need emotional harmony as a prelude to sexual enjoyment. When doubt enters into the relationship, you can become possessive and jealous to an irrational extent.

You are well suited to domestic life; in fact, you need it to operate most securely in all avenues of self-expression. You are a good provider, and you are naturally inclined to please others. This can cause you to lavish luxury and goods, along with affection, upon those you love. Harmony in the home might come after more than one marriage (see the 6 life number). Once the right mate is found, however, the home can be a source of joy to all who enter.

Careers and professions harmonious with the 6 can include nurses, teachers, counselors, artists and musicians, and they can be in the fields of cosmetics or apparel, medicine and service-related business.

Sixes are susceptible to stomach disorders from excessive worry and anxiety. When rejected, problems with the heart and blood might occur.

Personality Number 7

The 7 vibration is one of intellectuality, skepticism, wisdom, detachment and aloofness. Your wisdom lies within the memory of all you have been, and you prefer to go within for solace rather than turning to others. Your personality emits a strong sense of self-knowledge. Your temperament is judicial and stern, with very strong opinions about what other people are doing. People who are close by often intuit your attitudes—words are not always necessary when a personality as strong as yours asserts itself. You have a knack for appearing unable to understand exactly what someone else is saying, which keeps the other person off guard and makes it difficult for him or her to change your mind. On the other hand, you are a deep thinker and know how to project your beliefs with force and courage. You are logical, cerebral and honest and cannot be persuaded to deviate from your asserted position. The certitude of your attitudes makes you reserved and aloof when dealing with emotional situations.

Your reserved exterior can mask hidden talent and creative expression. Once you choose to reveal your creativity, you amaze friends and colleagues alike. Your originality is in your thinking. You can get caught up in causes or overlook practical factors if they become too intellectual, and this lack of practicality can hamper your aspirations in business, leaving you unable to inspire feelings of originality or worth in your employees. When handling personal relationships, you prefer to stay detached or indifferent; you often sense that you might be hurt by emotionally sticky attachment.

Your mind enjoys delving into the mysteries of life, death, the universe and virtually any question or problem that comes to your attention. Highly scientific in your approach to life, you sometimes overestimate mental knowledge and then become arrogant and snobbish. You can bring tremendous wisdom to light when you are willing to blend intuitive profundity with reasoned knowledge. Discipline and mental emphasis can prevent you from thoroughly enjoying superfluous or frivolous moments in life. You dislike noisy gatherings and party atmospheres. You are dignified and poised in public, usually garnering respect for your achievements. When discussing familiar topics, you are convincing and at ease. However, on other topics, you can impulsively shoot from the hip and regret your statements later.

The natural tendency of the 7 is to mentally control and regulate emotions, so you sometimes seek an outlet such as acting or role-playing to get a chance to release pent-up feelings. You do not like being pressed for personal information, yet you enjoy digging into others' intimate affairs. There are some hidden skeletons in the karmic recesses of your mind that you keep closeted in your subconscious. This makes you suspicious of (and sometimes cynical about) other people's motives. When out of control, you choose an extreme form of numbing yourself, such as alcohol or drug abuse.

Sevens approach romance almost as seriously as they do the rest of their lives. Intellectual rapport with their mates is an important ingredient to romance. When the cool exterior has been pierced by trust, 7s are loyal and capable of deep feelings. The nature of their love is enduring and sincere. Mental compatibility is a sought-after quality in the 7's marriage. As parents or spouses, 7s can be difficult because of their tendency to withdraw into detachment.

Professions in which 7s function best include scientists, analysts of all kinds, writers, educators and investigators, because they love to delve deeper into whatever occupies their minds. Their inquisitive nature often leads to rich new insights into the topic of choice.

Health conditions related to the 7 include glandular imbalance, pancreas and spleen problems and, in cases of severe cynicism and bitterness, cancer.

Personality Number 8

The 8 is the vibration of executive ability, financial success, power and leadership. This is a powerful personality, and it attracts respect from both other leaders and subordinates. You enjoy the competitive world and are at your best when in charge of a successful venture. You are driven by a strong inner will but have a sense of expediency that allows you to put on a tactful face at the most effective moment to get things done. You are materialistic, and vague philosophical speculation has little appeal to you. You have a knack for spontaneous enthusiasm, even to the point of passion.

You possess a distinctly independent belief in your ability to handle any situation, at home or in business. You tend toward conservatism in thought and have some fairly strong personal opinions about those who deviate from your conceptual beliefs. Since 8s derive influence from self-control, your success runs parallel to the amount of self-discipline you maintain. When you stumble, which is not often, it is because you become undisciplined and push fate too far.

You have an excellent insight into what motivates other people. This enables you to be an excellent manager but can also cause you to use others for personal gain (see the 8 life number for more insight about 8s and authority). You might find yourself attracted to the theater as a means of articulating your deep insight into human nature. When out of control, you can gamble away your own security and even the funds of others.

You have a great deal of pride and use it to hide your deeper emotions. You hesitate to demonstrate any form of tenderness for fear that others will see it as weakness. This could cause a loss of prestige and of the keen competitive edge upon which you thrive. When you are callously detached from emotion, your attitude toward others can become hostile, sullen or even intimidating. Your lack of regard can make you ruthless and can cause you to see other people as things to be used for your gain. This comes from an internal distrust of self that can make you overly suspicious of others and impossible to deal with rationally.

The evolving 8 is learning that money obtained just for wealth and power comes at great expense to self. When money is sought out of greed, you will encounter totally unexpected setbacks and forces that confront your will. As a result of the turmoil, you become increasingly aware of new laws of manifestation and management. Once in the flow of your authority, you demonstrate true mastery over self and situations; once harmony is acquired within, your life demonstrates integrity, influence and success. No matter what your interests are, 8s need a goal. Even in leisure hours, you are competitive. Relaxation is very important to your system to bring necessary rejuvenation.

Sometimes 8s seek romance and sexual activity to bolster a suffering self-image. This can be especially true of a man when his job or profession is not going well. An 8 seeks a partner of similar ambition as a spouse. In lovemaking, 8s can become mechanical. Although able to rise to the moment, the spell wanes quickly and it is back to work for the 8. Eights enjoy all the trappings of the good life, including the status symbols that are indicators of success. If out of tune, 8s are tyrannical in the way in which they run their home.

Positions compatible with the 8 include stockbrokers, executives, charity organizers, engineers, athletes, managers and vocational teachers.

Health factors relative to the 8 include ulcers, indigestion, hardening of the arteries and colon problems.

Personality Number 9

Nine is the number of sacrifice, generosity, tolerance, idealism and altruism. Nines are the dreamers and optimists who set a tone of hope and aspiration for the world; they live in an inner world of ideas, ideals and dreams.

You find it hard to be practical, and although you do not pursue material possessions, you seem to be provided with what you need. You are an idealist with a brooding awareness of the need for broader intuitive thinking and the expression of deeper feelings in this world as well as for more humanistic science. You are not at home in business unless it offers an opportunity to serve a greater cause for humankind.

There is a wholesome spirit of humbleness within 9s because of their awareness of the greater cosmic forces at work in their lives and in the universe. Your temperament is artistic, mystical and poetic. Your mind works in generalities rather than in details. You are emotionally impressionable and generous, which lets people impose upon your time and energy to their advantage. You must learn to overcome urges toward envy, spite and revenge by learning the law of forgiveness and release (see the 9 life number for more insight).

The 9s' extreme emotional sensitivity can lead to moodiness and depression. Your behavior will go from periods of elation, joy and hectic activity to listlessness and lack of initiative. When emotions become negative, you tend to take life too seriously and refuse to let go of the source of the trouble. You turn fearful and self-conscious. The idealistic tendency of the 9 can be your undoing. The presence of obsessive idealism about a person often cloaks previous abuse (often sexual) at the hands of someone placed unrealistically high upon a pedestal. Once you learn to let go and flow with higher consciousness, you can become an enlightened and inspired forebear of more elevated states of consciousness to come.

You have the chance to travel and experience life firsthand. Your opportunity for service is unlimited once you find the group to which you belong and the direction of your purpose. Your consciousness will have to grow with the coming tide of change on Earth, and you intuitively feel it coming like the uncertain calm before the biggest storm. If you do not fear the changes, you can awaken and prepare humankind for them through inspired art, music, writing, psychic wisdom or leadership.

You have come through much sorrow, disappointment, personal loss and perhaps illness. This can cause you to strive for such perfection that you can be frustrating to less demanding personalities. It has not been easy, but as the awakening of the soul and higher guidance touches the personality, you will move from self-centered aspirations to a greater understanding of the overall cosmic purpose. As you aspire to serve that purpose and let go of attachment to the world, your role gradually comes into focus.

You enjoy friends who are far-reaching, idealistic and sometimes unconventional. In romance 9s can fall in love passionately with an ideal, but as soon as the bubble is burst by reality, they plunge back into life and will soon be in search of another ideal mate. You seek the sympathy and praise of your lover and can be very giving in return. In marriage 9s have perhaps more difficulty than others, not because the cosmos has put a whammy on them, but because they search for the ideal of perfection. Too often 9s are disappointed when they discover that their mate is not who they expected, even though they themselves might fall short of their ideal image. Nines seek love and security but will experience unhappiness until they truly learn to "let go and let God."

Vocations and careers harmonious to 9s include speakers, inspired artists, fashion designers, humanitarians, explorers, inventors and ministers.

Nines are prone to nervous disorders and emotional fluctuations, and they have a tendency toward depression.

Personality Number 11

The 11 personality is similar to the 2 personality. Please review the description of the personality number 2. Some exceptions might develop as the 11 potential is awakened in consciousness.

The double 1 indicates the need to balance personal will with higher will, so you struggle to release ego in order to allow the higher self to take more domain. When out of balance, you use much adrenaline and effort to get your will done. If that fails, you can become complaining and angry toward both humanity and God. The 11 intensifies your desire to serve humanity, bringing reconciliation and peace to the world. You have a drive that often leads to positions of considerable influence and public prominence. When ambition and personal selfishness interfere with altruistic goals, you might suffer repudiation from the masses. Numerous famous politicians, evangelical leaders, entertainers and scholars have had the 11 prominently in their charts.

An 11 pursues ideals but at the same time can forget the human touch necessary to make idealism work. You can become fanatical about a cause and hurt people's feelings trying to make the world feel better. In extreme cases, this can lead to deception of the public and dishonesty.

Personality Number 22

The 22 personality is similar to the 4 personality. Please review the description of the personality number 4.

The 22s are often attracted to institutions or large movements that aim to bring humankind's greater cosmic destiny into form. The self can sometimes become greedy, lustful for power or aligned with darker forces who desire control over humankind by keeping the masses divided, confused and insecure. Your best inclination is to make a contribution to humanity's growth. You are working through highly constrained emotions, and it is easy to swing from steel cool to hysteria over the smallest incident, and your flair for melodrama gives you the persona of an actor. The rigors of research and science are intriguing outlets for the industrious 22 personality.

At their best, 22s are capable of uniting and working with people to bring a golden age unto the Earth. They might go through many menial and unimportant positions in their early years, but these can be tests to teach them humbleness and respect for those who will do the little jobs later under the direction of the enlightened 22s. By the end of their lives, they will likely be elevated to a position of considerable public influence. People with this number are often recognized for their work after death and can become martyrs for their cause.

The double 2 relates to both the inner and outer image. You are learning to connect with your inner directives, which raises confrontation with preconceived social and survival conceptions of the negative ego and the values and convictions attached to it. The structuring 4 can become overbearing in analytical weight and the 2s can give way to excessive worry. The 22 personality feels that he or she has some added responsibility. Until higher awareness is opened, 22s can wander around with a great feeling of self-importance and little to show for it.

Once in harmony, you develop heightened administrative skills and lead others with finesse and consideration. You address the social issues of the day with vivid detail and integrity, invoking a spirit of cooperation and desire for change within others.

Personality Number 33

The 33 personality is similar to the 6 personality. Please review the description of the personality number 6.

The double 3 indicates a search to unite the inner feelings and outer emotions of the personality. You see the ugliness and injustice around you and become very concerned, and you may not realize how much you suffer within. As you allow the joy of inner expression to come through, you blossom as a spokesperson and facilitator. There can be deep-seated resentment when you do not feel you have received your share of nurturing from Source. Then you become emotional and affective in your martyrdom and victimhood. Oftentimes inner, repressed emotions can be expressed through singing or acting. Another form of compensating for emotional deficiency from childhood is to want to give to others on a grand scale. This might be accomplished by dealing in big-volume business or perhaps in some form of information supply such as television or other media. Once aligned, a 33 is a delightful associate and emissary of light.

A 33 feels the suffering of the planet's population and is attracted to institutions and organizations involved with education, health, counseling and related fields of service. Very often 33s are involved in research, seeking better ways to make humans whole. Many 33s are becoming aware of unique psychic or intuitive abilities that they are unveiling in an effort to better understand the esoteric as well as the physical anatomy. Their contribution will shed light upon the inner gifts of Spirit with traditional forms of healing and counseling.

Thirty-threes can also be found in teaching and training. You are, in fact, present in all arenas of life, and you contribute to a better world by working to relieve suffering in whatever you do. Your need to communicate and work with festering emotions may lead you into public speaking, entertainment or writing. Whatever you choose, you will put your heart and soul into the endeavor.

Personality Number 44

The 44 personality is similar to the 8 personality. Please review the description of the personality number 8.

The double 4 attests to the challenge of using divine principles to build your foundation. Cosmologically, 4 represents the collection of atoms into the various crystalline archetypes that then become the building blocks of nature. The number 4 is essential in the exactness of and adherence to the laws of integration and alchemy, and 4s are learning to put their lives in an order that reflects discipline and appreciation of the laws of structure. They are often drawn into careers that get things done on a grand scale, and such careers could be in business, politics or possibly entertainment.

You have labored long and hard to reach a position of respect and accomplishment. As your influence expands, you will find yourself in just the right position to be of considerable service. You may very well acquire a lot of money during your lifetime. Whether you are in politics, business, education or other fields of endeavor, you assert influence upon those who can create a change in the world. You may be a philanthropist who supports enlightened projects.

You have studied the human animal well. Even though your profession may not be medical or healing by nature, you are very much interested in supporting healers and servants of light. You have an innate understanding of science and engineering, which filters into your management style and influences the insightful manner in which you inspire the best in others. Your knowledge of the laws of manifestation serves you well in giving the necessary push at the right time for the completion of important goals.

Personality Number 55

The 55 personality is similar to the 1 personality. Please review the description of the personality number 1.

The double 5 symbolizes the spiritual laws of life manifested in the outer world. You search to find the best dietary pattern of eating and the most efficient exercises for your physical body. You long for emotional balance and peace within. Your mind searches for the answer to the riddle of life and the cosmos. Your soul longs to return to the connection with Source that is so deeply embedded in the memory banks. You seek to fulfill the divine laws of life and honor the human experience. Your time has come to be a living example of the light within your being.

There is a lot of work to do to get the old addictive cells cleaned out and the compulsive behavior transformed into a natural lifestyle of adherence to inner direction. When these negative cravings take over, you can become involved in the trafficking of and indulgence in any number of possible drugs or vices.

You are known for your stand against injustice and your outspoken position against those who abuse the masses. Whatever your chosen calling, you are right at the front of groups who serve to awaken the higher light within all of humankind. You may be found in the research or exploration of outer space. Whether in outer space or inner space, your inspiration moves many toward a new level of awakening.

Your unabashed support for living life to the fullest can be threatening to institutions whose purpose it is to gain control over people and their behavior, and you meet resistance from them. Your enthusiasm for living leads you into activities of pleasure that can turn into profitable and/or humanitarian paths of service. Your humanitarian sensitivity gains you the support of many and rallies them to work against the organized oppressors.

Personality Number 66

The 66 personality is similar to the 3 personality. Please review the description of the personality number 3.

The double 6 represents purity of heart and purpose in the process of integrating the relationship with self. The symbol for the 6 is interlocking, reversed triangles that represent the trinity of deity manifested on Earth and reflected back to Source. The first step is getting the relationship between your own inner man and inner woman working together in a healthy manner. With that comes the integration of the divine feminine and divine masculine stimulus into the human personality. You are at the forefront of this integration process and will be helping many to develop further. You are a warrior who wishes to rid the planet of those who wreak tyranny and oppression.

You seek harmony, health and healing. Your drive to help humankind has taken you through a labyrinth of health modalities. You have learned that emotional harmony is central to the process of well-being, and your efforts are directed toward supporting those who specialize in this area of integration. You are drawn to harmonics, dance and movement as complementary components of any healing work, and you may also be drawn to working with crystals and their healing power.

Many 66s are very successful in business. There is a need to balance the emotional ledger, but you have difficulty dealing directly with emotions. As a leader, you seek to restore equilibrium to the many social and political imbalances that humans create, substituting goods and services for emotions. Your need to improve the lifestyle or quality of living of all humans is manifested in an almost compulsive drive to provide abundantly to the masses.

Your high energy and charm are positive assets when turning distractions into possible alliances. You are found where poise and proper protocol are honored and applied in human interaction. You radiate trust and stability, which helps you to dissolve tension between confrontational groups.

Personality Number 77

The 77 personality is similar to the 5 personality. Please review the description of the personality number 5.

The double 7 symbolizes the relationship between divine knowing and the process of logic and reasoning. Knowing comes from circular-intuitive-feminine receiving; reason comes from linear-logical-masculine processing. The well-developed, reasoning individual often accumulates a huge database of information within a given framework of belief. If the ego attaches to the belief system, it can get in the way of new information coming in from the intuitive planes. The logical brain will cancel out the intuitive information because it is illogical and inconsistent with the preconceived notion. As a 77, you are learning to trust the higher mind and allow the divine impulse to come into awareness. You can then devise logical ways to practically apply intuitively inspired ideas for human use. You could well be called upon to speak out in public, and you also have a chance to otherwise influence large numbers of people.

You are trained in the philosophies of humanity, and your heart is centered in the metaphysical philosophies of truth. Now you are concerned with bringing the latter to the former. You are logical and convincing when presenting your belief system. You are found in research environments, exercise organizations and life-performance centers where improvement of health is important. You have learned from time and experience that the mind does not function well without connection to the body. Dance, martial arts and other body-mind exercises are central to your teaching.

You mingle with some of the great leaders of human affairs and personal growth. You work to bring like minds together so the synergy of unity multiplies the power of the collective word. Your flair for drama can lead you into the public limelight, and you can be most entertaining in your manner of relating life experiences and lessons to other people.

Personality Number 88

The 88 personality is similar to the 7 personality. Please review the description of the personality number 7.

The double 8 symbolizes the divine power of Source implemented directly into the affairs of humans. It has been a struggle to accept your own power and to trust yourself with the implementation of higher force, and perhaps the process of trusting has not yet been accomplished. The breakdown of light into matter goes through many changes of vibration and levels of alchemical processing. You could become involved in the scientific study of light transference between different dimensions. Many of you will be attracted to mixing color, tone and rhythm in your music or other forms of artistic expression. Your pioneering efforts will bring reward and benefit.

You know how ideas manifest into reality, and you are found teaching these methods to souls whose intent is to improve the world infrastructure. Your reasoned approach to integrating the divine principles into matter makes it easy for the less gifted to learn this process. Number 88s are found in great laboratories, research and development centers and those institutions of learning that are positively reshaping the destiny of the planet. Whether it comes from the political podium, the science institute or the movie screen, your oratory leadership inspires in times of need and crisis.

You have had to work overtime to deal with the dysfunctional patterns of your childhood. You have taken excessive risks and gambled often to reach desired monetary goals. The transition from gambler to astute investor has taken much effort, but the learning cycle has paid off. Consequently, you are much more prepared in this time of troubled investment markets to help direct money wisely to worthy people and organizations.

Personality Number 99

The 99 personality is similar to the 9 personality. Please review the description of the personality number 9.

The double 9 symbolizes fulfillment of divine intent manifesting in the behavior of humans. You long for a perfect world and for people to act like cosmic grownups instead of rebellious children. You have glimpsed the pearl cities of heaven and the peaceful life of universal angels, and you long for such a life on Earth. You are learning to hold on to your fondest vision and inner dream. You can contribute to a better world. If you reach attainment and contentment within yourself, you lead the way for others to do so also. The downside of this need for perfection is that you become frustrated and cynical with the less-than-perfect world in which you live.

You are poised with your eyes and ears leaning toward heaven. Your clairvoyant or clairaudient sensitivities are central to your reliability as a translator of the inner-world realities. Your idealism is tempered with street smarts acquired from the school of hard knocks. You have struggled through years of abuse, victimhood and false martyrdom. This makes you wise to games of denial and gives you compassion for those still caught in the throes of denial. You seek to be an unconditional lover, and you long to live in a world where it is possible to be one.

You are found where the finest of artistic renditions are born. If you are not the artist yourself, you a benefactor to the arts extraordinaire. You seek refinement of character and life.

The Soul Number

Soul Number 1

The 1 soul works diligently on bringing the personality into accord with divine will. There is a strong inner drive to express yourself in original and individual ways. If your soul is restless, expect behavior and personal characteristics similar to the number 1 personality. You want to take charge of a situation and feel like you have a solution to everyone's crisis, an attitude that is more admirable than practical. The intensity of your willful drive can create the impression that you are lacking emotional sentiment. This is particularly true when your personality number is 7, 4 or 8. You have a strong passion for protecting the rights of the individual from misuse of authority.

Soul number 1 has an elevated feeling of self-importance—you *are* important—and when in harmony, this gives you the confidence to perform well. However, if the flow through the personality is impeded, this self-identification leads to conceit and intolerance of people who are deemed inferior. Long ago you chose this vibration for its thrust and initiative, which are necessary to accomplish innovation and renovation. Consequently, you are impatient with people who are resistant to change.

This life will bring you more than an average share of willful contacts. Now is the time to accept the will in others, so learn to unite your individuality with theirs into synchronized effort. Once you have attained a wholesome understanding of your will, there is little need to compare yourself to others' standards or to compete with their stipulations. Rather, your higher standard provides the most accurate indicator of success.

You have come to take action, so you will often walk alone among the many who live a life of reaction. How you channel and express this intensity of soul, of course, depends to a great extent upon your personality number. With a 7 personality, you are most likely an original thinker, and with an 8 personality, you might devise new business methods or ways of earning money. You possess the drive to accomplish much, and it is important for you to work with innovative people.

Soul Number 2

If 2 is your soul number, the emphasis is upon cooperation, companionship and the need to work harmoniously with others. Soul expression is modified as it manifests through the vibration of different personality patterns. For example, the soul energy may be more direct coming through a 1 personality number, whereas it might be softer and more colorful coming through a 3 personality number. The primary bridges of awareness you have come to establish are those between heaven and Earth, between the spiritual and the material realms. So it is particularly important for those of you with this soul number to find a quiet time to meditate each day. As you do this, you begin to construct the stronger bridge of cooperation between higher self and personality. Learn to listen to the inner voice of your higher intuition.

The 2 vibration is less aggressive than the 1 vibration, so your gains come from negotiation rather than force. You are careful not to give away your position until the exact proper moment. Because of your capacity for discretion, others of considerable power will rely on you to handle responsibility and influence behind the scenes.

Whatever your calling, you have the opportunity to bring people together and help unite the world by your contributions. Sometimes your inclination for tact prevents you from speaking your true feelings. This is a patient vibration, but if you are too complacent, people around you can get away with considerable mischief at your unsuspecting expense.

Twos can strengthen their natural spiritual and psychic sensitivity—which is already considerable—by a study of the symbolic and metaphysical sciences, and they usually are excellent channels and psychics. You may have some reservations about using these talents because of previous life experiences when you were punished for accurately foreseeing events and motives unfavorable to the powers that were in control.

Soul Number 3

The 3 soul seeks to express joy, hope and beauty for all. You enjoy the pleasant side of life and strive for a beautiful and colorful environment in which to express it. You have a natural touch for creative expression. The work, hobbies or avocations of your life reflect the added little touch you give to each circumstance passing through your life. As a 3, you benefit from an in-depth study of the yin and yang energy patterns. You have a knack for recognizing what is needed to bring harmony and balance into any situation. You intuitively know how to meet someone's needs and are a natural host or hostess.

Threes are artists on canvas, with the written page, in music and on and on. Many artists with the 3 soul number are entering into an inner-plane awakening, producing psychic or cosmic art. This can include portraying symbols of the soul or of inner-body energy patterns such as the aura or chakras, or producing musical pieces that are in resonance with the inner consciousness.

You have come to use the word. You must work diligently to eliminate the subconscious blocks that prevent you from using the word to its fullest glory. Let a strong inspiration from your heart be a prelude to your speech. Clear your mind of doubt and resistance to the guidance of the soul. The spoken word from the heart has healing qualities that may produce unrecognized benefits to those around you, and the most important place to measure your improvement is in the home and with those closest to you.

You respond to life from the heart and can be hurt easily. However, because you are a well of perpetual optimism, life will seldom keep you down for long. You are entertaining and love people, pets and children. Company and close friends are important to your well-being.

Look to your personality number for channels of your creative potential. With a 7, for example, the act of looking within is creatively natural for you, and your creative talent may be more scientific. Or if your personality number is 8, you might do very original work in advertising or sales.

Soul Number 4

The 4 soul is learning to appreciate the value of a job well done. You are known for your reliability and pride in your work, and you can sacrifice much personal time and effort if you believe in the work you are doing. As a 4, you will work for the benefit of others, even if it means giving up your own aspirations.

When 4 is your soul number, you increasingly feel the need to find your inner work. Deep within yourself, you feel something compelling you to seek out the work that you can do—with the quality of your work above everyone else's—to serve the plan. This inner conviction may lead to work that is not glamorous or likely to attract much public attention. However, in the end, you could never be happier than when you perform your destined calling. No one else can do this for you, nor will anyone else be able to help you. Others can point the way and shed light upon the experiences through which you have passed, but inner work is an individual process. When you follow the guidance of your soul and higher self and pass the outer tests, you will come under the tutelage of inner-plane teachers. The preparation includes riddance of self, ambition, pride, sloppiness, laziness and those qualities that interfere with perfected labor.

Fours are natural administrators and you obey, to the letter, the commands of your superiors. Be careful not to be misled. You are methodical and thorough in your labor and take pride in work well done. If anything, there is the need to incorporate a more open attitude of flexibility and change.

You are loyal and dependable to family and loved ones, a faithful companion. However, sentiment and emotions can be difficult for you. You do not care for lying or deception in any form and are discouraged by those who fall to pretense and flattery. As a result, you are awkward when it comes to handling situations that involve subterfuge or deception.

Once you have a goal in mind, you are tenacious and persistent. Sometimes you hide your personal insecurity by pushing too hard in your work. This can become an obsessive-compulsive syndrome, and your underlying insecurity should be recognized and released. As with the 3, your soul cleansing will bring a new peacefulness.

Soul Number 5

"Let freedom be!" cries the heart of the 5 soul number. Participation in life is very central to your evolution at this time, and you are here to accomplish a lot of living. When 5 is your soul number, it is particularly important that each lesson of each experience be incorporated, understood and then released for still further growth.

Freedom is a requisite to free will, and through the opportunity of free will, we can choose to ignore, defy or cooperate with divine law. The soul at this juncture is caught between the dicta of the law of self and the desires of the personality, or lower self. This position is one of working out lower desires through the test of life. The temptations of the flesh are strong; the temptations of the mind and its desires are intensified and challenge the soul. Now is the time to learn the lesson of desire and to leave those desires in order to hear the higher self. In a way, it is time to leave the body behind.

When you understand this, you will no longer strain for mental domination over the soul or seek sensual experience for personal gratification of the lower self. Rather, you will learn the laws of acceptance—that is, you will learn to call up the divine self for proper experience. Once you learn to accept that opportunity, you can utilize it in loving appreciation for the Creator, who is the provider of all that is to be experienced. Then you will inherently desire to use your experiences for the glory of the Creator and share them in a manner that assists in the awakening of others. Zeal is your forte.

The tremendous range of activities encountered by 5s makes you indispensable as a teacher and lecturer. You draw from personal experience to accentuate your lessons and instruction, making them come alive in a witty and anecdotal fashion. You roam the world working with all classes and races of humanity. Much of your wisdom comes not from scholarly studies but from your personal contact with people in all walks of life. Such contact keeps you flexible, progressive, restless and anxious to participate in yet another phase of your growth.

You have a responsibility to share your growth, even though it is not easy to take on an intense involvement with others. But you are learning to stay with each relationship long enough to receive and share the entire lesson associated with that relationship. Be generous with the strength and knowledge you have to share.

Soul Number 6

The 6 soul number focuses life upon the home, family and the company of close friends and loved ones. You work best when sharing the responsibility of your assignment with others. You feel deeply and are concerned with those who suffer needlessly in their home life or through personal circumstance, and you spontaneously respond to assist others when called upon. Empathy marks your every relationship.

People are comfortable around you and can turn to you with confidence to discuss their conflicts and suffering. This is probably because you are a natural counselor—many 6s are, and will be, opening their inner awareness as counselors. Often you can tap the akashic records to help with recognizing past-life trauma that still troubles the subconscious. Even if your awareness has not led you into the akasha, most likely you can still get inside another's consciousness to help relieve discomfort.

Marriage and home are central to your unqualified harmony. You seek a perfect mate and can be disappointed when any sort of flaw shows up. Often it is metaphysical students who seek such a union. However, it is very likely that you may have chosen a spouse who is not favorably disposed toward—and, in fact, may even be antagonistic to—your pursuits of soul. But there is a purpose in this madness. You have chosen your husband or wife to fill some need. If the two of you were completely compatible, it would be so easy to say, "Aren't we so spiritual and perfect?" That could be true, but too often such couples slip into a self-righteous habit of patting each other on the back while failing to grow. On the other hand, when there is challenge on some level, both mates grow rapidly if they are sincere and searching. Each assists the other, often through adversity, to better define and recognize personal needs. However, if you see only weakness and rebel prematurely, a beautiful chance for evolvement may be overlooked.

Your intellectual outlook is broad and flexible, but your lifestyle and emotional makeup are inclined toward the conservative and traditional. You want to correct all the abuses around you and make up for the wrongs that have plagued humankind for eons. There is a good chance you will help many this time around.

Soul Number 7

You prefer to be left alone to seek the quiet and wisdom deep within your heart and soul. Your rejuvenation comes from tranquil interludes of meditation and introspection, and it is good that you take this time to, as philosophers have said, "know thyself." Within your inner self is a vast storehouse of evolutionary knowledge. You have come at this time to tap these memories and to bring the deepest secrets of humanity and the cosmos to light.

The 7 soul is learning to set aside the rational, concrete mind of the lower self—not totally, but long enough to hear communications from the universal mind. The concrete mind must be patiently instructed on its proper role of waiting to support and digest the promptings of higher mind. True meditation is simply listening quietly to the soul and higher self. The mind will assert all sorts of hindrances and tirades in its attempts to prevent losing the dominance it has held for ages. The reasoning mind need not be disdained, but it should become an adjunct to the soul and universal mind.

As a 7 soul, you enjoy probing the deeper realms of psychology, religion, science, philosophy or metaphysical studies in an attempt to solve the deepest mysteries of humanity and the universe. You often possess a tremendous inner wisdom or gift of spirit, and you will enjoy the invitation of your soul to recognize and mature this exceptional spiritual gift for the glory of God and the benefit of humanity.

The clamor and noise of the hectic world outside are distracting and irritating to you in your quest for wisdom. Those closest to you often see you, a 7 soul, as distant and unfeeling, so you may have to work diligently to establish a way of presenting your wisdom in an entertaining and humble manner. You have very strong opinions about your wisdom, which can surface as arrogance. You find it uncomfortable making "small talk" for the sake of convention.

You benefit from being out in nature frequently to recharge your batteries. You are slow to change your attitude and way of living. It will not be easy for you to learn to express emotions and to trust your feelings—subconscious emotional blocks must be overcome in order to accurately tap the intuitive mind.

Soul Number 8

You are best deployed where power, money, management or material challenges are concerned. When you learn to accept the laws of manifestation and work with them, you will attract money for beneficial causes. If you seek money purely for selfish gain, it will likely slip through your fingers as fast as it comes. Look at your attitude toward money. Does the possession of wealth mean more to you than other values in life? Do you feel superior to those who have less? Does material wealth affect your attitude toward friends and acquaintances? Once you let go of the need for money and accept the universal flow, you will have as much as you could possibly need. There should be no anxiety and no fear of loss. By learning to give and use money with love for the divine supplier and with love toward all who share in the flow, you begin to manifest the divine law of supply!

Eights seek power. When the ego is attached to money, it is tempting to use money for power, control and manipulation of others. Once you let go of the ego's attachment to power, the next step is to become empowered from the higher self. Higher direction will guide you through the complex decisions necessary to become an inspired leader. The world will then recognize your inspired leadership qualities.

You have the stamina, poise and confidence to achieve anything you set out to do. You are generous to those you feel have earned it, but you do not give handouts. You dislike weakness and inefficiency. You have an opportunity to pass on your skills and thus enable someone else to develop confidence and competency in his or her calling. You have an excellent ability to recognize potential in others, and life will bring a chance to determine which way you will use this gift, selfishly or genuinely, to assist in the awakening of another person's potential.

There is definite potential for executive leadership in large organizations. Your calling may come in business, community work or government. Whatever it is, you will take control and leave the situation greatly improved by your effort. You have the vision and leadership required to handle the demands leading into the new era.

Soul Number 9

You must learn to let go of every need, and only then will you have all you could want. You have come to serve God and humanity in whatever capacity the higher self directs. Learn to visualize yourself acting as the higher self would have you act. Then, as you perform the duties of life, you will soon find yourself naturally acting in accordance with inner guidance.

Nines dream of a world where there is no misunderstanding, no criticism, no ego threat, no other cause of disharmony and distrust. It is possible to be part of such a world, but one must let go of those human characteristics that underlie these discords. You have the chance to lead the way by living this dream. How can you free yourself? You can do so by visualizing yourself cutting loose from the hang-ups and traps of the personality; and by applying forgiveness and acceptance of grace, the process of cleansing can be accelerated to further enable you to attain detachment.

Nines often develop into inspired artists, poets, inventors or psychics. As a 9 soul, you are blessed with a tolerant, sympathetic and understanding viewpoint, and once the personality no longer distorts higher consciousness, you can develop very accurate intuitive prophetic abilities. However, your generous and emotional nature can put you into predicaments because of an almost inviolate gullibility.

Satisfaction in personal love does not come easily, because you are learning in degrees to move toward an impersonal, universal love. The paradoxical counterpoint of this is that old adage, "When you stop trying so hard to have, it will come." Emotions can be unsettled as you strive for the final release of personality.

Nines dream of a utopian world. Despite the less-than-perfect current world condition, you should not give up your dreams. After all, your message and inspiration may well be the spark to move many others into an awakening of the new dawn. Follow your intuition, follow your dreams and the world will follow you.

Soul Number 11

The 11 soul is similar to the 2 soul. Please review the description of the soul number 2.

The awakened 11 soul possesses the capacity to work on the inner planes and to consciously bring information back for useful application. It can be very easy for you to be so inwardly focused that you function impractically in the everyday, mundane world. At best you function intuitively while keeping your feet grounded in the social reality of our world. You will find yourself concerned with major issues that involve vast numbers of the population.

Many of you excellent channels and psychics have 11 prominently in your charts. You may work consciously with devic beings or inner-plane guides, thereby bringing knowledge or guidance. Awakening others to the many possibilities of life gives you joy, and this inclination attracts you to publications or other media opportunities that allow you to reach out to vast audiences. You may share the suffering you experienced in your own life with others as a means of awakening and healing the masses.

Your idealism can become so saturated with zeal that you lose touch with the individual on your way to aiding the people. Once you have a cause, you are very sure it is the best, which can make you less than tolerant of those you are attempting to convert. You need to be careful not to overpower your converts with excessive initial information. It is a highly kinetic energy that gives you the ready intuition and inventive ability that let you anticipate social trends and public opinion. With your great capacity to inspire the populace, it is quite likely that you will find yourself in a position of prominence at some period of your life.

Soul Number 22

The 22 soul is similar to the 4 soul. Please review the description of soul number 4.

This combination makes 22s inspired dreamers and builders. They are often able to read the etheric and inner-plane blueprints and prepare a foundation for the golden cities of an advanced culture. Once in harmony, 22s attract the financing necessary for laying the foundation for their utopian dreams.

An awakened 22 consciously discerns the inner-plane forces and can then learn to acquire the skills necessary to control subtle inner-plane forces and energies. You recognize other lightworkers and work with them on both the inner and outer planes toward fulfillment of the divine plan on Earth. Your mental foresight and discipline allow you to be part of the forces molding humankind's evolvement. Your inner world of emotions is contained and intense, so you may choose to act out hard-to-express feelings in some form of dramatic outlet. At the same time, your disciplined nature lends itself to the rigors of science, and very accomplished athletes are often a product of the 22's ability to train and organize as well. No matter what field you choose, you are likely to be involved in large organizations or humanistic movements that integrate practical idealism into the real problems that face society.

Prior to the call to higher service, you might hold positions in many types of work. You have learned to build a solid foundation by paying attention to details and learning from each step of progress. As you complete each lesson, it seems like the task becomes less demanding and you move on with growing confidence. Your inner self knows you are an important soul with a masterful task, and you may wonder why the world does not recognize this. Until you have earned the right (through study and application of higher instruction) to know your true work, you tend to suffer with feelings of inferiority, underestimating your worth and diminishing your own capacities.

Soul Number 33

The 33 soul is similar to the 6 soul. Please review the description of the soul number 6.

The 33s serve as counselors and teachers not only to individuals but to mass consciousness as well. To the awakened, this can bring access to the akasha and the inner records. In preparation, you would benefit from a good, solid investigation into the secret teachings and world history from the esoteric perspective. With such a historical perspective, you could assist in reawakening the memories of past civilizations on Earth. Eventually, you may find yourself becoming preoccupied with certain past civilizations that reached great heights of accomplishment before their demise. It could be empowering to both you and those you will teach to bring forth this ancient history.

The natural inclination of the 33 soul is to seek balance and understanding for humankind. Whatever endeavor you choose, you will most likely put much passion and expression into it. Because you hold in your deeper feelings so much, it is difficult for others to grasp what it is you are feeling and what it is you want. Although this can be true for your interactions with those close to you, it is particularly true when you are in social or public situations. An outlet for your efforts at giving to others might be going into a large business venture or expressing yourself through creative interests such as drama or song.

Perhaps you choose to act out a lot of emotions through physical exercise and athletic expression. Whatever you choose, you are driven to do to your utmost ability. As you live true to your inner feelings, your outer manner of expression is an inspiration to all. Your work with large organizations flourishes as you come into an understanding of the inner teachings.

Knowledge of crystals, herbs and the etheric body anatomy is probably a part of your healing repertoire.

Soul Number 44

The 44 soul is similar to the 8 soul. Please review the description of the soul number 8.

Your managerial accomplishments and discipline of faith will serve you well as you are given more and more responsibility and leadership. Perhaps you have struggled to accept your personal power. The presence of this number suggests a strong likelihood of misuse of power in past lives. You will likely encounter situations in this lifetime where you are once again tempted to misuse power or authority. The choice is yours: Will you give in to this temptation or will you become a source of empowerment for others? Many of you will be called upon for your survival skills and common-sense approach to solve problems during a time of major crisis.

The enormous amount of discipline and coordinative talent of the 44 may be channeled into research or practical engineering. You are highly interested in body discipline and balance. You have an enormous amount of bottled-up emotion and energy that you find difficult to articulate and share with others, so acting or entertainment may work as a conveyance of your talents. Another area that would be a natural outlet is the motivational field. As a leader, you strive to see that the pie is distributed equally among all of the children in the kingdom. You are prized for your ability to break things down into component parts and then put them together in such a manner that things get triumphantly done.

You could be called upon to raise money for altruistic groups and endeavors. Your convictions and solid reputation assist in making this successful. Your mastery of form and ritual allow you to bring forth energies from the etheric dimensions. You are an excellent teacher of the art of manifestation.

Soul Number 55

The 55 soul is similar to the 1 soul. Please review the description of the soul number 1.

You have studied the academic theories of humanity as well as religion and the arcane teachings. When you combine your academic studies with your esoteric knowledge of humans, you have a compelling mixture of disciplines, and you will be called upon to teach the relationship of these two disciplines to growing numbers of students. Your expansive range of human experiences gives you a vast reservoir of practical wisdom that you apply in your dealings with others, and your mastery of dance, martial arts and exercise provides an excellent framework from which to teach the subtle energy systems.

There is a saying that "we are what we eat," and you would be a natural in the realm of diet and nutritional counseling. Many people with the 44 are drawn to singing, dancing or theater as a means of communicating their emotions to others.

Your chance of succeeding on your chosen path is quite good. You strive to know the higher will and are at the forefront of techniques and rituals that accelerate humanity's preparation for acclimation into the next dimension. You may be drawn into preparing for travel into outer space. If not, you are a pioneer of travel into inner space.

Soul Number 66

The 66 soul is similar to the 3 soul. Please review the description of the soul number 3.

As you delve more deeply into the ancient wisdoms, you become more humbled and reverent about life. You have learned to heal and counsel others and have established a connection to your Source that is reliable and profound. Helpers of light counsel, guide and assist you in your progress.

You can often become frustrated dealing with the mundane issues of this planet, because your grasp of the divine principles of balance and harmony makes it difficult for you to put up with the incredible emotional instability that many humans display. On the other hand, your inner patience and sensitivity allow you to bring peace and inner harmony to those who seek your help.

Your radiant aspirations are channeled into wonderful works of art and design. You have a talent for color and decoration. You may find yourself working to improve the health environment of buildings and institutions. The desire to find a more perfect world may lead you into the realm of science and research as you seek the remedy or solution for discomfort and disharmony. You are a spokesperson for methods of emotional clearing and balancing.

Soul Number 77

The 77 soul is similar to the 5 soul. Please review the description of the soul number 5.

Because of your mental curiosity, you are inclined to investigate the nature of humans and their spiritual aspirations. Perhaps you were raised in a conventional religious environment but you find that the answers you seek do not come from the old dogmas. As a result, you may remain as an inspired spokesperson within the system, or you may seek an institution that reflects your emerging need for inner contentment. The mystical and esoteric teachings mean much to you.

Along with your well-developed mental package of talents, you have a grasp of structure and integrative techniques to bring ideas into form. You analyze and derive solutions quickly and at best brilliantly, which makes you a sought-after consultant in the field.

You enjoy the physical body and have probably been indulgent to excess along the way in life. Over time and with growing wisdom, however, you have become interested in the fields of nutrition and a naturally healthy diet.

You have an innate sense of knowledge that is not intellectual, but it is wise. You will be active among groups trying to open the minds of the masses.

Soul Number 88

The 88 soul is similar to the 7 soul. Please review the description of the soul number 7.

You find yourself among some of the elite thinkers and policy makers of commerce and education. On the other hand, your inclination toward the alternative also introduces you to those with radical theories of change and reformation. So you work quietly to bring the two divergent circles of thought toward an exchange of information. Your knowledge of subtle energies has helped you persevere through times of skepticism and ridicule.

Underneath a mental umbrella of consciousness, you have a powerful trust in your inner guidance and are able to inspire others even under the most trying of circumstances. You have learned to trust your inner self and encourage others to develop that same inner connection.

Often 88s are blessed with exceptionally developed skills in science, engineering, math and any field of construction and architecture. They want to create a physical environment that reflects the glory of sacred geometry and archetypal building blocks of the cosmos.

Soul Number 99

The 99 soul is similar to the 9 soul. Please review the description of the soul number 9.

People will say you spend so much time with your head in the clouds, it's hard to understand how you stay grounded. A lot of your time is spent tapping into the higher realms of the inner worlds and it is not easy for you to stay grounded, because you have seen the open doors of heaven and it is so inviting to be there.

Along with your loving and sensitive qualities you have some fundamental skills of leadership and organizational acumen. You are a dynamic and magnetic leader when in harmony with inner spirit and outer cause. Having learned the laws of prosperity, you can be an excellent money manager or an outstanding fundraiser in the most positive sense. No matter what talent or career direction you choose, you will always be somehow trying to make it easier for the masses to open their awareness to the glory and beauty of cosmic design.

Integrated-Self Numbers

Integrated Self 1

You are attuned to divine will and flow in rhythm with both the divine and the human aspects of will. By now you have learned to work with all your brothers and sisters and you no longer need to dominate, nor are you intimidated by expressions of will in those with whom you interact. This does not mean that you will be totally at ease with everyone you meet, since some vibrations simply do not touch each other in total compatibility. What it does mean is that you have a healthy respect for individuality and no longer need to be angry or judgmental about another person.

Your keen sense of originality and innovation is an inspiration to many, and your ambition is to awaken originality in all you contact. You meet greatest success at the forefront of endeavors, and you will be called upon to lead, direct and manage. Your powers of concentration and visualization are very keen—others know this of you. You are strict about habit and behavior but are willing to change to improve yourself. Once you have set your sights on something, your concentrated focus enables you to complete the job quickly and fully.

In social matters, 1s are inclined to be independent, rebellious and at the forefront of reformation and change. They are usually outspoken, freethinking and quick to note miscues by those in a role of leadership.

The qualities of originality and independence are the 1s' strengths in business and commerce. You are inventors and innovators. Your independent streak very often leads you into enterprises of your own rather than being held at the mercy of someone you feel is less able or qualified.

In science and academics, 1s are rarely content with the status quo in whatever endeavor they pursue. You are constantly turning over stones to find new and improved ways of doing something. You encourage independent thinking and rally around freedom of study and research. You may start heading in several directions before settling into one specific discipline or study.

In matters of art and entertainment, the 1 is often at the forefront of pushing for change and attempting productions previously unheard of. You are not content to rest very long with something that does not work—or something that *does* work. Your flair for inventive thinking makes you appreciated for seeing how something can be done differently when others think it cannot be done at all.

In sports the 1 is proud to be the leader or best performer on the team. You relish the limelight of success and, by nature, are extremely competitive. As a performer, you are usually quick, dextrose and willing to take risks.

Integrated Self 2

You are comfortable functioning between both worlds, inner and outer. The ease with which you tap the inner planes provides you with an almost uncanny foreknowledge of events affecting your life and the lives of those nearest you. You are able to perceive inner-plane cause, producing outer-plane effect.

Your role is one of mediator, bringing heavenly decrees to humankind on Earth. You also serve as a peacemaker and mediator between factions of disagreeing humans. You seek personal tranquillity by delicate persuasion rather than by force. There is a charm of character that causes others to be at ease in your presence. You give tenderness and sympathy and need the same in return. Your innate intuitive insight enables you to know just what others need—which might be a kind word or the appropriate bouquet of flowers. You work best in association with others and benefit from growing through group consciousness.

In social matters, 2s are arch supporters when it comes to seeking world peace and community harmony. They are noted for their negotiation skills and diplomatic aplomb. Often they believe in sacrificing individual rights for the benefit of the collective population.

In business 2s flourish at middle-management levels and wherever merging or restructuring is taking place. Because they can see both sides of an issue, they are able to find solutions that make both parties feel like winners. Patience and tact are assets that help 2s go a long way in their professions.

In scientific environs, 2s are often found in the areas of administration, public relations and communications. As researchers they are careful with detail and meticulous in their procedures. In academics they are frequently found in administrative positions or in the area of communications; if they are instructors, they often teach literature and social studies or liberal arts.

Many philanthropists and patrons of the arts are people with the integrated-self number 2 prominent in their charts. As artists they often portray a message of sympathy and compassion toward humanity. They find the universal threads of life that are common among all people and seek to encourage harmony through their expression.

In sports 2s are often coaches, motivators and assistants. They are able to grasp the principles of their chosen field and find strategy as important as ability in competition. They prefer teamwork to individual stardom and will willingly make needed sacrifices for the team.

Integrated Self 3

You are a constant source of joy, spreading your good news through words, music, painting or writing. Your inspiration and vivid imagination are apt tools for bringing greater light into a weary world. You can get across an important moral in your teaching by using popular thought and language. You have overcome hesitation and inhibition of your creativity. This allows you to express a full range of creative interests wherever your higher guidance leads.

Your previous learning lets you flow through life experiences, balancing comfortably in the expression of both your masculine and feminine self. This innate attunement gives you insight that enables you to help others you perceive as being out of balance. Your artistic and creative work stimulates the upper chakras, thus elevating the aspirations of humankind. Your natural integrity and cheerful disposition are like a healing tonic. In friendship you are sincere and patient. As your creative fire is elevated into the higher chakras, you may experience a waning of sexual drive. Consider it a growth rather than a loss; you are compensated by increased creativity above the sexual plane.

Threes are the consummate socialites in the best meaning of the word. They love to make others feel comfortable and at home. Their gift for speech finds them active around social issues and in spreading the word of enlightenment around the globe. They mix, mingle and travel among all races, creeds and mixtures of human society, bringing the message of life and joy to all.

In business threes are frequently the communicators of the industry. They are found in sales, promotions, public relations and educational formats of all kinds. They are creative and relish opportunities to bring new ideas and untried programs to the forefront of application. They lobby for freedom of speech and individual expression.

In the world of academics, 3s are found among both the communicators and the instructors. They enjoy being at the front of the classroom or symposium. More often they are the reporters and spokespersons for science rather than pure research scientists. However, that does not exclude them from research. Here they are innovatively and imaginatively involved and are often at the forefront when it comes to identifying outdated methods and ideas.

The 3 is the archetypal number of the artist, so you are right at home being involved in any form of artistic expression. In an effort to expand humankind's self-understanding and self-expression, 3s are an inspiration to many because of their ability to spontaneously and comfortably reveal feelings and emotions. As artists they convey feelings through their art that other people feel but are unable to recognize or articulate. Through exposure to their artwork, the viewer is provided with an outlet through which to experience and communicate awakening revelations and sensations from within. Imagination and articulation of pure feelings are the vanguard of a 3's way of life.

In the sports world, 3s are found around the promotion of sports and wherever aesthetics are involved. As athletic performers, they are graceful and articulate in the expression of their chosen sport. They enjoy the pageantry and ceremony of the sport perhaps more than just the pure competition.

Integrated Self 4

You know what your inner work is and you proceed happily in the performance of your role in the plan. Others may encourage you to take time out to have fun, but they do not realize the great enjoyment you experience when you are doing your assigned task to the best of your ability. Fours at this point in consciousness can tap the universal blueprint to comprehend the design for Earth. With higher inspiration, you become the builders of form on Earth, working to establish the kingdom on Earth.

You are a natural organizer, but your systematic and methodical nature may appear too cumbersome to the more rapidly vibrating numbers. Once you have set a deadline, you will work feverishly to complete your project on time. Your work is an extension of your word and trust—you take pride in what you do and it shows. You are recognized for your grasp and effective usage of factual data, your dependability and your endurance. Self-control and discipline are central to your lifestyle, and you expect the same from others.

In social matters, the 4 is more often than not active around the more conservative issues of public interest. You are ardent about law and order and believe it is an individual's responsibility to make something of his or her life. Although you will lend a hand to help others help themselves, you will not do something for them.

The 4's inclination is to be conservative, taking each step only after the previous one has been properly completed. In business 4s are known for their steadiness and for being dedicated to long-term organizational commitment. They have the patience to see a project all the way through and do best in a military setting or in one with prescribed rituals and protocol.

In academics and science, 4s can be demanding and perhaps a bit ponderous in their manner of expression. They ask much of themselves and expect much from others. They enjoy the solidarity and prestige of earned degrees and credentials, and they strictly adhere to the rules. Curious about the foundation of life and the nature of matter, 4s want to better understand natural laws and then work to find how to be more efficient at putting theoretical knowledge to practical use.

The pure 4 is not as frequently found in the arts as some of the other numbers. Artistic expression may be an avocation or hobby rather than the prime profession. When they are active as artists, 4s are usually late bloomers because of the time they take to master a chosen field of expression. Fours are frequently found as patrons of the arts or as investors in that arena.

In sports 4s are often prominent in the areas of training, bodybuilding and coaching. They are steady performers and may not be superstars as often as some of the other numbers. However, they are good coaches, managers and trainers. Fours emphasize the importance of the body and its health, nutrition and well-being.

Integrated Self 5

You have finally released the shackles of life and live ebulliently in your complete state of freedom; you have learned that freedom comes from natural adherence to divine law. The temptation of the senses and cunning of the lower mind you have mastered; your consciousness has expanded the inner senses and curiosity of the intuitive mind. Through projection of inner being, you can travel and explore happenings throughout the world on many levels. This capacity for extended sensory awareness makes you a valuable source for new ideas, rapid solutions and alternative methods of dealing with the innumerable changes and challenges coming in the transitional years just ahead.

You will have opportunities for travel, mingling with people from diverse backgrounds and viewpoints. Your ability to draw upon these human encounters for storytelling enables you to be most effective as a lecturer or teacher. You are in touch with your dharmic guidance and are free to move with all your life experiences in confidence and joyous anticipation of each event that takes place.

In business 5s keep things hopping. Their restlessness can be helpful to offset routine and complacency, and their glib tongue and smooth manner make them good sales people. They are drawn to the fields of entertainment, travel, sports, advertising and working with the public. When attracted to law, they defend personal rights and fight against abuses. They excel in speculation and chance, but this can get out of control and bring loss to themselves and/or their clients.

In academics they make excellent instructors and lecturers. Fives are often drawn to areas such as psychology, religion, the humanities or other fields that help people learn more about helping themselves. They enjoy the encouragement of self-awareness and teach from personal experience rather than dry intellectual detachment. In science they enjoy integrating ideas from various disciplines of thought. Fives tend to be eclectic, blending the old with the new to integrate variances of cultural ideologies through time.

As artists 5s are often multitalented, mercurial, witty and light. In particular, they make good satirists and mimes. If they are not in the spotlight, they are found in the arena of creative public venues. As artists 5s draw from rich personal experience and project that into their media.

In sports 5s are characteristically known for their flair for excitement and participation. They are good team members, often doing several things well rather than being a superstar at one specialty. They are usually quick in body and excel at sports requiring dexterity and agility.

Integrated Self 6

You have come into an understanding of the role you have chosen to serve humankind. Each day the pleasure of rendering assistance echoes through your heart in thanksgiving for this chance to serve God and humans. The hours may be long and material rewards meager, but the struggle of selfless services pays rich dividends on the karmic ledger sheet.

Family, home and close friends are paramount in your life, and you seek an ideal home and spouse. You live in accord with higher ideals that many find impossible to accept, let alone attempt. When fully integrated, the 6 individual has learned to accept self and others; only then are these ideals truly available to him or her.

You are a natural counselor and guide and are sometimes referred to as a cosmic mother or cosmic father. You are generous when rendering assistance and have learned to give with no expectation of receiving anything in return. You benefit from incorporating your knowledge of music, color and vibration into your emotional counseling of others.

In society 6s are the helpers and healers. They are attracted to causes that help eliminate the suffering they see in the world around them. They are sought after for their counsel and guidance. Loyal friends and caring associates, 6s are the glue that helps hold society together.

Sixes in business are very often found in service-oriented commercial enterprises—more often than in areas requiring purely competitive efforts. They seek to bring information and comfort to a world in turmoil. Often they are the whistleblowers and are among those who speak out in moral indignation against injustice and abuse.

In academics and science, 6s are often found in medical research, anthropological fields or areas of study that seek to solve the riddle of human nature. They strive to alleviate disease and disharmony. Their compassion and concern for humanity can find them active in the areas of literature, religion and psychology.

Sixes are drawn toward artistic ways of expression. They are often supporters of the arts, they are practicing artists. The 6 artist brings out the depth of the expression of human feelings and struggles with issues of social evolution.

In sports 6s are frequently associated with injuries and maintaining the athletic body (that is, they are doctors, trainers, physical therapists). They may be concerned with nutrition and other special needs of athletic competitors. When involved as athletes, they are team-oriented and very meticulous about training and health issues.

Integrated Self 7

Your inner perception and meditative nature let you delve deeply into the future of humanity. Your far-reaching insight enables you to ponder and prepare philosophical ideas that are literally ahead of their times. You may be left very much alone in your thinking, but a few will grasp your advanced concepts. Expect to be appreciated only occasionally for ideas ahead of their time.

You prefer to keep to yourself and should make more of an effort to share your thoughts—after all, you can be a convincing and articulate spokesperson on abstract matters. You are scientific and thorough in your intellectual interests, excelling in specialty work of a scientific, abstract or metaphysical nature. You work quietly behind the scenes, preparing the 4s and 8s with the necessary foresight to get the concrete work done. You can see long-term plans clearly, thus enabling the more practical to better prepare for the future.

Sevens are often detached commentators and observers of society and its endless intricacies, and they discuss, analyze and theorize on how to make it better. However, they are somewhat reluctant to get their hands wet and therefore just participate in social matters. Frequently 7s are loners and isolated personalities.

In business 7s make excellent strategists and analysts. For better or for worse, once you have made up your mind to do something, it is difficult to persuade you otherwise. Your detachment can be valuable when more emotional types of people plunge impulsively into a bad situation.

Sevens are frequently found in the halls of science and academia. You are natural scholars who wish to turn over every possible stone in the exploration of truth. You dig and delve relentlessly into the laws of nature and the mysteries of humanity. You are natural detectives and investigators of whatever mystery intrigues you.

Oftentimes 7s are art critics and analysts. When practicing as artists, they strive to reveal the depth and seriousness of humankind's search for self-understanding and truth. Frequently 7s are sculptors or express themselves in some other artistic form. Literary 7s are inclined toward in-depth novels or philosophically-based treatises.

In sports 7s are frequently found as commentators and analysts. When involved in competition, they are often specialists in intricate types of athletic performance.

Integrated Self 8

People naturally turn to you for leadership, and they respect your decisions. You have learned to exercise authority according to higher guidance in conjunction with divine plan, so life will automatically put you into positions of authority, even command. As long as you see the one Source as your commander, your success will be unlimited.

You are a living example of how to work the laws of manifestation through proper visualization, expectation of divine assistance, appreciation for that received and application for the greater good of humankind. Once in this flow, all your mystical and spiritual needs are met at exactly the right moment. You are a master on all levels of expression, and you will have the chance to help many more work toward that.

You give your skill and leadership to humankind purely for the goal of building a better world. Eights are often called into situations that have broken down and need revitalized leadership, and you like nothing better than meeting such a challenge while allowing others to find faith and confidence in their own potential.

In social matters, 8s can be found leading fundraising or charity drives. They enjoy the limelight and public plaudits as much as they enjoy the protocol and rites of lodges and sororities. Eights also support practical philosophies and self-help teachings.

Eights prefer a stable environment where they can attain their desired goals. This might include being a part of large organizations in commerce, the military or the government. Wherever they serve, they almost always end up in positions of supervision, management or leadership. They are good troubleshooters and relish the challenge of detecting inefficiencies within a system and then making improvements. Their savvy at dissecting and assimilating information makes them good in the boardroom or at handling reports and presentations. They make excellent money managers, such as investment brokers or real-estate agents. On the negative side, 8s can become unscrupulous and overbearing.

If drawn to science, 8s are often inclined toward practical application, such as engineering, rather than research, since they like to apply the laws of science to practical matters.

In the arts, they are more often patrons and administrators than practicing artists; they more often own a gallery than show their paintings. As artists their abilities come naturally, and they may not seem to need as much training or discipline as other artists. Individuals with this number often achieve success and recognition by the public.

In sports the 8 likes to take command and is a fierce competitor; 8s make excellent coaches and managers. An 8 is more likely to own the team than be a player on it.

Integrated Self 9

You have come to a turning point in consciousness—you have had the opportunity to accumulate the mastery of each vibration, which allows you now to serve as a universal helper. The lessons of this number are particularly difficult to learn, because they involve the process of letting go of the attachment to ego and personality. That is, you must learn to be *in* the world, but not *of* the world. Your intuition tunes to the utopia blueprint being prepared now in the inner planes, and you will have a part in making these dreams become reality in your world.

When you have learned to let go of the need for possessions, power, wealth and self-gratification of the lower self, all of the above can come to you easily and appropriately. You share your universal love and gifts generously, help the poor and hindered, assist others with their responsibilities and give encouragement to the downtrodden.

The 9 as the integrated-self number is a highly intuitive, inspired and artistic vibration. You are poetic and prophetic in your use of words and other expressive modes. Your eye for beauty and your standards of perfection give you a disposition that reaches for the stars, and there is a good chance you may become one of the first to catch one.

Socially you seek the high road of service and are attracted to causes that seek to benefit humankind. Your idealism leads you through many philosophies and ideologies in the hope of discovering a way to a utopian world. You are found among the eccentrics and unusual personalities of the world.

The visionary aspect of the 9 carries over into the business world: You see possibilities before others do. You sense the need for a product or service before the time for that product or service has come. However, you may not be as practical as others in the implementation of ideas and therefore do well surrounded by a team of well-grounded and sensible associates.

In academic settings and scientific arenas, 9s are often intent upon creating a utopian world, regardless of what branch of study they follow. They dream of improving the world so that humankind can live in a better environment. They enjoy the abstract philosophies and poetic literatures of the world.

Nines make sublime artists and entertainers. Their natural creative talents are abundant, and they are often leaders in the fields of imagination and presentation of new forms of expression. They capture the drama, delight and despair of human growth with a rich appreciation for archetypes and universal metaphors.

In athletics and sports, 9s are usually high-strung and finely-tuned instruments of their chosen endeavor. Their enjoyment stems from the success that comes out of team effort, out of the merging of personalities to accomplish collective goals.

Integrated Self 11

You are driven by the notion that you have a particular destiny to serve the human race. No one can dissuade you from your course once you have recognized the way. Develop caution and discretion to keep on the newfound path. Even the most idealistic of efforts can go astray when working with the mass consciousness.

People will seek you out for counsel, because you can supply them with logical, common-sense information blended with intuitive insight. Your impersonal perspective enables you to provide solutions without becoming involved in emotional entanglements. You can see that considerable improvement is possible in the world and work tirelessly to bring about needed change. There is a strong likelihood that you will reach a level of public recognition, but you are content to serve in the role God gave you, no matter how meager that role might appear to the world around you.

Integrated Self 22

You have probably worked in many different positions and jobs in your lifetime, always feeling within your heart that someday you would have a particular task to fulfill. Now you have begun to see your role in the plan and can start the inner work on your evolutionary sojourn. You can see into Earth's plan, perhaps deeper than most of humanity. With that access to inner design, you are a part of those constructing the future institutions and organizations that will soon serve jointly with the hierarchy and angelic hosts to reestablish God's plan on Earth. You could well find yourself attracted to large groups or institutions that seek to benefit humanity. By the end of your life, you may have acquired so much personal wealth that you become the one to support such benevolent endeavors as being a patron or philanthropist.

At the appropriate time, you will be joined by other lightworkers, and by inner illumination, you will know them and they will know you. You are truly a master mason who has a chance to participate in building a new world, stone by stone, following divine order with each addition of etheric mortar.

Integrated Self 33

When you reach this level of self-growth, you will finally be freed from restraints and will be able to serve humankind without limitations. It is like a fond dream coming true. You will be part of an organization or group whose work it is to care for and heal thousands. There will be little time for you to think of yourself—even the inclination to do so is gone.

You would be wise to accumulate as much knowledge as possible about the divine origin and history of humankind from direct experience with the akasha. This research will be useful for your teaching and counseling. Since much of your work will be involved with the astral or emotional level of humankind, you would also benefit from a thorough knowledge of the esoteric anatomy, particularly in relation to the feeling nature.

Integrated Self 44

You have struggled long and hard with issues of authority and rigid personalities in high places, and your accomplished sense of integration and personal empowerment allows you to face such people on an equal footing. An excellent administrator and organizer, you now find yourself working to elevate the consciousness of the commercial or academic leadership.

Your financial skills are particularly appreciated in times of down markets and reverse monetary trends. Few may be aware of the amount of time you have spent incorporating the deeper arcane teachings into your being. You are an excellent example of one living the law without having much to say about it out loud.

Integrated Self 55

Your passion for life and your unbridled enthusiasm for learning are an inspiration to all who meet you. You walk on the path of the masters and yet say little that would indicate this. Your mysterious nature piques the curiosity of the masses and attracts seekers to you like a huge magnet. You enjoy being a conduit of information and willingly direct those who seek an appropriate path, but you do not relish the thought of having a following or being a guru figure.

You find yourself around spokespersons for fitness, health and diet. Your knowledge of esoteric anatomy is thorough, even though you may choose not to reveal such in public. Your own regimen of developing extended consciousness is simple and awesome, and you share with a trusted few some of the higher dynamics of the energy dance.

Integrated Self 66

Your life is enriched by connections and friendships with accomplished personalities of numerous talents and professional achievements, and you move among a crowd that has considerable impact upon mass consciousness. You lend support to those who aspire to heighten the awareness of humanity through elevated art and education.

Your environmental concerns are echoed by a rapidly growing number of world citizens. You live in close touch with the elemental kingdoms and inner-world helpers of light, and your knowledge of communications allows you to spread the message of awakening to a cross section of culture.

Integrated Self 77

You have studied many religious and spiritual philosophies of the world, and you have found a spiritual practice that fills the need of both mind and soul. Many approach you to inquire as to why your life appears to be so meaningful and at ease, and you are glad to share your truth with sincere seekers. You are active in academic circles that are open to exploring the planetary transition into expanded dimensions of awareness.

Your own personal journey into mind expansion has taken you through some pretty rough roads of misuse and overuse. You are an outspoken crusader when it comes to informing the public about the multigenerational damage from drug and alcohol abuse.

Integrated Self 88

You have accomplished much in the material world of trade and competition. The laws of prosperity that once eluded you have become second nature in your drive to success. It is, however, your humanitarian instincts that have led you to seek an accomplishment that is greater than fame and money. When called upon to take charge, you can be an inspiring and uplifting leader, and your organizational and administrative skills will be recognized. However, you have taken time to withdraw from the frantic world of business and reflect upon the business of spiritual empowerment.

Your mind struggles to grasp the nature of the awesome might contained in the spirit of humankind. You seek to comprehend the nature of the universal laws of cohesion and structure while trying to unlock these forces in a positive and efficient manner. You can be attracted to communicating these principles through writing or research. You sense the drama of the human struggle and seek a way to make life easier for others. You may well attract enough money to become a benefactor of humane causes. You are a supporter of science and research that is on the threshold of bringing the universe to our doorstep.

Integrated Self 99

You have suffered much and have overcome many hardships on your road of life. You had a lot, and it burdened you; you had a little, and it troubled you. Then one day you let go of everything, and since then you have had everything you need. Your eloquence and refined manner attract respect from the dignified and cultured. When frustrated you may adopt a slightly sarcastic manner of communicating your message to others, and this negative side leads to cynicism and doubt. You are equally at ease with the casual and common as you are with those upon thrones. As a philanthropist and community activist, you are known for your patronage of the arts and the creative genius in humankind.

Others may not know as much about your own accomplishments in the arts, because you are selective about the people you introduce to your inner world. Those of you who become known will be popular as icons of taste and refinement of character. Your awareness of the evolved ones in other dimensions is maintained with discretion and care, and you know when the time is right for a more open revelation of your secret doctrines.

Changes in the Name

The beginning student of numerology often has many questions regarding the change of a name and the numerological implications. The full name at birth along with the date of birth make up the natal chart for numerology, much like the date of birth is the basis for the natal chart for astrology. It remains the underlying foundation and does not go away with the use of a different name later in life. The numbers of the integrated self, soul and personality remain a permanent influence, just like you remain the same underneath even if you put on different garments to change your appearance.

The change of your name does, however, have much meaning, and its ramifications should be taken into serious consideration. When you change the name, for whatever reason, you do change the vibrational pattern you emanate. Recent university studies have proven that people react differently to different names. They respond differently to Jimmy than to James; they expect different behavior from Sara Jean than from Peggy Sue.

The use of a nickname, an entertainment name or a married name does change the vibration. However, it does not eliminate the presence of the natal influence. When changing a name, it can be important to consider these underlying vibrational patterns along with your desired goal.

Throughout my career, television personalities, movie stars, organizations, artists, singers, businesses and people from all walks of life have consulted me on the numerical vibration of a new name they have chosen. The first rule when creating a new name is that the name has to stand on its own: If it is going to be for promotion or accomplishing positive results, it must have a "ring" to it that produces a positive response in the given social context. Numerology cannot make up for an ill-chosen name.

When working with a client to determine a name, I try to get to the client's real motive and intent. We work together to get a name that is numerically appropriate and at the same time has a nice vocal rhythm. Consideration is given to the client's natal name so that the new name resonates harmoniously with the original name.

There are doubts and ethical questions regarding the naming of a child by numbers alone. I personally do not pick names for children, since I believe that is a matter between child and parents. However, I will give insight regarding potential names that parents may present to me. Remember the old saying, "Be careful about what you ask for because you may get it"? When parents select a name numerologically, they usually do not see the unconscious nature of the selection they make. Later, as the child gets older, certain unconscious patterns of behavior emerge that disturb the parents right in their psychological blind spot.

I do believe that if you select a name numerologically, you will attract a soul seeking to act out that pattern. I did name my first child with heavy numerological expectation. With the next one, I was working toward a specific numerical combination when I came across a name that did not fit the numerical parameters. However, the name appealed to both my wife and me and I never got around to achieving the desired numerical intent. Time will tell the outcome of these ramifications.

When calculating the numbers for any name other than the name given at birth, I use a different terminology that gives a better indication of the meaning of secondary names: the outer you, the inner you and the accomplished you.

The Outer You

The number of the outer you gives a clue as to the face you present to the public. It is your outer persona. It is the outer garment you have put on to present a certain image. You can gain some insight into the meaning of the number by looking at the characteristics of the numbers given in Chapter 4 or, if it is a master number, in Chapter 5.

To determine the number for the outer you, first add the numbers for all the consonants in the new name—that is, the name that is not the full name given at birth. Reduce this number to a single digit, except when master numbers appear.

The Inner You

The number of the inner self—the inner you—reveals your introspective nature, what is going on inside of you. It sheds more light upon how you see yourself (not always accurately) as a result of this identity, and it gives clues regarding the internal processing going on as a result of your new name. To get a feel for this number, you can read the equivalent karmic accumulation number in Chapter 10. They are not the same, but they are close enough in dynamics to give you a starting point to work from in your interpretation.

To get the number of the inner you, add the numbers for all the vowels and reduce the sum to a single digit, unless it is a master number. Remember that this applies to all names other than the full name at birth.

The Accomplished You

The number of the accomplished you provides clarity as to what you want to attain as a result of taking the new name you have chosen. It defines goals and aspirations. To better understand the meaning of this number, read the appropriate section on the personality number in this chapter. The two numbers are not the same, but the personality number gives you a sense of the dynamics of the lesson.

You have probably figured out by now that the number of the accomplished you is the sum of the numbers for all the letters in the new name reduced to a single digit, unless the sum is a master number.

An Example

Here is a sample chart utilizing these three numbers:

M	E	G	R	Y	A	N
4	5	7	9	7	1	5
Accomplished you: $4 + 5 + 7 + 9 + 7 + 1 + 5 = 38 = 11(2)$						
Inner you: $5 + 7 + 1 = 13 = 4$						
Outer you: $4 + 7 + 9 + 5 = 25 = 7$						

A quick glance tells us that this star has worked hard to look natural and be charming. The success she has attained is apparent to all. Very often superstars have 11s in the chart. The 3 and the 8 accentuate her charm and suggest she has the potential to make a lot of money. You can look more closely at the appropriate interpretations to further investigate this chart. You can also find her natal chart in Appendix A.

The Planes of Expression

The letters of the alphabet can be delineated in yet another way, to give us further insight into the interpretation of a numerology chart. Here the letters are arranged into four categories that reveal the fundamental tendencies of your intellectual or mental character, your emotional temperament, your physical proclivities and your intuitive or spiritual inclinations.

To determine the placement of the letters on the appropriate level, use the chart below:

Physical:	D, E, M, W (4)
Emotional:	B, I, O, R, S, T, X, Z (8)
Mental:	A, G, H, J, L, N, P, (7)
Intuitive:	C, F, K, Q, U, V, Y, (7)
	= 26 Letters of the Alphabet

As a rule of thumb, when a preponderance of letters appears on the physical plane, the individual is practical, focused on mundane issues and concerned with material needs in the world. Those with a high number of emotional letters are creative, artistic and react to life more on an emotional basis rather than a factual one. If the letters in your name lean heavily toward the mental plane, you are intellectually oriented, using your head for business, teaching, leadership and related fields. When the greatest number of letters appears on the intuitive plane, the consciousness is inclined to be more psychic and artistic, and the individual often lives in a realm of idealism and imagination unless other factors in the chart help to ground his or her lofty speculation.

Note that the descriptions in the following pages are broken into three descriptive phases. Use these as a guideline by which you can measure your own manifestation of attitude. When you recognize excesses, you can bring about change through self-discipline or methods of self-help. By studying the tendencies indicated through numerology, you can become aware of many new avenues of developing and expanding all facets of your life.

Here is an example for determining the planes of expression for a name:

BARBARA ANETTE KNOTTINGHAM: 25 letters total	
	Numbers on the Planes of Expression
Physical:	E E M (3)
Emotional:	B R B R T T O T T I (10)
Mental:	A A A A N N N N G H A (11)
Intuitive:	K (1)
	= 25 letters

Counting the letters at the beginning and at the end is just a way of confirming that your addition is accurate.

Following is a more detailed description of how the numbers on the planes of expression influence you. These are just brief sketches, and you will want to add your own observations as you become more experienced in the use of numbers.

1 on the Planes

Physical

Assertive: Restless, enjoys athletics and competition, starts many projects without completing things, overactive, dislikes delays, has headaches.

Passive: Procrastinates, careless with material goods.

Harmonious: Can be a starter or leader, original in hobbies and vocations or work, knows how to kindle interest and get others started, prefers work with variety and change.

Emotional

Assertive: Is fickle and emotionally unreliable, attempts to dominate or manipulate others' feelings, puts on a rough exterior, is restless.

Passive: Is afraid to engage in emotional relationships, demands attention without giving in return, has difficulty trusting feelings.

Harmonious: Enjoys meeting new acquaintances, is enthusiastic, does not care for subterfuge, is optimistic.

Mental

Assertive: Needs to win arguments and debates for ego's sake, forces own thoughts upon others, is stubborn.

Passive: Is unsure of where he/she stands, makes decisions after it is too late, is easily talked out of personal beliefs.

Harmonious: Is an original and quick thinker, likes to solve new problems, follows own beliefs and opinions.

Intuitive

Intuition hits like a lightning strike; with 4, 7 or 8 on the mental plane is likely to follow logic rather than trust intuition; original ideas need to be developed into reality. May inspire new directions.

2 on the Planes

Physical

Assertive: Can get too involved with minor details of dress, work and so on; chooses personal items to please or impress others; enjoys sports of strategy rather than of power.

Passive: Lacks courage to take self-initiative, wants every detail in order before making a move, holds on to worn-out or useless items for sentimental reasons.

Harmonious: Works well with others to get the job done, is able to see the needs of others clearly, enjoys dealing with factual information to make a point, enjoys dancing and artistic hobbies.

Emotional

Assertive: Is hurt readily by criticism, speaks impulsively and critically to others when everything does not go just so, is overly self-conscious.

Passive: Has negative moods, worries excessively, withholds complaints, relies heavily on another's support, uses acerbic speech.

Harmonious: Has a good feel for evaluating people and making decisions; gives encouragement to others; is naturally at ease with various types of people; is calm, patient and poised.

Mental

Assertive: Becomes encumbered with too much detail, manipulates statistics to support own opinion, is unyielding and has fixed attitude, can pursue needless incidentals to extreme, distorts logic, is rhetorical.

Passive: Is unwilling to consider varying viewpoints, is intolerant, is unable to communicate personal ideas, needs others' support when stating a position.

Harmonious: Sees both sides of a position fairly, has good judgment when reviewing facts plus accurate gut feeling, is a storehouse of knowledge and meaningful trivia, is logical and factual, is firm but fair with decisions.

Intuitive

Needs to trust intuition and gut-level feelings, is psychic, has unusual ideas and visions, is sensitive to inner moods of the mass consciousness. Intuition may help solve personal conflicts and yield clues to enhance cooperation with those close to you.

3 on the Planes

Physical

Assertive: Scatters talents in too many directions, neither systematic nor disciplined; is oversexed; cannot make imaginative ideas work practically; has gaudy taste in dress and decorum.

Passive: Squanders potential talents and creative abilities, is asexual, may have problems with creative organs, has difficulty putting feelings into form.

Harmonious: Has lovely voice, is artistic and has creative ability, dislikes restrictions, likes beautiful attire and home, enjoys nature and natural products, travels.

Emotional

Assertive: Overreacts to someone else's criticism of his/her work or ability; is impulsive, superficial; emotions overcome reason under pressure, has variable emotions.

Passive: Feelings are hidden under fears of criticism; has repressed emotions; is unable to plan ahead; is listless; is vain about personal dress and belongings; is oversensitive to criticism, whether real or imagined.

Harmonious: Is expressive, a good friend, pleasant; spreads joy; is adventurous in personal affairs; works for appreciation and needs recognition; is intuitive.

Mental

Assertive: Ideas and thinking may be too imaginative to have practical value, is unable to convince the masses to see his/her personal viewpoint, colors facts with personal feelings and opinions, has controversial ideas.

Passive: Is unimaginative and dull, thinks things out but acts on impulse, exaggerates ideas and facts to compensate for fears of inferiority, is confused by emotional issues.

Harmonious: Is creative and imaginative in thinking, many feelings go into decisions, is not too serious, takes life as it comes, is colorful and lighthearted when discussing philosophical ideas and concepts.

Intuitive

Artistic in comprehension of intuitive and psychic impulses, inspired in art or speech, must overcome sexual guilt to best receive impulses. Intuitive side may open up or reveal clues to possible outlets for various talents.

4 on the Planes

Physical

Assertive: Overworks self, is harsh as a boss or supervisor, overestimates skills to compensate for poor self-image, takes work seriously, can pay too much attention to procedures without getting the work done.

Passive: Is stubborn about alternative work procedures, is lazy, feels work is below his/her dignity, is uncoordinated, must work hard to discipline body.

Harmonious: Is dependable, loyal employee; executes others' directions well; is capable; is economical, dislikes waste; does job well.

Emotional

Assertive: Possessive with personal relations and personal belongings, domineering, controls emotions, resents regulations and authority, has conflicts with aggressive people.

Passive: Temper builds slowly and explodes when pushed too far, dislikes restriction, is uncomfortable unless in control of emotional relationships, forgets to consider others.

Harmonious: Is loyal and patient, overcomes others' negativity, has difficulty enjoying spontaneity of feelings, is generous and warm-hearted with family.

Mental

Assertive: Studies long and hard so he/she will not be shown up, has too much pride of thought, has to be shown to believe, dislikes speculation.

Passive: Has fixed, opinionated ideas and prejudices; refuses to change mind even when facts prove his/her opinion wrong; hesitation and excessive caution causes him/her to miss opportunities; is envious of those who are successful.

Harmonious: Is thorough and exacting, is analytical, has managerial ability, has technological ability, can carry a project through from idea to finished product.

Intuitive

Is uncomfortable with mystical and intuitive experiences, does not follow through on inspiration unless practical, prefers conventional religion and studies, has inventive ability. May shed some light upon new career or work opportunity.

5 on the Planes

Physical

Assertive: Is on the move often; cannot stick to a job or to personal responsibility; seeks escape in sex, alcohol, drugs or gambling; suffers from nerves; takes chances.

Passive: Fears change, does not like to perform in front of many people, is always tired, has difficulty making new friends, has sexual problems.

Harmonious: Has good dexterity and physical prowess, enjoys travel and people, has sales ability, benefits from working with many people, is adaptable to changes in circumstances, is a good speaker.

Emotional

Assertive: Dislikes getting too close emotionally, has many types of adventures, can misrepresent feelings, is overly frank and brusque, seeks risks for kicks, has disregard for others.

Passive: Has difficulty letting go of outworn relations, uses others and then leaves, can be cruel and cold, is unable to enjoy and benefit from life experiences, has unpredictable outbursts.

Harmonious: Can be comfortable with different people and make them feel the same, is able to adjust to different temperaments, likes to probe and analyze others' feelings, is impatient, has variable moods that are superficial and short lived.

Mental

Assertive: Cannot stand monotony, is deceptive, uses intellect to prey on the less fortunate, likes to study bizarre and unusual subjects, changes opinions frequently.

Passive: Has sluggish mind, prefers pat answers and social norms to independent thought, needs to learn mental discipline, is repetitive.

Harmonious: Is flexible, curious and witty; is a mercurial thinker; needs to get out of set routines; investigates many subjects but none very deeply; is quick to catch on to things.

Intuitive

Can tap deep, cosmic mysteries of the universe and humankind, is a natural occultist and metaphysician, can become a crusader of some inspired revelation, is inventive, is artistic, may lead one to inspirational literature or ideas.

6 on the Planes

Physical

Assertive: Gets in other people's way, worries more about something than actually getting it done, is exacting, has poor taste in clothing and home decor.

Passive: Is upset with less than perfection in self and others, takes shortcuts, overevaluates own importance to boost ego, is usually somewhat physically frail, must work diligently to build body strength.

Harmonious: Often displays artistic touch, chooses career of service or assistance to others, is willing to handle responsibility, enjoys pets and plants, works for human welfare and justice.

Emotional

Assertive: Is too concerned about little setbacks in own and others' lives, remembers embarrassing experiences longer than necessary; feelings are hurt easily; is irritable and cranky.

Passive: Worries about potential pitfalls and misfortunes, can be a hypochondriac, gets touchy about certain personal issues.

Harmonious: Knows how to work effectively with other people's problems and worries, brings harmony into the home and working environment, can keep another's trust, has high integrity, is calm.

Mental

Assertive: Is sensitive to criticism about ideas, carries many imagined and unnecessary burdens, lets world conditions and suffering upset his/her mind, meddles in others' business.

Passive: Has callous disregard for another's situation, is self-centered in thinking, is unable to solve problems effectively, is lethargic.

Harmonious: Handles responsibility with efficient and confident ease, is a problem solver in personal or business matters.

Intuitive

Is inclined to be conventional, has personal religious experiences and faith; must learn to live and express own ideals rather than living by someone else's standards; may have breakthroughs in understanding how to serve humankind; may show the best way to serve.

7 on the Planes

Physical

Assertive: Is timid, prefers to be reclusive, analyzes all events rather than accepting and enjoying them, prefers individual activities to team sports, is rigid, does not accept things at face value.

Passive: Does not prepare endeavors thoroughly; takes too much time to make decisions; can become aloof, rude and critical.

Harmonious: Is analytical and thorough in work conducted, is scientific in nature, is reserved, is usually conservative, does not enjoy crowds or noise.

Emotional

Assertive: Is reserved and aloof, has difficulty establishing new friendships, stays in the background on social occasions, is disgruntled.

Passive: Has difficulty making conversation with new acquaintances, is very secretive about personal feelings and experiences, overanalyzes feelings, represses emotions.

Harmonious: Has deep and long-lasting feelings although not easily expressed, is loyal, uses discretion and caution, struggles to make thinking and feelings compatible.

Mental

Assertive: Analytical mind is so intense that everything goes through the mental microscope, leaving very little spontaneous enjoyment of life; isolates himself/herself and is reclusive; is overly aggressive with personal opinions.

Passive: Weighs everything analytically and then acts on impulse, holds resentment too long when intellectually humiliated or embarrassed.

Harmonious: Is an excellent technician, scientist or analytical advisor in many fields; likes to examine and investigate ideas and situations with scientific precision and thoroughness, can communicate ideas well when discussing a familiar topic, enjoys quiet and peace.

Intuitive

Can tap deep cosmic mysteries of the universe and humanity, is a natural occultist and metaphysician, can become a crusader of some inspired revelation, is inventive, is artistic. May lead one to inspirational literature or ideas.

8 on the Planes

Physical

Assertive: Has to dominate any situation, uses money for selfish and greedy ends, can be dishonest, is competitive in sports and hobbies, wants recognition even if unearned.

Passive: Has no desire or ability to make money, has fear of taking leadership and responsibility, does not like to depend on others.

Harmonious: Has natural ability to determine potential in others, has executive ability, knows how to make and use money productively, is often successful as leader in a large corporation or in government, can achieve considerable recognition.

Emotional

Assertive: Wants to dominate all relationships, has unpredictable outbursts, is stubborn, does not admit errors, is satirical and caustic.

Passive: Worries about possible losses and misfortunes, is self-conscious around those deemed superior, needs to appear invulnerable, wants symbols of success for ego gratification.

Harmonious: Has deep and loyal feelings, takes charge in a crisis, enjoys being needed, works hard for family.

Mental

Assertive: Does not like to lose an argument or debate, wants to dominate others' thinking, is belligerent, is a powerful leader, is frank and outspoken.

Passive: Gets right to the brink of success and makes mental errors, gets things organized but does not carry through, has overgrown pride that seeks recognition, is disloyal when not given recognition.

Harmonious: Is a good organizer and leader, has sharp business and commercial acumen, works hard to improve skills and profits, is an excellent financial or business counselor, works hard for success.

Intuitive

Enjoys leadership roles in church, lodges and/or metaphysical organizations; applies intuition directly to leading and business; at best, is a highly inspired leader of awareness; can aid in decision making, organization or leadership.

9 on the Planes

Physical

Assertive: Pursues less aggressive careers, is an artist and/or poet, has colorful styles of dress, enjoys radical and unconventional friends, gets interested in work because of ideals, is impractical.

Passive: Can grasp broad ideals but needs direction when dealing with details, has difficulty reconciling ideals to reality of the world condition, has fluctuations in emotions that hinder attainment.

Harmonious: Is artistic and colorful in conducting work, likes to work for an ideal objective, is generous and tolerant.

Emotional

Assertive: Emotions fluctuate from feeling good to feeling depressed with little apparent reason, dreams and worries keep consciousness unsettled, feelings are hurt easily, is overly dramatic.

Passive: Becomes discouraged without approval and support, seeks others' attention, has difficulty relating personal feelings, emotions confuse reason, is withdrawn.

Harmonious: Is inspired, is highly intuitive, has fluctuating moods, is colorful and poetic, is idealistic in love, is tolerant and compassionate, seeks to assist humankind.

Mental

Assertive: Extreme idealism can prevent finding realistic solutions, needs to plant feet on firm soil, is gullible, plans far ahead, is selfless in giving ideas and assistance.

Passive: Mind tends to wander, which makes it difficult to keep in touch with the work being done; worries because he/she cannot change the world situation; is unconventional in thinking and habits.

Harmonious: Is an original and inspired thinker, is a visionary, can see future plans clearly and inspire others to make them become a reality, likes broad plans and ideals rather than details.

Intuitive

Is highly inspired, can tap inner planes and symbolism thereof, needs to discipline consciousness to be effective channel. Awareness can help awaken humankind. May bring entirely new visions for serving and uplifting human needs.

0 (Zero) on the Planes

When no letters appear on one or more planes (rarely on more than one), this does not mean you are without body, feelings, mind or intuition. Rather, it often indicates that you will have to consciously work to harmonize attributes on the particular level where letters are absent. In other words, it means that subconsciously, you are blocking the attention needed for that particular level and must purposely determine a method for dealing effectively with it.

Physical

Wants to dream and speculate; avoids hard work, getting hands in soil and physical discipline; tires and bores readily.

Emotional

Has difficulty both communicating feelings and accepting own emotional nature; is lacking in patience, sympathy and tolerance.

Mental

Cannot reason confidently, distrusts pure unfeeling logic and cold facts, lacks curiosity and inquisitiveness about life.

Intuitive

Distrusts intuition and vague abstract impressions, is self-centered in own belief structure, would benefit from meditation and consciousness expansion techniques.

More Than Nine Numbers

In some instances, such as with very long names or when there are two middle names, more than nine letters can occur on a plane of expression. In such a case, the double digit is reduced to its single-digit value for interpretation, and the concentration of energy on the particular plane will likely show an achievement in life of extraordinary proportion. For example, if a double-digit number appears on the physical plane, it may indicate a great leader; on the emotional, a teacher-healer or counselor; on the mental, some area of genius; and on the intuitive, an inspired teacher or inventor.

Working with Foreign Names

On occasion, the student of numerology may be requested to construct a chart for someone born in another country where the name was given in the native language. This can create some perplexities for the aspiring numerologist, considering that texts written in our country deal with only the English alphabet.

To construct a natal chart in a foreign language, set up the chart in the native alphabet using the numbers 1 through 9. Give the first letter a value of 1, the next a value of 2 and so on, through the number 9. When you come to the tenth letter, go back to number 1 just as you would do when calculating in our alphabet.

Many cultures have an alphabet that does not lend itself to using the 1 through 9 numbering system. Oriental systems and Arabic systems are such examples. In such situations, it would be more appropriate to do the chart in the numerical system of that culture.

The next alternative is to do the chart using the name given at immigration or the name the person is currently using. The numbers will tell you what lessons are emphasized in the chosen culture. In such a case, you are working with the numbers identified as the person's accomplished you, outer you and inner you mentioned earlier in this chapter. Although this approach will not provide the depth and nuance you get from using the natal chart, it can still be of assistance in dealing with the vibrational lessons of the moment.

Your Chosen
Life Path

T he date of birth provides one of the four most significant calculations when interpreting the natal chart. From the number you derive from the birth date, you can determine the life number, which yields insight into the reoccurring lessons the individual will attract into his or her life experience as well as into how that person will likely react to the circumstances life offers.

The life number provides a clue as to what fate has in store for us. It tells us which particular lessons will be repeated and given most attention until they are learned and integrated into the soul memory. Proper utilization of numerological information can provide guidelines and can help us adjust more readily to the lessons of life.

If you take conscious responsibility for your potential, you can better understand yourself and considerably accelerate the learning curve of life. With understanding comes the foundation upon which effective actions are based. Right action releases us from the wheel of karma and rebirth, furthering the evolution of soul so we can continue our journey onto higher spirals and planes of existence.

It is my personal belief that the date of birth is determined by the soul and higher self of the incoming child. Every mother has the experience of knowing that when the child is ready, birth occurs. It seems only proper that the soul does the choosing, because the life number indicates the types of opportunities, challenges and destiny that life experience will bring to assist experiential evolution. However, it is not necessary for you to accept this opinion to appreciate the meaning of numbers. Whatever the process of selection, it is the birth date that defines the life pattern.

The Life Number

The life number is derived from the sum total of the numbers in the month, the day and the year of birth. The total is then reduced to a single digit, except when dealing with master numbers.

For example, the birth date of July 21, 1931, is calculated as follows:

7	21	1931
$7 + 2 + 1 + 1 + 9 + 3 + 1 = 24 = 2 + 4 + 6$		

Note: Calculating by adding each number in consecutive order is the preferred method and is considered the pure number.

Secondary systems for calculating the life number help find potential master numbers and can be used as the basis for other interpretive derivations. Here are two more ways you can calculate the life number using the same birth date as the one above.

7	21	1931	
(7)	(3)	(5)	$7 + 3 + 5 = 15 = 1 + 5 = 6$

Or:

7	
21	
1931	
1959	$1 + 9 + 5 + 9 + = 24 = 2 + 4 = 6$

Here is another example:

11	22	1984
$1 + 1 + 2 + 2 + 1 + 9 + 8 + 4 = 28 = 2 + 8 = 10 = 1 + 0 = 1$		

Also:

11	22	1984	
(11)	(22)	(22)	$11 + 22 + 22 = 55\ (1)$

In the above example, the day and month are master numbers, as is the sum for the year 1984, 22. Since these are master numbers, they are not reduced to 2 or 4, respectively. Whenever a master number appears in the birth date, it is generally left in that form for purposes of calculation and is not reduced until later, when we start subtracting.

Or:

11	
22	
1984	
2017	$2 + 0 + 1 + 7 = 10 = 1 + 0 = 1$

And here is one more brief example:

11	21	1934	
(11)	(3)	(8)	$11 + 3 + 8 = 22 \ (4)$

Note that regarding master numbers, the concept of a pure number has been introduced in this book. Other methods of adding numbers have been used in numerology, and I was influenced by some of them in my early years and still watch for them. These methods can help pull potential master numbers into recognition. Following are some examples for deriving pure numbers to help clarify the process:

In the birth date November 22, 1901, you could add $11 + 22 + 11 = (44)\ 8$. The second 11 comes from adding $1 + 9 = 0 + 1 = 11$, which is not reduced.

Or:

For the birth date August 13, 1953, you add $8 + 1 + 3 + 1 + 9 + 5 + 3 = 30 = 3 + 0 = 3$ to get the pure number. A variation on this would be $8 + 4$ (the reduced 13) $+ 1$ (the reduced 19) $+ 53 = 66\ (3)$, or $8 + 4 + 1 + 53 = 66$.

And here is one further example, with a birth date of July 12, 1950: $7 + 1 + 2 + 1 + 9 + 5 + 0 = 25 = 2 + 5 = 7$, so 7 is the pure number. Or you can get a master number: $7 + 12 + 19 + 50 = 88\ (7)$.

Some numerologists would argue that this is stretching the system to find master numbers, but it is one of the ways that have been used to calculate numbers. There is a legitimate rationale for splitting the numbers this way, and I do feel that this approach can reveal a potential master number. In the end, it is still up to each individual person whether or not he or she wants to take on the vibration and responsibility of the additional force in a conscious manner.

Note: Interpretations for the life numbers and personality numbers are in many ways similar, and with an understanding of the nuances of their differences, they can be interchanged.

1 Life Number

A person choosing the 1 life number has come into this lifetime to learn individuality, self-reliance and proper expression of will (both human and divine). Very often the person with this life number is born into a family with a very domineering, interfering or willful parent—or parents. This creates early tension and a conflict of wills between parent and child. The resentment reaches a boiling point in the late teens or the twenties, and once the child leaves the home environment, a period of rebellion transpires. The 1s need to learn that pure rebellion, a lifestyle of pure opposite reaction, does not necessarily establish independence and self-direction, since they are still controlled by the person against whom they are rebelling. By the thirties, the life number 1 individual usually starts to recognize and release the rebellion, overcoming it with a healthy independence. Having grown into an appreciation of self-identity, the 1 learns to more fully value individuality in others. Only now can he or she cooperate and grow.

In other cases, parents may simply express indifference (passive abuse) toward the child's growth and personal interests. They do not take an active interest in the child because they need interest in themselves and do not like the presence of competition. This lack of attention leaves a feeling of inadequacy within the child, which can be so severe that it causes difficulty with initiative in later years. Lack of confidence and willingness to properly attain wanted necessities can lead to a pattern of using gambling as a means of quickly acquiring wanted commodities.

Those of you with a 1 life number may encounter supervisors, ministers, schoolteachers, relatives or spouses with whom you experience an intense conflict of wills. You may spend more of your life in combat with partners rather than in harmony. You repeat the pattern of finding people who you feel are domineering or intimidating rather than supportive and helpful. Realize that the tension and anger you stir up in these conflicts are reflecting back to you a closer look into your own unconscious willfulness. As you have sown so shall you reap! The karmic implication of this cliché applies to all the life numbers. Qualities seen in others represent qualities that you have likely expressed in an earlier life or lives. You are learning to overcome the tendency toward too much self-importance and replace it with cooperation and harmony.

Ones who have not worked out their subconscious conflict of wills will often marry a person of extreme ego and/or willfulness. The 1 is finally berated, intimidated or ignored by a partner for so long that he or she runs away to "do his or her own thing." This flight pattern leads to many premature divorces or separations. Sadly, it often takes the death or divorce of the spouse to awaken a 1 into self-reliance and acceptance of the fact that he or she is learning to be respectful of the individuality of both partner and self.

A very consequential nuance of the life number 1 has become more evident in recent years: the adjustment from human will to divine will. Many advanced seekers of light have come to a conscious turning point in their growth when they have made the decision to put their lives into harmony with divine plan and divine will: "Thy will, not mine, oh Lord, my God." The higher frequency of the number 1 symbolizes divine will, or the Father's will. Every living human soul eventually lives through the challenge of clashing wills, both human and divine. However, those with the number 1 (not necessarily just in the life number) usually have an ongoing life struggle with this issue, ultimately leading to the process of dissolving the domination of ego and transforming the will into attunement with the intent of divine will.

On many occasions, individuals may reach their forties, fifties or later years before they overcome their resentment and resistance from a life with a domineering parent (particularly Dad) for the first time. With added years, the pattern may become more ingrained, but other than that, age makes little difference. The seeker is joyous and confident at having truly found a greater awareness of self-reliance and strength.

Perhaps the one who is seeking has been studying metaphysical philosophy for some time and has made an effort to know and follow the Father's will. Consciously, this may all be well and good; however, subconsciously, the mind is saying, "Here I am, just starting to find my own will and becoming free, and now I have to become subservient to another's (the Father's) will." Thus a subconscious battle rages, and the balancing of will continues. Each time we expand higher in awareness, we go deeper into the subconscious to rework conflicts and karmic blocks. This battle for balance between self-will and higher will is an ongoing challenge for all of humanity.

In the case of a well-balanced chart, 1s may grow up in a very supportive and congenial atmosphere that fosters self-esteem. Because they will have reached balance early in life or in a previous lifetime, they are securely self-aware and free to live prosperously and productively. Those with the 1 life number are often at the forefront of crusades and reformations.

Ones have come to be leaders and pioneers in their calling. As such they are independent and are best left alone to complete a task. They become owners, supervisors and managers. They have a tendency to think that no matter what their lifestyle, it is superior to others'. They have difficulty taking orders and can become bossy and opinionated.

As a 1, your life is characteristically full of adventure, travel and exploration. You are inclined toward active pleasures and competition. Challenging nature and overcoming obstacles are the reasons why you enjoy the outdoors. You are oftentimes active in sports and can get into extreme sporting ventures.

Originality, invention and courage are native to 1s, but you can soar to varying degrees of overconfidence and egocentricity. Once a goal is sighted, it is easy for you to concentrate your attention. Paradoxically, 1s must be wary of their tendency to start a project, become bored and go on to something new before they have completed the first project. This tendency can be the result of rampant ambition. More often, however, it is caused by the 1's restless urge to get on to something new and different.

Ambition is a significant driving force for you, and you are determined to succeed and be productive. Overcoming obstacles and limitations presents an exhilarating challenge to you, and once you learn to cooperate without losing your identity, the sky is the limit to your productivity.

2 Life Number

Twos come into this life to learn tact, diplomacy, sincerity, teamwork and neatness, to mention some of their key lessons. Their natural inclination is to want to get along and live in harmony with everyone around them. The 2 life number places emphasis upon learning to gather facts accurately and to present them with impartiality. At best they are sensitive, considerate and refined.

Those choosing the 2 life number very often come into a family environment where a parent—or parents—is prone to pettiness, contrary opinions and criticism. The child is seldom complimented or given reinforcement for personal accomplishments; rather, the child is more often reminded that he or she could have done better when, for example, he or she got a 95 percent instead of a 100 on a school exam or came in third place instead of first in a contest. Living in such an environment can undermine self-confidence and heighten the inability to cope with criticism in later years. One likely result is that the 2 will find it hard to make decisions, for fear of being wrong or for fear of criticism.

Very often those with a 2 life number carry the brunt of seemingly unjustified or unwarranted gossip or criticism, especially in school and during the early adult years. Such uncomfortable accusations may occur in any aspect of social situation. Often the accusations are untrue, and the victim asks, "Why are they saying this about me?" Twos may be caught in the very sort of pettiness that they themselves created in a previous life or lives.

If you, the 2, respond with anger, hurt or vengeful behavior, you perpetuate the karmic pattern. It is important to remember that criticism comes from the other party and that it is the other person's problem. When you react with negativity, it becomes your karma also, and you link yourself to the instigator. Learning to release judgmental, self-righteous and critical attitudes is a key lesson for you. When 2s become tormented and overridden by negative emotions, it can be easy for them to turn to drugs or alcohol as an escape.

At your best, 2s are natural diplomats who bring change through persuasion rather than force. They are more often found in the middle ranks of business, lacking the drive of the 1s. When a 2 does achieve the highest position, it is by influence, diplomacy and finesse. You do well helping others reach their goals and are best at team efforts, not solitary endeavors. You are attracted to cultural events of refinement and artistry. Your enjoyment of nature comes from finding the subtlety and intricate beauty amid the power and splendor of her forces. You enjoy the intricacies of different cultures and search for the common traits among diverse groups.

Twos work well when it comes to bringing groups or people with divergent attitudes into a unity of understanding. Their talents emerge when articulating and developing an idea that may have originated with someone else. However, it is important that 2s pay attention to details in all endeavors. A 2 may often be the person doing the real work for those who capture the headlines. Such patient service pays off, and all proper effort is someday rewarded on the wheel of destiny.

Whereas the 1 relates to the father and male-energy archetypes, the 2 relates to the mother and female-energy archetypes. Perhaps your mother was not happy in her marriage and constantly complained, or she might have tried to live her life through you. Either way you did not receive the healthy nurturing that is so important to a child's early growth. Your life will bring you into contact with feminine personalities who directly reflect back to you the issues you are working on with your heart and soul.

The 2's unconscious belief system about women is a reflection of the relationship with his or her mother in early years. Many people never resolve these issues and are controlled, on an unconscious level, by the very parent they so deeply despise. One of the most frequent unconscious reactions to such underlying animosity is to become sweet and nice to a fault. This is a very frequent pattern with men who have underlying anger against their mother. Although syrupy sweet and seductive with the women in their lives, they nurture deep resentment and oftentimes rage.

The esoteric side of the 2 is opening the door between heaven and Earth. Twos are excellent at integrating intuitive guidance into day-to-day experience and capture glimpses of inner realism more readily than some of their contemporaries. This is particularly true for 2s who have an 11 master number. Twos are happiest when the door to the soul has been opened and the higher light pours into their lives.

3 Life Number

Threes have come to learn beauty, charm, grace, enthusiasm, creative expression and joy, to mention some of the primary lessons. Often 3s are found in entertainment, the creative arts, public media, sales, crafts, writing and related endeavors, since they have come into this life to create, to radiate beauty and harmony and to express self. The expression of the creative ability and the opportunity to apply it in life may come naturally for many who have 3 as their life number, and this is especially true when indicators in the whole chart show balance and flow.

Often 3s are born into families where they encounter considerable inhibition, resistance or indifference to the artistic or creative skills they possess. It is possible that in a previous life or lives, the 3 had developed pronounced abilities and failed to discipline them to highest virtuosity or became superficial about the gift. Now once again the 3 may have the potential, but this time life has thrown obstacles in the way of development. This could be because the gift that is truly earned is more respected, appreciated and expressed with dedication. Here are a few hypothetical situations:

A young lady strongly desires to play the piano and has shown ability at a school tryout, but she lives in a family where money is scarce and her parents are unable to afford the instrument. Or there is a young man who has shown outstanding proclivities toward acting and singing. His father is from the old puritan work-ethic culture, and the thought of having an effeminate milquetoast artist as a son is overwhelming to his male ego, so the son is intimidated and forced to pursue "manly" occupations. A three-year-old child creates a particularly colorful, symbolic and aesthetically pleasing finger painting. Unfortunately, it is done on the new kitchen cabinets, so she is severely punished for her creativity. As a result, the spontaneity of creation becomes associated with chastisement and pain, and it may not surface again for many years.

You as a 3 enjoy the aesthetics and diversity of expression among the different nationalities of the world. Your fascination with nature takes you to different climates and variations of season and splendor. Your joy of living leads you to dance, sing and celebrate among people from numerous religions and social classes. You enjoy sports for the improvement it brings to the body and to the appearance. Your sense of fashion and grooming brings you great delight as you shop and search for just the right piece of clothing or makeup. You enjoy presenting a favorable appearance. Your abilities as a host or hostess bring both the famous and the unknown to your door, but whether well-known or not, they all are almost always interesting characters.

Three is the union of 1 (male, father) plus 2 (female, mother), resulting in the expression of universal creative energy. All creative acts result from releasing the creative force, or kundalini. The same creative energy expressed in the physical act of creativity (sexual intercourse) can be channeled into other levels of expression, be it job creativity, artistic creativity, intellectual creativity or soul creativity.

Very often early childhood awakening to sexual curiosity or outlet is associated with feelings of guilt, shame, embarrassment, chastisement or confusion. Incidents such as self-exploration, childhood sex games, sexual abuse, stimulation from a family member, petting, foreplay or guilt-ridden early sexual relations leave a scar of guilt, fear, shame or confusion in the subconscious attitude toward creativity on the sexual level. When the adult commences a new creative endeavor later in life on another level (work, art, soul), the subconscious conflicts become activated, and the individual will react to the subconscious stimulus by terminating the project prematurely. A 3 with this conflict may become involved in a multitude of creative diversions but will fail to truly excel in any of them. One may find several incomplete paintings, poems, stained-glass fixtures or projects of every creative nature underfoot in this 3's home.

Each time we expand our consciousness higher and outward, we go deeper into the subconscious to release deeply hidden blocks. This conflict with creativity may also apply when 3 appears elsewhere in the chart, as the personality number for example, or as letters in the name, day or month and so on.

A 3 yearns to investigate the laws of creative energy and work to release it sensibly in harmony with all other factors in consciousness. On the esoteric level, 3 is the word spoken, the Christ consciousness manifested. Despite the conflicts they must outgrow, 3s are the heralds and spokespersons preparing humanity for the dawn with the illuminating inspiration of their works. When the struggle is won, life is glorious for 3s. They are naturals as hosts and benefit from socializing with other seekers and creative personalities. At their best, they are imaginative, inspired and able to tap deep emotions. They are gifted with the ability to use words but must be careful not to slip into pettiness and superficiality.

Misguided—or perhaps a better word is "unguided"—3s are very capable of speaking endlessly and having very little to say. They need to discipline their energies and avoid spreading their talents too thinly. Threes often run with the "in" crowd and the jet set and, when out of harmony, can squander away talent in self-indulgence, luxury and pseudo-sophistication.

4 Life Number

Four is the number of work and discipline. When 4 is their life number, individuals often feel like they have some special work to do, and their life work and career will be very important to them. Some people know early in life what they want to do and prepare their whole life for it. More often with the 4 life number, though, you will find yourself experiencing several types of work or career directions before discovering the real desired work of the soul. You may plan relationships and residences around your work, as opposed to others who plan their work and residence around family or relationships.

Fours are often born into a family where one (usually the father) or both of the parents are hard working and unavailable. It is often that the father is a workaholic and is never available to the young child as he or she is growing up. On an unconscious level, the child begins to resent the father's work. Once such children become adults, they often develop a pattern of sabotaging success or the opportunity to do work that they would really love to do. This is because of unconscious resentment toward the father and his work that always kept him away from home so that he was not available to love and give of himself to the child.

Work is associated with loneliness, pain and anger. As that child becomes an adult and gets closer to success or important work, the old subconscious pattern kicks in and undermines the possibility of getting a good job or finding successful work. People with this conflict will go through several jobs, always just getting to the threshold of landing a really good one—and then they bail out and move on to start all over again. Once it is understood and resolved, this pattern can be broken, and they will find it easier to discover and thoroughly enjoy the work they choose.

Fours are the workers of the world. They must strive diligently and with dedication to achieve their goals. In most instances, things will not come easily for them but only through effort, because they may bring a tendency toward laziness or avoidance of work with them from a previous life or lives. When that is true, 4s may begrudge the work at hand and become irritated in their labors.

When you resist learning the lesson of the 4 vibration, you tend toward the unconventional and refuse to honor custom or social norms. You decidedly dislike routine and system and want to pass detailed and monotonous requirements on to someone else. The result is a constant seeking of shortcuts and ways out of duties. When this attitude prevails, a 4 may get to a point of success, but eventually, the individual's whole world collapses. At that point, the 4 has to start again, step by step, brick by brick, from the solid foundation to the well-earned heights.

On the more positive side, 4s are loyal, intense and dedicated workers. When they are given an assignment, they will carry it out, meticulous to the nth degree. However, they may lack imagination or originality when it comes to making any needed adjustments to a job. The 4s' disciplined nature can carry over into other areas of their lives. They may prefer activities that are routine and predictable, and it is easy for them to stay around the home or in the neighborhood to find their recreational activities.

As was touched upon at the beginning of the discussion on this life number, 4s may experience several diverse occupations or professional fields before settling into one in which they are content. They handle money well and tend to keep a small reserve for fear of not having any resources. When a 4 attains a position of wealth, it is from hard work and persistence.

A 4 needs facts and must be shown the practical side of a new project before starting. The 4 gravitates toward administration, engineering and mechanical and technological pursuits. A 4's inclination toward life is conservative and protective; he or she has to know the whys and wherefores before taking any risk. Fours are not prone to superficial interests and must work on developing a lighter side in their attitude toward life. This approach may manifest in concern about financial stability.

Fours nurture a strong sense of dignity and worthiness about their lives. They tend to help all who are in need, but their conservative nature limits their friends and associates—admittedly an odd combination of traits. In a supervisory position, they expect equal dedication and effort from their employees and are inclined to become overbearing and bossy, to the point of personal severity. The 4s' natural tendency is conservative, but when desperate, they can turn to uncontrolled gambling or illegal measures to meet their needs.

On the esoteric side, awakened 4s have come into this life to build the form for establishing the divine blueprint on Earth. Once they have recognized the inner work of the soul, 4s are truly inspired workers toward the light. Once content with their direction and purpose, they become more patient and tolerant of the awakening souls of mass consciousness.

5 Life Number

Fives have come into this lifetime to experience the Earth opportunities more thoroughly. The lessons for 5s include versatility, freedom, embracing humanity and curiosity. They profit most from contact with others; therefore, they should seek every opportunity to mingle with the endless variety of people.

Five brings change, movement, travel and opportunity. Very often a child with the 5 life number is born into a family where a parent has a career that forces the family to move frequently. An excellent example would be a military family where reassignment is the way of life. If 5s do not have the opportunity to move, travel and get out to explore the world during the childhood, they will get that chance later in their lives.

Fives learn best from contact with other people—and they have much to learn. The karmic suggestion here is that in a previous life or lives, they have expressed some prejudice and intolerance of certain nationalities, ethnic groups, religious sects or political persuasions. Most likely, previous life patterns are heavily intellectual, and lofty, rigid intellectual biases were formed toward select human classifications. This time around, the 5's soul and higher self chose to be born into a situation that somewhat coerces that individual to work with people, some of whom he or she distinctly dislikes! The 5s will have the chance to deal with all types of people, including the rich and the poor; those of different races, creeds, religions or colors; and those of varying political, philosophical, moral, ethical and economic persuasions. Such powerful dichotomy cannot help but provide a learning experience.

Let us say for example that a 5 has come into this life with an intense prejudice against left-footed Latvians. It is likely that as a child or later he will move next door to a left-footed Latvian family. It may turn out that this is the only family on the block with a child who is his peer. Over a period of time, a friendship develops on the day-to-day human level. The 5 eats left-footed Latvian food, plays with left-footed Latvian toys and learns left-footed Latvian history and family tradition. Sooner or later he realizes that left-footed Latvian people are the same as all people: some are good, some perhaps are not. The whole point to learn is to accept people for who they are, and experience is the best teacher. It shouldn't be avoided.

At their shallowest, 5s have a tendency to try a little of everything but learn from nothing. They become superficial and are unable to create sustained or responsible relationships. On the other hand, 5s are often experiential extremists, becoming involved in an experience to such an overwhelming extent that they are unable to break loose to try a new opportunity.

There is a tendency toward excessive self-indulgence. A 5 strives to learn the balance of knowing when he or she has learned from a life experience and needs to move on to something else. When out of balance, 5s will seek excitement and stimulation in sexuality, drink, drugs or other sensual indulgences—or they will go to the other extreme and be afraid to try anything new or different. They vacillate between too much and too little.

Many a seeker of self-awareness has previously been in a life of asceticism, abstinence and impoverishment, quite possibly as a nun or a monk in earlier religious or esoteric sects. In such lifetimes, they avoided contact with mundane human desires and frailties. Now, as 5s, they have chosen to come back to make up for experience previously avoided. They find themselves caught between strong, pent-up physical urges and the dictates of family morals and mores, religion or society.

Fives have come in this time to find a proper balance within self in terms of the correct expression of their sensual and sexual needs. They have a tendency to disregard and flout social norms or entice others to act inappropriately. Conversely, they may cling obsessively to the law (religious, social or civic) as a means of dealing with uncontrollable desires and urges. Once they have achieved a harmonious lifestyle, though, 5s know how to respect the norms of society while independently and unobtrusively pursuing the right lifestyle for themselves.

This is the number of humanity and free will; as the dualistic counterpoint to freedom, 5 is also symbolic of divine law. Those seeking the esoteric wisdom of 5 realize that eventually, the course of proper action comes from within, and they learn to follow the voice of dharma, a complex eastern concept. Very roughly translated, it means the performance of an action that is precisely proper for the participant at his or her moment of evolution. To react any other way at that moment would create imbalance (too much—too little) and more karma. As we listen to the voice of dharma, it will direct us in a manner that most efficiently balances out karma. To consistently tap the dharmic directive, we must learn to bring our life, personality and soul into balance and under the direct tutelage of the higher self.

6 Life Number

Sixes have come into this lifetime to learn the lessons of domesticity, responsibility, humanitarianism and service, and one of the greatest challenges for them is establishing emotional balance and security. Often they are born into a family where dissension and disharmony exist between the mother and father, in many cases leading to separation and divorce. The strain leaves a strong emotional insecurity in the child's subconscious memory. People with the 6 life number frequently experience difficulty adjusting to the responsibility of home and family, and they often go through more than one marriage.

The karmic implication in the 6 life number is that in a previous life—or lives—these individuals had difficulty adapting to home, family and the personal responsibilities of marriage. They may have been irresponsible or unyielding and caused grief for those nearby. In this lifetime, 6s experience emotional suffering, just as they generated it in earlier patterns.

The 6 is the archetype for codependency, and those with this number must watch themselves carefully when entering into relationships, because they can so easily become enmeshed in unhealthy and toxic bonds. On the other hand, the 6 life number can also be indicative of having harmonious lifelong relationships, which is especially true for those who have worked through the many issues of their codependent nature. Remember that consideration must always be given to the entire chart when analyzing each segment.

Sixes have usually come into this life to be of service to others. They are at their best when what they do directly benefits the lives of those they serve. Ministers, doctors, nurses, teachers, counselors and social workers often have the 6 prominent in their charts. Frequently 6s enter these types of service with an unconscious desire to alleviate their own inner hurt and pain, compensating for this with the assistance they feel they are giving to their clients or patients. Once their own inner conflict is resolved, they can be some of the most effective counselors and healers.

The karmic suggestion is that in an earlier existence, 6s have developed a tendency to disregard or interfere with the lives of others. A 6 may have intimidated others intellectually or used power to keep them insecure and under control. A 6 is here now to balance the scale by assisting and caring for others. The key here is probably learning to know when to take responsibility for self. After all, the most important relationship is with our own self, and once we have established a healthy relationship between the inner man and inner woman, we can then be a most loving and endearing partner or mate.

As a 6, your inclination to compare yourself constantly to others can become a big distraction in any relationship, no matter how casual or intimate. Once you have found security within and a direction that satisfies, you will find your life becoming more harmonious and content. Once you have learned to set standards based upon realistic appraisals of your personality and its components, you will be a most desirable partner and associate to those with whom you share your life.

A 6's idealism and desire to serve create some very strong opinions as to what is best for others. You should also be careful about others taking advantage of your generosity and imposing upon you for assistance. They work upon your karmic subconscious memories of having neglected others in a past existence, perhaps even in your current life. By working upon the guilt, they make you feel obligated to give when you should be getting. Because of your idealism, you set very high standards for both yourself and others. Your demanding nature can make it frustrating for would-be friends and lovers to try and match your elevated expectations. It is very easy for you to see the faults, weaknesses or shortcomings in a prospective mate without even giving thought to that person's many positive attributes of personality.

You will have to work hard to find tranquillity in the home, but once you are content, your surroundings will be tasteful and harmonious. As a 6, you can succeed at anything when you are truly helping and serving others, so in business you tend toward assisting others rather than excelling in completely competitive professions.

Sixes are excellent when helping to mend the body, emotions, mind and soul. They are often self-made martyrs. But 6s can also be instruments of a greater cause and sacrifice themselves for humanity. Then, when they truly are martyrs in the best sense, they give of themselves nobly.

7 Life Number

Sevens come into this lifetime to learn the lessons of thoroughness, analysis, follow-through of logic, discernment and inner conviction. Those with the 7 life path are constantly searching for a deeper understanding of themselves and the world around them. They analyze, investigate and probe for hidden information, no matter what their calling. Their love of study and introspection makes them intense and attached to their beliefs and conclusions.

They have accumulated a vast storehouse of wisdom from previous lives and lean toward a cerebral and intellectual life. For some, higher education or specialized professional training is not available or is difficult to attain. It is likely that 7s have pursued the intellectual route many times, and this time, life is directing them to use their knowledge in a practical expression rather than to emphasize yet another cerebral endeavor. It is also possible that a 7 has to struggle to derive perspective and appreciation for the role of intellect in the growth of consciousness.

Those of you with the 7 life number tend toward a lonely life of introspection and aloofness. You find strength from within self and are reluctant to open up to others for aid or guidance. Although you want intimacy like any other person, your suspicion makes you fear betrayal and deceit. You long for the complementary mate who brings a sense of completion, but at the same time you are reluctant to open up in a way that allows for true intimacy and union to occur. When you feel threatened or betrayed, you are a master at mind games and ruses of distraction.

Because of their tendency toward specialization, 7s often lose perspective on simple personal needs and the ability to enjoy lightheartedly the trivial events of social living. They prefer to wear a mask and play a role rather than be caught up in the pettiness at hand. The paradox is that the detachment is a role. In extreme isolation, 7s can turn to drink or drugs to keep the body numb and ignorant of the feelings within.

Dedication and a scientific attitude often enable 7s to accomplish much and attain considerable success. Most importantly, 7s need to balance compassion and human sensitivity with knowledge. This combination inspires wisdom and a deeper search through the occult mysteries and metaphysical studies. You will find that the inner search for deeper mysteries of life and knowledge of your true self will be the basis of your primary drive throughout your life. Although you are capable of great accomplishment and achievement in the outer world, you will find your greatest satisfaction in the reverie and discovery of profound mystical and intellectual revelations that come from the depth of soul and highest levels of divine expression.

When awakened to inner realities, the 7 investigates intricately the deepest mysteries of humanity and cosmos. As we advance closer toward higher awareness, many with the 7 life path are coming into such a period to bring a special spiritual gift or teaching. Conversely, negative 7s can become skeptical and cynical toward life. They then enjoy playing with rhetoric and games of subterfuge. Sevens can use excessive analysis and intellectuality as an escape from feelings they are repressing. There is so much that 7s keep bottled up inside that they are frequently on the edge of emotional explosion. Some of the world's greatest actors and actresses have learned to put this force into their roles on stage or in movies, not having been able to find a direct path of expression in their daily lives.

The karmic suggestion is that too much attention has been given to intellectuality in past life patterns, so heart and feelings need to be integrated into your being this time around. When these become united, your opportunity for spiritual growth is enormous. This is the number of meditation, introspection and self-examination, and through these avenues, the 7's mystical side is awakened.

Sevens tend to value their intellectual ability as a tool for power and control. They can intimidate others with their intense reasoning capacity and cool recitation of the facts. When ego and pride get in the way, they are cunning and deceptive in nature.

As a 7, pride and dignity are natural to your reserved attitude, and your conservative trend makes you selective of friends. Your natural inclination is to trust your own ideas and judgment. When linked to your intuition, this combination leads to decisions of impact and strength that enable you to reach your predetermined goals. You are learning to trust your decisions and, most of all, the wisdom coming in from your finely tuned intuition.

8 Life Number

As an 8, you have come into this lifetime to learn the lessons of power, efficiency, authority, money and leadership—this is the number of management and executive skills. The 8 life number indicates opportunities that can lead to attainment and success.

Those with the 8 life number often choose a family where one parent—or both parents—is severe in the administration of authority. Another frequent situation is a child born into a family heavily burdened by religious, ethnic or intellectual dogma. Both these possibilities place the 8 into a position of having to struggle in finding his or her own true sense of authority and inner wisdom.

At best you grasp the inner laws of abundance and reap from the very best things in life. When you are in harmony with Spirit, abundance flows. When you become insecure and fear loss, you can be cold and calculating in your disguised plots to get something. You are also quite capable of intimidation and aggression to get your way with other people. Once you are secure within the laws of abundance, you can be most generous and helpful in assisting others to reach the same level of prosperity in all ways.

In the early years, 8s become very resentful of incompetent supervisors who, in spite of poor skills, do it their way because they are boss! Your inclination as an 8 is to say, "I could run things better." And you probably could. The karmic implication is that in a previous life or lives, you misused authority because of money, ego or pride. So in your youth, you will feel the discomfort of being at the lower end of the totem pole, carrying the brunt of abuse where leadership is misdirected.

At their best, 8s have an uncanny knack of sizing up another's potential accurately and quickly. They may manipulate this talent for selfish purposes or to attain purely self-centered objectives. They are outstanding executives and can handle personnel effectively with this ability. Eights seek the symbolic trappings that suggest success—the large home, the big car, expensive decor, the club membership or whatever the appropriate symbols are in their culture. They need to appear successful.

In a woman's chart, the 8 life path usually suggests a tendency toward a business career or professional pursuits. This is not to say that she disdains being a wife and mother but that her need is to prove herself in the outer world. In most instances, the woman has experienced circumstances in early childhood where she has denied her feminine identity and built a strong masculine subconscious focus. This enables her to compete and excel in her chosen field.

As one enters into expanded realization, the 8 vibration is taking on a new significance. Eights who are aware of higher laws will be leaders but must tap their divine guidance and execute authority that is based upon universal law. Instead of manipulating and being fearful of helping others develop authority, the awakened 8 will educate others to draw out their authority and skills. Such a more enlightened leader will help administrate the raising of divinely ordained cities, governments and cultures. Whereas unawakened 8s keep others dependent in order to hold control and domain, the enlightened 8s are never fearful of someone taking their position, for they know that as they enable others to find confidence and self-authority, they themselves will also greatly expand and unfold.

Eights are here to learn the proper value and utilization of money. They can attract money more easily than any other number. When wealth or esteem is the only ambition, they may find it slipping away until the proper balance toward money is learned. Out of control and desperate, 8s can turn to gambling and unscrupulous investments.

If you are an 8, you most likely will be put into positions of leadership and control. Industry, large institutions and government are attractive to 8s. You are at your best executing others' dreams, in sound managerial fashion.

9 Life Number

Nines are the dreamers of all generations. They have come into this lifetime to learn to work toward the collective welfare of all humankind. The lessons for 9s include learning compassion, being unselfish and altruistic, following their fondest dreams, creating and exploring the higher realms of consciousness. They bring a sense of idealism, tolerance and compassion to humankind and dream of perfection in their marriages, in society and within themselves.

Individuals with the 9 life path often possess eloquence, charisma and oratorical brilliance. When called upon, they are masters at inspiring and giving encouragement to the masses. They may find themselves falling short of their own lofty ideals and of living those ideals in the day-to-day-activities of their lives. Once they learn to live the truth, however, they will find themselves to be far more efficient in their ability to inspire others toward the lofty goals humanity aspires to attain.

At times 9s are naive in their enthusiastic outlook toward others and life itself. As they reach their more adult years, this idealism is dissipated by the harsh reality of imperfect and often terribly troubled behavior. In their early years, 9s are oftentimes exploited by someone using their blind idealism as a lure to get a more nefarious act completed. After having used the 9, the exploiting party then frequently drops him or her cold. A 9's obsessive idealism about a specific person often masks an abuse committed by that idealized person. In the extreme, such idealism frequently turns to disillusionment and despair in later years, and the 9 becomes inclined to depression, bitterness, cynicism and anarchy.

This is the finishing number, and when 9 is the life number, it indicates a significant turning point in evolution. It represents the ending of one stage in growth and an opportunity to make a major leap into a next loop in the spiral of growth. Consequently, 9s have come to let go of the things of this world. The paradoxical lesson is to let go in order to have. As 9s cling to anything less than the eternal, it will eventually weigh like an anchor upon their ship of growth. There is a metaphysical saying, "Let go and let God," and this could hardly be more appropriate than to an individual with the 9 life number.

If you attach yourself to things of this world for your security, it is likely they will eventually be removed by fate until you seek security within the inner self. Let's say you need lots of wealth for security. All of a sudden, the stock market may plunge or your property may become valueless. Or maybe you are dependent upon your marriage partner and death or divorce occurs. The more tenaciously and fearfully one clings, the more intense the life suffering becomes. Stubborn, clinging 9s may experience death of loved ones, major illnesses, financial losses, accidents, divorce and on and on. Finally their anguish becomes so deep they reach out to soul and higher self—and reach equanimity and balance.

This does not mean that life must hold suffering for 9s. For those who have learned to let go, life is often rich in all ways, with divine supply. Because it is a finishing number, life will often be full of adventure, bizarre and wonderful people and events, inexplicable happenings, invention, artistic achievement and creativity. Once need no longer exists, supply comes in abundantly.

Because of the outreach of the consciousness, there is a strong tendency to fluctuate between emotional highs of ecstasy and lows of depression. As the inner light is established within, this roller-coaster syndrome dissipates, and 9s then enjoy an enriched and full life.

Nine is also the number of dreams fulfilled. When the cobwebs of ego have been cleared, the aspiration of the inner self comes to the surface. Or to put it in therapeutic jargon: Once you get rid of your stuff, good things start to happen. The aspiration for perfection can lead to extremely unrealistic expectations for you and from others. Once you truly know yourself and live your truth, it is possible to have your fondest dreams come true, within the boundaries of being human with all of the human frailties.

11 Life Number

The 11 life number is similar to the 2 life number. Please review the 2 life number at this time.

Elevens tend to be drawn to movements and organizations with idealistic aims. In a balanced chart with other power factors, they are likely to gain public attention and influence. Many 11s work in the psychic, healing and metaphysical fields and can be excellent channels for the light. They are often attracted to theatrical, religious, communications, sociological, political, ecological or metaphysical organizations. When their zealousness overrides discretion, they get caught up in fanatical cults, religious sects and fringe movements.

In the pursuit of an ideal, 11s are prone to overlook delicate personal considerations and sensitivity. When this occurs, they may alienate the very people they wish to inspire. It is very important to be a living example of truth, and 11s must trust and follow the inspiration of intuition, yet maintain contact with the other planes of consciousness.

Since the 11 is also a 2, it relates to society and public events. People with the 11 life number frequently become public figures, and many well-known entertainment, political, media and artistic people have 11 in their charts. You may not become world famous, but there is a good likelihood you will become known publicly for your efforts.

22 Life Number

The 22 life number is similar to the 4 life number. Please review the 4 life number at this time.

The 22 has tremendous power for organization and establishment of institutions that are resonating with higher-plane guidance and inner-world archetypes. Although you may not lead the work, your contribution will be vital to success, even if the role appears insignificant by worldly standards.

In times of quickening human consciousness, humanity becomes more interested in establishing cities, governments, spiritual institutions, art centers and educational facilities that reestablish conscious cooperation between humanity and the lords of higher worlds. Twenty-twos of awakened spiritual consciousness are working (often as yet unwittingly) to prepare the foundation for those institutions of a more enlightened global population. They must use their mental strength in harmony with body, emotion and soul. When all levels become spiritually directed and disciplined, they become the master builders for a new and more evolved world.

33 Life Number

The 33 life number is similar to the 6 life number. Please review the 6 life number at this time.

The 33s have come to serve humankind in a grand fashion and affiliate with groups or institutions whose primary aim is to relieve the suffering of humanity on Earth. Such institutions can be related to health, religion, education, science, entertaining or charity. Avenues of communication that can contribute to social reform and awakening attract the 33s, and this can lead them to careers in entertainment, the news or education.

In an earlier life, many 33s were part of a group that created frustration, confusion or pain for large numbers of people on the planet. Consequently, they come back laden with a compulsion to help. At their worst, this compulsion is ingratiating, even obnoxious to those who see the 33s as self-righteous to a fault.

Thirty-threes frequently have very complex and deeply rooted emotional conflicts to resolve before they are best able to assist other people. They may compensate for emotional deficiencies in childhood by creating a big business or developing communication for many, such as through television or some other form of media. They can also be drawn to acting or singing. Of course, first of all, they must see their own self-righteousness. Once the heart center is functioning harmoniously, 33s become excellent healers, counselors and instructors. Then they truly are able to alleviate the woes engulfing so many on the planet in this era.

44 Life Number

The 44 life number is similar to the 8 life number. Please review the 8 life number at this time.

Often 44s possess excellent organizational skills along with an outstanding knowledge regarding the mechanics of getting things done. They may be trained in (or, as is often the case, have innate knowledge of) areas of engineering, business management, physics, mathematics and other professional fields related to construction and architecture. These are the visionary artists who create lofty structures that emanate sacred geometry and glorify the dynamics of universal laws in structure.

When attracted to the arts, they organize, choreograph and provide financial support to drama, music or any artistic endeavor that inspires humans to seek a deeper understanding and relationship with their Creator. They are often articulate and powerful orators who can inspire thousands at a time into working for a righteous and venerable cause.

55 Life Number

The 55 life number is similar to the 1 life number. Please review the 1 life number at this time.

Fifty-fives are frequently attracted to the ministry or spiritually oriented groups that emphasize adherence to divine regulation and contact with God. If not directly spiritual, they are also interested in humanitarian organizations that teach self-reliance and individual responsibility. They can be extraordinary dancers or masters of the martial arts. Their curiosity leads them into the more pragmatic philosophies rather than the abstract and speculative.

You as a 55 are often active in companies that are at the cutting edge of technology or in any form of research that pushes frontiers and the limits of reason. You can be found leading reform movements and human rights activities. Your ability to appeal to basic human needs makes you popular to the masses—and sometimes a threat to the establishment.

66 Life Number

The 66 life number is similar to the 3 life number. Please review the 3 life number at this time.

Sixty-sixes are attracted to the media, entertainment, religious movements, human rights and animal rights movements, charitable organizations, causes to reduce human suffering and self-help education, to name a few. Your inner concern and outer flair for charisma often take you to the forefront of your chosen path. This does not necessarily mean that you will be known publicly, but rather it speaks to the effort you put into your chosen cause.

You are closely connected to nature and often work consciously with the angelic kingdoms. You bring an added ray of hope to the gloomy environs of darkness and despair, and it is very likely that you become a part of social groups or reform movements concerned with domestic violence, abuse and exploitation of children and adults. Your tireless effort and sacrifice gain you respect by those you benefit.

77 Life Number

The 77 life number is similar to the 5 life number. Please review the 5 life number at this time.

Scientific or medical research is attractive to 77s, since they see such research as directly improving humans' living conditions. They are often found in areas of theological debate, physics, cosmology, metaphysical thinking, international negotiations, sports and fitness, to mention a few. Their enthusiasm and elevated thoughts for living give others the confidence to overcome the doubts of daily life.

As a 77, you stretch the limits of logic and challenge your more conservative contemporaries with expanded thoughts of new technology, human feats of consciousness and utopian plans for living together. Because you so frequently leap into other worlds of being, you're a fighter for the freedom of all to pursue their life dreams in harmony with divine precepts for living.

88 Life Number

The 88 life number is similar to the 7 life number. Please review the 7 life number at this time.

Eighty-eights are attracted to such interests as engineering, metallurgy, architecture, philosophy, corporate management, academics, money management and legalities, to mention a few. You are found at the forefront of science and technology that apply speculative research along with the traditional laws of mechanics. Your combination of intellectual finesse and logistical acumen allows you to see options where others only come to a dead end.

Those 88s in the performing arts often demonstrate skills that seemingly defy gravity or the limited mechanical potential others see in the physical body. You love the application of mathematics to the solution of everyday problems. You may be found arguing a landmark case that changes the course of human events. You choose to use your vast earnings to support educational institutions of enlightenment and epistemological persuasion.

99 Life Number

The 99 life number is similar to the 9 life number. Please review the 9 life number at this time.

As a 99, you are attracted to the fine arts, humanitarian organizations, groups with global concerns, philanthropic societies, spiritual groups and communications, to mention a few examples.

Your idealism and love for humanity may find you getting involved in important medical research, promoting inspirational music, channeling other worldly philosophies. Serving in some type of charitable work may be another option.

The Personal Year

Personal years repeat in a nine-year cycle. Each time the cycle is renewed, it provides the individual with the opportunity to face the lessons, challenges, opportunities and pitfalls of that vibration. As the cycle comes around again, there is another chance to move up a notch and face the lesson again if it has been unattended. On the other hand, if the aspirant has been doing well in the growth school of life, the lesson is there to be faced once more but on a higher level of the archetypal learning scale. At first this can be a difficult concept to grasp.

Each nine-year cycle is replete with innumerable chances for added self-understanding and wisdom. If one faces and overcomes the challenges of the cycle, new opportunities enter into the life path. However, if one fights, ignores or overreacts to circumstances, the same situations or very similar ones will reoccur. Therefore, this concept is well worth holding in one's mind. Knowledge of your personal year can be invaluable for accelerating your development in consciousness.

To determine your personal year number, add the month and day of birth to the universal year. Let us say your birthday is January 24. To find the personal year for 2005, add your month and day of birth to the universal year (2005 = 2 + 0 + 0 + 5 = 7). So you add 1 + 2 + 4 + 7 = 14. This is the pure number. Then add 1 + 4 to get 5 for your personal year number.

Here are some more examples:

Birth Month and Day	Universal Year	Calculation	Personal Year Number
September 10	1994	9 + 1 + 0 + 1 + 9 + 9 + 4 = 33	33 (6)
October 22	1956	1 + 0 + 2 + 2 + 1 + 9 + 5 + 6 = 26 = 2 + 6	8

Consider the following examples:

Birth Month and Day	Universal Year	Calculation	Personal Year Number
November 14	1917	1 + 1 + 1 + 4 + 1 + 9 + 1 + 7 = 25 = 2 + 5	7
November 14	1918	1 + 1 + 1 + 4 + 1 + 9 + 1 + 8 = 26 = 2 + 6	8
November 14	1919	1 + 1 + 1 + 4 + 1 + 9 + 1 + 9 = 27 = 2 + 7	9

In the above charts, I followed the rules for the pure number. For example, for the birth date of October 22, 1956, the pure number is displayed as 1 + 0 + 2 + 2 + 1 + 9 + 5 + 6 = 26.

The advanced student may wish to calculate master numbers as complete units to determine the potential for master numbers in the personal year (see the beginning of this chapter). Using the abovementioned example of October 22, 1956, such an alternative calculation using the master number would be as follows: 1 + 0 + 22 + 1 + 9 + 5 + 6 = 44 (8), which would be a master personal year. This is one of the areas of numerological research that needs further investigation.

The personal year should be scrutinized carefully, as it is one of the most significant cycles affecting consciousness. It is particularly important to watch those years that cross over the life number, personality number, soul number, karmic indicators and stress patterns. For example, if your soul number is 3, passing through the 3 personal year stimulates the yearning and restlessness of your soul to be one with its life goals. How you react to the annual vibrations is very indicative of the progress you are making in your journey of personal growth

1 Personal Year

The 1 personal year is the first of the entire nine-year personal year cycle. Therefore, it is easy to see the importance of getting off to a good start. This is the time to get in motion the things you want to get accomplished. Clear planning and thorough goal visualization add to the likelihood of success. If you delay changes in the 1 year or ignore the chance to expand, the steam might be taken out of the entire nine-year cycle. It is very difficult to break an apathetic or listless habit that is established during this year.

The 1 year is a time to convert ideas, aspirations and dreams into physical action. It often opens new opportunities in the job or business and is therefore a good time to add to your business or expand into wholly new facets of your profession. If you see no future in your present employment, the 1 year is the time to investigate the market for other possibilities. There may be a move to a new residence; there may be a fresh start. Take advantage of favorable opportunities that are presented at this time.

The 1 year intensifies the masculine energy patterns, emphasizing individuality, aggressiveness, courage and self-reliance. In a man's chart, the 1 year activates subconscious memories and conflicts related to early childhood, particularly those relating to the formation of his masculinity. Conflicts with his father, brothers, male schoolteachers, ministers or his own masculinity that have their origin in very early years (or prenatal time) are triggered. Once set loose, they flow into the stream of daily consciousness.

For instance, a boy may have had a father who did not want children and was unable to provide his son with confidence and support at key points in the building of his male identity—the first year in school, at puberty, when competing in a sport and playing in a key game, at his first job and so forth. Later in his adult life, that boy (having become a businessman) is faced with an excellent opportunity to start a new business venture. Professionally and intellectually he has all it takes to succeed, and consciously he knows this. However, subconsciously he may want to get back at his father's lack of concern by not wanting to give him the satisfaction of seeing his son become a success. Therefore, this businessman subconsciously finds reasons to delay the venture and creates critical mistakes that prevent a sure-fire business from developing. An awakened consciousness is needed to counter such an aversion to growth.

The 1 year attracts activities and situations that put pressure upon an individual to face the masculine conflicts within self. When such conflicts exist, the person's attitude can become hostile, overly assertive and defensive. This can be true for a woman passing through the 1 year. For instance, let us say her father (perhaps both parents) did not want a girl at the time of her birth. She feels angry and rejected on an unconsciousness level and compensates by trying to be the little boy (later man) Daddy wanted. This creates a false yang, or false animus energy. Rather than being assertive, she is aggressive. Rather than being strong, she is intimidating. Rather than moving with confidence at the right time, she forces the issue and tries to prove herself in almost exactly the same way as a man who is insecure within himself. This is an excellent time to get in touch with your own true male energy and release the rebellion that has been going on for much of your life. The 1 energy out of control often manifests in rebellion rather than confidence.

Passive traits of the 1 may come out as indifference, lethargy and stubborn resistance to opportunities. This is the passive side of willfulness: getting back at the parents by not doing anything to remind them of how badly they did their job. The unconscious message is, "You failed to prepare me properly for life, so now I am going to prove it by failing."

2 Personal Year

The 2 personal year is a time to nurture that which was started in the first year. This is a cycle of elaborating on and developing any ideas and new endeavors that you have initiated. If you resorted to negative resistance last year and did not take assertive steps with prospective opportunities, be ready for emotional trials that can take you deeper into the emotional roots of unconscious blocks and complexes. This is a time to pay attention to details and fine print, and your appearance and presentation will be particularly highlighted during this cycle. The downside is that this year can be one of gossip and behind-the-back criticism. Remember that what you send out comes back.

Cooperation with self and others is stressed, so it is time to expand friendships and contacts in your life. This is the time to be with compatible and supportive people who are on the track toward success. The spirit of sharing prevails. Diplomacy and timely pauses are characteristic of this time, which is in contrast with the assertive push of last year. Expansion and refinement of the things at hand are encouraged and socializing increases, so this can be an excellent time to meet important new contacts in your networking activities.

The 2 year relates to the feminine energy and stresses relationships with your mother, aunt, grandmother, as well as with the female teachers and supervisors in our life. As you pass through this year, old issues with this polarity of self will be stimulated, and where unresolved issues are uncovered, the emotions and conflicts of the past will arise with even more intensity. You will find yourself attracting relationships that act out old negative patterns related to childhood conflicts with your mother. For example, a man will enter a relationship with a woman who is very similar to his mother, which will often result in him acting out old negative patterns in a new relationship. If both parties are aware of the issues, it can be a major time of healing and recognition.

This year activates intuition and trust of inner awareness. It is a time to trust those deeper promptings and develop intuitive skills. Sometimes men can be uncomfortable developing the creative intuitive side of self because, in a man's world, it is not "macho"; he fears that the development of the feminine side will overwhelm his masculinity. Such fear is often related to memories of a domineering mother. For a woman, this time stirs up many old social and family attitudes about women and their role in the house, in society and in certain positions of business, politics and so on. She may start to remember painful experiences during her puberty or the discomfort of maturing into her feelings as a woman. This can be a time of active social reformation and speaking out about the injustices to women in modern society.

The number 2 is very much related to our public persona or social "image" and so indicates a time for recognizing the image you created to survive in your dysfunctional environment. Once this is done, you can cultivate a new image based upon your true identity and aligned with the inner self.

3 Personal Year

The 3 year is one of creativity, new ideas and self-expression, where the masculine 1 and the feminine 2 merge into a marriage of creative manifestation, and artistic and aesthetic proclivities are awakened. It is a time of flirtation, romance and being with good friends. Your natural charm is at a peak, and you radiate enthusiasm and joy. This time includes activities related to communications, media, entertainment, writing, public speaking and all forms of self-expression. Home decorating, beauty work, possible travel, involvement with luxury items and gardening are a few of the activities you might pursue.

As you pass through this year, you may well find yourself stimulated to develop artistic or aesthetic abilities. The 3 indicates a time of inspiration and expression, and dancing, painting and writing are some basic artistic skills that might come alive. For those in business, it might mean the creation of a new marketing strategy or product, and for those in science or a more technical arena, this could be a time of developing a new theory or hypothesis in your field of endeavor.

The 3 year emphasizes the trusting feelings and learning to be more honest with self and others in our relating of feelings. As it unfolds, you will most likely run the whole gamut of feelings and emotions from highs to lows, in a cycle that encourages the process of differentiating between emotions and feelings. You may experience a mystical-like connection of joy and love that comes from Source.

On the other hand, the 3 year may also find you plummeting into the depths of self-loathing, deprecation and despair. Be willing now to face the dark thoughts that threaten you and get to the source of their origin and force. You may want to seek a trained or professional helper if things get to be overwhelming. A trusted and honored support group is truly valuable to have at this time.

Three is related to creativity and sexuality. Very frequently, memories of past abuse surface in the 3 year. Promoting a creative product or idea can be difficult because of conflict regarding sex and creativity—the unconscious does not differentiate between the two. Sexual guilt or shame can manifest in hesitation to promote creative aspects of yourself, because you are afraid that someone will discover the truth of your lurid sexual (creative) past.

This is a favorable year for forming long-term relationships and/or marriage. The most important marriage you will ever experience is that of your inner man and your inner woman, and the 3 indicates a most auspicious cycle to heal the wounds from the past that are associated with your dysfunctional parents. By doing just that, you open the door to the possibility of integration of your anima and animus—the inner man and woman.

4 Personal Year

This is the year to roll up the sleeves and concentrate on the work at hand. Business matters, career and life work are important, so now is the time to build a solid foundation preparing you for the next move in your life plan. Put your best foot forward, and try to avoid complaining at work, as you may be under scrutiny by someone in a position to help your future. If you determine objectively that you are at a dead end, it is an excellent year to consider a new vocational direction.

If you are unwilling to make a timely move to further yourself, fate and circumstance may force you into a change—perhaps your company will downgrade and your position will become redundant. Circumstances may force you into considering something different and, in the end, probably more satisfactory.

Be aware and don't get yourself stuck in a workaholic pattern where you are avoiding more intimate life matters by staying busy on the job. Perhaps when you were young, your father or mother was a workaholic and constantly absent. As a child, you missed that parent very much and on an unconscious level blamed the loneliness and increasingly angry feelings of abandonment upon the father's or mother's work. Now, as an adult, these repressed feelings start to surface as you work harder and harder. Suddenly you manifest behavior that is embarrassing or sabotages your future; the angry inner child is trying to get back at the neglectful parent.

Another possible scenario is the father or mother who may be unwilling to change jobs and do something he or she would really like to do in order to keep a secure job that feeds the family (and specifically the unborn new child). The child in the womb senses this and begins to feel guilty for preventing the father or mother from doing something he or she really wanted to do. Later in life, such children will sabotage opportunities to do something they would really like to do, as a form of self-punishment by the guilty inner child.

On a spiritual level, the 4 year (especially after the twenty-eighth year) can stimulate the desire to do the Father's work, or the work of the soul. Where there is residue of resentment and anger toward the Earth father, there is anger toward the divine Father. (With working mothers, the same pattern develops, only the resentment is more focused upon lack of nurturing from the feminine side.)

This is an important time for contemplation and searching to get in touch with your inner work. The soul may be excited and unsettled, because it senses the approach of an important opportunity. The subconscious, however, distracts and diverts you from a core spiritually aligned course.

This is a time of loyalty and support for and from good friends. Be careful not to get in any kind of rut, emotional, mental or physical. Be willing to listen to new ways of improving your efficiency. As this year passes, you have the opportunity to elevate and expand your productivity and contribution to humankind.

5 Personal Year

This is a year of growth, change, freedom, travel and fun; especially travel is accentuated, to near and particularly to far-away places. Open yourself to new philosophies and ways of looking at life; mix and mingle among the many diverse cultures and subcultures of our world. The 5 is the number of the senses and of humanity. It encourages exploration of your sensuality and sexuality, and you may discover previously overlooked opportunity for pleasure and restoration. This would be an excellent time to further explore alternative healing methods that can improve health and tone up your body.

The desire to change the situation at work, which became noticeable during the past year, turns into an excellent opportunity for change of employment; perhaps the change comes in form of a move to a new department or a promotion. Either way, you will find yourself more able to use your diverse abilities that had become stagnant, in a more congenial atmosphere.

Impulsiveness, impatience and restlessness abound as you go on through the months. It is time to tap that nervous energy and put it to constructive use, time to get out of restrictive relationships and environments that no longer offer progression. However, be careful not to run prematurely from unfinished business, or you will find yourself stepping right back into the same type of situation.

Your desire for experiences can lead to dangerous participation in alcoholic, drug or toxic sexual indulgences. It is easy during this cycle to seek escapism through such potentially addictive behavior.

The 5 year accelerates lessons regarding moral, ethical, religious and social issues, and as people pass through this year, it often feels like they are reliving their teenage rebellion all over again. Therefore, you may find yourself struggling to disengage from rigid beliefs forced upon you in childhood. For instance, let's say you were raised in a strict religious environment where everything was sinful; let's say dancing was considered a major sin. Now you find yourself starting to enjoy dancing, but at the same time, you have deep feelings of guilt and shame for doing something your subconscious considers to be immoral. The 5 indicates that now is the time to learn, from experience, what is your own truth.

Five is the number of humanity, and it is the number of the divine laws of life. You can ignore the laws, you can defy the laws, or you can live in dharma and harmony with the laws. This is the time to know the difference and establish your imprint on life with relish and gusto.

6 Personal Year

The focus this year is upon home, marriage, responsibility, service, sacrifice and resolution of personal antagonisms, and for the single person, this can be one of the most fortuitous years for entering into a long-term relationship. Your need to serve may find you volunteering for a church or charity program, and you may find yourself called upon to render help to others with little notice. You are more concerned with health issues. It is also a year that might prompt you to decide to initiate the study of art or to pursue some other creative interest.

The 6 year seems to offer little time to satisfy personal desires. Friends and neighbors come over or call for advice, the job seems bogged down, or the children have more sickness and arguments that need attention. Bills get out of hand, relatives seem particularly troublesome, unexpected repairs arise and the spouse is less than cooperative.

Struggling marriages often come to an end during the 6 year. Most couples act out their parents' unconscious patterns, but aware couples are learning to separate from old, unconscious family patterns. The 6 is the archetypal number for codependency, and as you pass through this year, the tests of codependents will reoccur frequently if you have not begun to face and work through those issues, so this might be a good time to seek marriage counseling or professional help. The 6 cycle encourages establishing and maintaining a healthy relationship.

This phase in consciousness acts as a test of altruism. You accomplish most by putting others first at this time and resolving the immediate crisis. Yet it is also an easy time for false martyrdom: "Oh, look at all I've done for others, with no appreciation" is the oft-spoken plea during the 6 year. Forget the drama and face the demands; it is time to serve unselfishly. Be careful, however, lest others take advantage of your desire to be of assistance.

And herein is the flip side of the lesson. Being altruistic also means honoring yourself. The 6 year takes you through the lessons regarding boundaries. Because it is easy to get so involved in someone else's problems that you lose yourself and your identity in the process of serving another person, you need to learn that unselfishness includes a little of benign selfishness, that is, you need to be as good about caring for yourself as you are about caring for others. Then, when the call for help comes, you are clear of your own mess and able to serve totally and willingly when it is appropriate.

7 Personal Year

The 7 year is a time of meditation, introspection, study and self-examination. The year encourages philosophical searching and intellectual delving into the nature of universe, humanity and self. Your search for self-discovery may lead you to deeper investigation of psychology, scientific research, religious or metaphysical studies. No matter what path you choose, it leads to the understanding of life's great mysteries during this time of calm after the activity and upheaval of the past two years.

In many respects, the 7 year can be a lonely one, and as long as that's the case, you might as well learn to be comfortable with yourself. You seek quiet, tend to shun noise and raucous social gatherings and therefore may appear to be detached, aloof or indifferent. It might be a good idea to put a little extra effort into not ignoring others' sentiments.

You find time now to elevate your consciousness. Those of you who have been working for many years on expanding your awareness may be blessed this year with illumination from within. You may find clues that help you put your destiny into perspective; you may find cosmic clues as to the purpose of existence. You may experience revelation and the unfolding of your inner gifts of Spirit. At a minimum, you may get to hear a whisper of the small, still voice within.

The fickle finger of fate may throw the 7s who seem unable to slow down and take a look at life for a loop; they may find themselves involved in an accident or illness that puts them in bed and forces them to be quiet. So by knowing the cycles, 7s can work in harmony and make mishaps a less likely probability.

Many adults use intellectualism as a means of avoiding feelings and inner emotional turmoil, and they are not "there" in the day-to-day home activities even though they are present. If you were a child in such a home, you may find yourself becoming depressed and angry as the 7 year progresses, since the loneliness and pain of having been intellectually abandoned comes to the surface. The good news is that now you can do something about it.

Each time we expand upward in awareness, we also delve deeper into the recesses of our subconscious motivation and, as a result, some of the residue and debris stirred up the past few years may surface at this time. You may find yourself moribund, cynical and skeptical of anything promising a better life. Do not let repression or confusion disturb your ability to find inner peace. A tempestuous sea may rage around you; however, your keel is set, and the inner rudder should be firm enough to conquer the threatening currents of mass skepticism, doubt and discouragement.

8 Personal Year

The 8 year places emphasis upon themes of advancement, social status, finances, executive ability, power, authority and business interests. If you spent time in the 7 year working on self-integration, you should find yourself ready to reenter the social environment with greater confidence and inner strength. It is time to live fully the newly found truth and wisdom you acquired during the past year.

The world will recognize your potential and skills, and the year brings promotions, advancement and recognition for your achievements. Go slowly and cautiously with this newly acquired power and authority and be aware that 8s very often feel they have deserved the attention or promotion for a long time. The inner hostility and resentment from injured pride has been simmering, and finally, when the recognition comes, the pride and ego needs dictate some vengeful or rash behavior. Avoid the evils of false pride in this year and enhance your natural ability to inspire and lead.

On the dark side, along the same vein, the year can also bring frustration with authority. Perhaps your parents held strong moral, political, ethical or social bias, which were unjustly or abusively administrated. The unconscious still retains resentment and anger toward the misused authority, so you may find yourself constantly thwarted by coworkers, spouse, friends or relatives. These people help bring to your attention the underlying issues that can be released. They will challenge your word on everything, from how to fry an egg to celestial cosmology. Watch your reaction to confrontation, since herein is the clue to your growth opportunity: If you attempt to win every argument; refuse to listen, nod politely and later criticize; or quote endless sources as support to your thesis, something is awry. It is time to flex a little and be willing to learn from others. It is time to let go of institutional domination, social pressure, family dictates and subconscious tyranny. See them for what they are, and relax.

This is the year to recognize and live by the dictates of higher authority. Power should be balanced with compassion and consideration of others. This does not justify breaking the laws of society, but it may require an active participation in restoring divine law to man's affairs. You may become critical of church, political or civil authority. Supervisors or leaders in your department or business will receive the wrath of your opinions. This year is a reminder that the misuse of power and authority you see in others, which troubles you so much, is simply seeing yourself. It is very likely that in a previous life or lives, you have committed those very transgressions.

Dealing with money is particularly important this year. A proper perspective should be encouraged that recognizes the rightful energy exchange involved with monetary transactions. You can increase your earnings and cash flow this year, so concentrate on your sense of dollar worth. Many students of the light have an aversion to earning money, especially when this is associated with spiritual work. There can be old vows in the unconscious from a time when spiritual people had to take the vow of poverty, so now you are afraid that if you have money, you will not grow spiritually.

This is a good time to study the laws of prosperity and work through poverty consciousness. As long as we live in a monetary society, it will take money to sponsor the institutions and businesses of light. Money earned through greed and unethical practices may slip through your fingers, but money acquired through the application of divine principles can yield rich rewards to be used for the building of a better world. This is a most favorable time to reap the rewards of abundance.

9 Personal Year

This year brings a nine-year cycle to its finale and closes one way of living while offering the prospect of a renewed and revised style of living ahead. The 9 is all-inclusive, containing all of the previous vibrations, so this year will bring a variety of life events. It is a finishing cycle and, with few exceptions, it is not the time to enter new business, marriage, jobs or partnerships. However, if you feel that you want to initiate a new commitment, such changes are more likely to prove successful after September of a 9 year.

Often overlooked in numerical interpretation is the importance of the reality that 9 is also the number of our deepest wishes and dreams come true. If we have been doing our cleansing and following the cycles of personal growth in a healthy manner, the 9 year can bring a culmination of great fulfillment and contentment. If you have truly balanced the karmic ledger and gotten your "stuff" together, this can be a year to enter a dreamed-of relationship or marvelous business venture. The key to knowing is through the settled heart and inspired brain.

This is an excellent time to sort through the psychological framework and get rid of remnants of your growth and breakthroughs of earlier years in this cycle, recognizing immature emotions, negative thinking and other restrictive behavior patterns. This can be one of the easiest times for release of the negative if you cooperate with the cycle. In therapeutic terms, we say this is a good time to get rid of old "stuff." Those who tenaciously cling to the past may have some heavy going this year, because the 9 year can be one of depression, illness and constant frustration when nothing works. It is time to let go. That which should be eliminated now becomes a burden if carried over into the new cycle next year.

The 9 year is full of mood swings and unexpected happenings. Friendships, marriages and partnerships that have been floundering will face a point of reckoning during this cycle. Loss of a loved one can open old wounds and inner searching. Be willing to let go of relationships that are no longer in touch with the changes taking place in your life, and let new contacts and acquaintances enter your life to infuse new vigor into the life stream.

This is a year of letting go of selfish needs and giving birth to the altruistic inspiration within your heart and soul. It can bring greatly increased intuition and artistic inspiration, and psychic sensitivity grows stronger. Open your heart to the possibility of having your fondest dreams come true. Balance the ledger and be ready for the new cycle ahead.

11 Personal Year

The 11 personal year is very similar to the 2 personal year. Please review the 2 personal year at this time.

A heightened religious, mystical and psychic awareness can lead you into a deeper investigation of this phenomenon, so this is a time to develop latent spiritual gifts. The year stimulates inspired thinking, originality, invention and breakthroughs of awareness that could bring you into social prominence. You could be called upon to speak out publicly about a controversial social situation, which can stir up old fears of public embarrassment or rejection. Be careful of fanaticism and becoming overzealous.

22 Personal Year

The 22 personal year is very similar to the 4 personal year. Please review the 4 personal year at this time.

The year opens the door to a greater understanding of your soul purpose, and you may find yourself in a situation where you must choose between a secure position and opportunity to do something that thrills your heart. This year may present an opportunity to serve on a greater scale, and you may find yourself involved with institutions or organizations that deal with crises and rebuilding the infrastructure after disasters; interaction with administration of projects affecting large masses of people is emphasized. Use this time to turn the directives of your soul into tangible realities.

33 Personal Year

The 33 personal year is very similar to the 6 personal year. Please review the 6 personal year at this time.

This year may bring about a very difficult sacrifice of personal time to get involved in a life-saving effort for others. For example, you may find yourself in the middle of a life-saving medical effort. The theme this year focuses upon large-scale efforts to improve the welfare and health of many people, so you could find yourself in the middle of an epidemic or unknown health threat to the population.

If you are an artist, you may find your method of expression rising to a new level and dimension of expression. The tuned-in musician now hears a symphony of the spheres amid the raucous noise of popular tunes. Your emotional instincts are heightened and on alert.

44 Personal Year

The 44 personal year is very similar to the 8 personal year. Please review the 8 personal year at this time.

This is a time of enormous effort, with the offer of equal rewards. You could be called upon to serve on a large project or task. Your academic training and specialized education pays off handsome dividends at this time. You may be taken away from family and friends for a long period of time and find yourself among a team of well-trained specialists working to meet a timely and life-saving deadline. You could be promoted because of your intellectual solidity and timely intuitive discernment.

55 Personal Year

The 55 personal year is very similar to the 1 personal year. Please review the 1 personal year at this time.

You may now find yourself arguing with God and angels about the messy predicament you have been called upon to clean up. You are bold, courageous and full of determination to overcome almost impossible odds. Despite the things you must relinquish, the opportunity to learn miraculous new things makes the trouble more than worth your commitment. You may be challenged in such a way that it makes you stand up for your highest of ideals.

66 Personal Year

The 66 personal year is very similar to the 3 personal year. Please review the 3 personal year at this time.

Your range of emotional swings can be more intense at this time. You go through an internal purging of past memories of emotional misjudgment and abuse. As you continue through the year, an opening of the heart takes you into a never experienced level of forgiveness and release. You connect with the right people at the right organization, where you improve your skills that help others to improve their lives.

77 Personal Year

The 77 personal year is very similar to the 5 personal year. Please review the 5 personal year at this time.

Much of your searching and forays of curiosity are rewarded during this year as you put together a system of living that optimizes growth and development of human potential. You are able to more clearly explain your philosophy to others, and many come to hear your ideas. You find yourself preparing a new avenue of research into mind realms of time and travel. Your most important journey this year may be to a new realm of existence.

88 Personal Year

The 88 personal year is very similar to the 7 personal year. Please review the 7 personal year at this time.

You find yourself amid a laboratory-like setting of investigation and research. Your skills of science and math come to the foreground now to help solve a problem that will result in relief to thousands of souls. For the artist, this time brings into focus a long-elusive search to put into form a cherished vision of light. You are promoted to the forefront of a powerful team of professionals who are on the verge of linking science and spiritual concepts.

99 Personal Year

The 99 personal year is very similar to the 9 personal year. Please review the 9 personal year at this time.

You are excited, ecstatic and on the verge of enlightenment as this year progresses. As the heart opens, you feel the need to serve on a larger scale. Your creative energies are alive and functioning at the finest level of perception. You see a greater plan on Earth by which humanity can live in greater peace and harmony. Selfish needs are put on hold as you are called upon to take on the needs of many troubled souls.

Personal Month

To calculate the personal month number, simply add the universal month to your own personal year. If, for example, you are calculating the month of June and you are in a 7 personal year, you add 6 (June) + 7 (personal year) = 13 = 1 + 3 = 4 personal month. The calculation using pure numbers applies to determining the personal month.

An alternative method is for more experienced practitioners who wish to make the calculation using master numbers: Let's say you are calculating the month of November and are in a 22 personal year. In this case, you could add 11 (November) + 22 = 33 (6) personal month.

The interpretation of the personal month is similar to interpreting the personal year, but it is slightly scaled down to fit the month. The experienced numerologist will already know how to do this. For those just getting started, some brief interpretations follow.

1 Personal Month

Initiate new projects, record ideas, be willing to change and stand up for individual rights. Overcome procrastination and laziness, passive anger, egocentric pride, defeatism.

2 Personal Month

Be of assistance, harmonious; get details out of the way, build network, recuperate. Overcome pettiness, gossip, overreaction, neglecting of details, projecting blame.

3 Personal Month

Promote artistic skills, make time for good friends, enjoy entertainment, express joy, make time for romance. Overcome moribund moods, extravagance, envy and jealousy, scattered energies.

4 Personal Month

Get organized, finish work project, cultivate loyal friends, teach practical skills, be prompt. Overcome stubbornness and laziness, envy of others' accomplishments, self-defeating attitude.

5 Personal Month

Travel, excitement, sexual exploration, meeting new people, open to diverse ideas, new experiences. Overcome prejudice, addictions, compulsive sex, avoiding experience, fear of travel.

6 Personal Month

Attention to family and children, public service, music and art, new relationships; redecorate. Overcome codependent relationships, fierce idealism, fear of commitment, poor living habits.

7 Personal Month

Take time out for rest and quiet, examine things thoroughly, don't force issues, enjoy reading and contemplation. Overcome social anxiety, detachment from feelings, mental arrogance, cynicism.

8 Personal Month

Assume management role, increase earnings, organize environment, resolve legal issues, follow inner guidance. Overcome abuse of power, dubious investment offers, fear of taking charge, overspending.

9 Personal Month

Nurture compassion, look at global picture, refine artistic aptitudes, find support group, find strategy for realistic dreams. Overcome naive idealism, prejudice, wasteful fantasizing, depression.

11 Personal Month

Develop intuition and esoteric knowledge; public service; nurture a new idea or invention; public speaking. Overcome being overcritical, fear of social rejection, misuse of psychic talents, false idealism.

22 Personal Month

Involvement in worldwide movements, practical mysticism, esoteric ritual, education of children, big business. Overcome workaholic pattern, repressed anger, black magic, fear to speak out against impropriety.

33 Personal Month

Administer to the many, apply healing skills, listen to the angels; interdimensional art; expand support group. Overcome compulsive caretaking, sexual fears, unrealistic expectations, self-importance.

44 Personal Month

Trust guidance in leadership role; training and wisdom come together; work escalates; apply sacred geometry. Overcome fear of power, rigid methodology, fear of trusting higher guidance, quick-fix schemes.

55 Personal Month

Follow inspiration; creative mind yields profitable concept; your leadership inspires; share higher laws with others. Overcome egocentricity, fear of leadership, hesitation to present ideas, fear of God.

66 Personal Month

Bring music of the spheres to others; blend medical and alternative healing methods; cultivate voice; spread joy of Spirit. Overcome self-effacement, sexual guilt, fear of trusting others, worry.

77 Personal Month

Share esoteric wisdom at the right time; research yields secret truth; additional schooling is helpful; take lead in educational training. Overcome preconceived dogma, mental defeatism, addiction to books, exploitive schemes.

88 Personal Month

Integrate sacred math into the equation; become the living truth; raise money for altruistic cause; establish a sacred group. Overcome black magic, arrogance, fear of authority, get-rich schemes.

99 Personal Month

Be open to channeling higher guidance; record archetypal visions; join the greater cause; release inspired artwork. Overcome rigid heart, defiance of higher laws, fear of losing ego, rejection of body.

Personal Week

A cyclical pattern other authors have not mentioned but that I have found to be very useful is the weekly cycle. The personal week number is determined independently from the personal month and day, although it is very intimately related to the personal year.

To determine the personal week, start with the number of the personal year and add it to the weekly number. For example, the week of June 26 to July 2, 1977, is the 26th week of the calendar year. Add the 2 and 6, which makes 8 $(2 + 6 = 8)$. Then add the 8 to your own personal year. Following the personal week cycles is important, and I have found it rewarding when helping people make decisions. To determine the number 1 week of the universal year, you start with the first week that has a Monday.

Personal weeks with master numbers can be calculated both ways, as a reminder of the added potential. Rules regarding master numbers are the same as indicated for the life number at the beginning of this chapter.

By now you should have a feel of the cycles so you can make your own interpretation for the personal week. If in doubt, use the personal year and personal month information and tone it down to fit the shortened length for the week.

Personal Day

To determine your personal day number, add the appropriate calendar date to your personal year. Let's say you want to determine the personal day for August 29, 2002, and you were born on December 21, 1966.

Your personal year is calculated as 1 + 2 + 2 + 1 + 4 (for the universal year 2002) = 10 = 1 + 0 = 1. Then add 8 + 2 + 9 + 1 = 20 = 2 + 0 = 2 personal day.

Here is another example, for someone born March 23, 1972: Add 3 + 2 + 3 + 4 (2002 universal year) = 12 = 1 + 2 = 3 personal year. Now add 8 + 2 + 9 + 3 = 22 (4) personal day.

Rules regarding master numbers are the same as indicated for the life number at the beginning of this chapter.

For interpretations of your personal day, go to the sections for the personal year, month and week. Study the meaning of the numbers and apply them to the given day.

Triune Cycles

The triune cycles help to delineate three major phases of one's life—education, maturity and reflection. The duration of the cycles is approximately twenty-seven years, based upon the equation of 9 (completion) times 3 (creative expression). The triune cycles reflect things going on within the individual. The pinnacles, which we will look at later, are more indicative of external factors impacting one's life.

To determine which number governs each phase of the cycle, you need the month, day and year of birth:

1. The number of the month governs the first phase of the triune cycles.

2. The number of the day determines the number of the second phase.

3. Finally, the number of the year of birth determines the number of the third phase.

To compute the beginning and end of each phase, start with the month, day and year of birth. The first phase is, in effect, from birth until the 1 personal year closest to the twenty-seventh year of age. The second phase goes from there until the closest 1 personal year to the fifty-fourth year of age. The third phase continues until the end of one's life. Here is an example:

The date of birth is December 11, 1934, so this person turns twenty-seven in 1961, which is a 4 personal year. Calculate back to 1958, which is a 1 personal year.

As a reminder of the added potential, you can do the calculations with master numbers. Rules regarding master numbers are indicated at the beginning of this chapter.

1. The first triune phase (1 + 2 = 3) is in effect from 1934 to 1958. The 54th year is 1988, another 4 personal year. You go back to 1985, which is a 1 personal year.

2. The second phase (11) goes from 1958 to 1985.

3. Finally, the third phase (1 + 9 + 3 + 4 = 17 = 1 + 7 = 8) goes from 1985 to the end of life.

1 in the Triune Cycles

The 1 cycle is a time of testing the development of individuality and will. During the passing of this cycle, you can anticipate being tested by encounters and confrontations with strong-willed souls similar to yourself, but with differing agendas. You will be forced into circumstances that push you to express your own identity and take a stand regarding your convictions. You will be challenged to live your truth and be an example of your inner wisdom. You are learning to grow beyond the lessons of survival and into the process of learning to participate in life.

During the first phase, you will most likely encounter domineering or willful parents (or a parent), who may try to impose their agenda upon your life without taking time to notice what you might be here to do. You will have to stand up to teachers, bosses and other authority figures who can be intimidating and overwhelming. This is a test of individuality and inner strength where the challenge is to grow and mature without being overridden with rebellion, anger and devious avoidance of issues. The lesson also includes learning to respect the individuality and will of others.

During the second and third phases, these lessons can become less confrontational and more developmental of mature response and growth. You are inventive, creative and dynamic as you grow. You take initiative with confidence and self-assurance after finding yourself at the forefront of reform, revision and recharging society. The tests of the second and third phases have to do with making the transition from personal will to trust in divine will. Your spiritual faith and trust in higher principles become the focus of learning.

2 in the Triune Cycles

During the 2 cycle, the lessons are of learning to find your own true identity and self-image. In the first phase, there is the likelihood of living with parents who are attached to presenting a specific public image to the neighbors (society). Usually, something is being hidden that has occurred in the family past and as a result, there is a fixation on appearances. You could be forced to live by that measurement, with little attention given to developing your true nature. There can be oversensitivity to criticism and controversy. You are not taught to stand up for yourself but to appear the way others expect you to. The result of living according to these mixed messages is confusion of identity and frustration in being natural and comfortable with self.

During the second and third phases, you have a chance to establish your own identity and work within the framework of society to bring about more integrity to institutions that serve the collective consciousness. You can be direct and tactful at the same time, and you are learning to refine your behavior and establish an etiquette that is appropriate without selling out your foundation of principle. You will be placed in a position to negotiate and bring together people and groups with opposing or divergent beliefs and points of view. The final test of this lesson is to be centered within your true image of divine self.

3 in the Triune Cycles

This is a time of dealing with true feelings and expression of heart and soul. The first phase of the cycle is characterized by living in a family where emotions are stifled and repressed and where an environment of coldness or threat exists. You may have to hide your spontaneous joy and natural childlike gaiety. With time you learn to seek your own joy and leave the fear-based family pattern. Honesty of feelings is not welcome in a dysfunctional family setting, and potential talents and creative interests can go ignored or discouraged.

During the second and third phases, you have the opportunity—and it becomes easier—to shout out loud the great joy of life within your being. You want to dance, sing, write, type and tell all of living life fully and completely. Your talents blossom and you bring your full range of artistry into light. Three is the Christ word spoken; when in harmony, you speak with the voice of angels and dance like the sprites of the forest.

4 in the Triune Cycles

In the first phase, you may be living in a family environment with an overdriven or workaholic parent, and as a result, work ethic is associated with pain, anger and denial, causing you to avoid the pain by avoiding work. Or perhaps your lesson revolves around a parent (or parents) who has no discipline and is unable to give you any sense of definition or direction to life, so you are aimless, undisciplined and lost, and you may have trouble being motivated and consistent in work habits. Either way, it could take time for you to find your path of passion and purpose. You can easily become stuck in stubborn patterns of belligerence and unproductive repetition.

During the second and third phases, there is a more positive trend. You find it easier to discipline your life and the work of choice comes into your life naturally. You are directed and dutiful in your profession of choice, live by the highest ethics and are admired for your accomplishment and clarity. As you come into harmony with soul and self, you connect to the real purpose and work of your true being.

5 in the Triune Cycles

The 5 stresses lessons related to sensationalism, sex and the senses—you have come to learn to live. The early years of your life are spent in a parental environment that distorts the life pattern, for example, you may be born into a family dealing with addiction and indulgence that is out of control. The paradoxical side is that you may be born into an early environment of fear and unwillingness to participate in the activities of living. Perhaps it was a strict religious doctrine or rigid social rules that governed the household activities; or perhaps your parents were intolerant and prejudiced toward certain nationalities or cultures. You are learning to determine your own healthy lifestyle and interaction with humanity and yourself.

In the second and third phases, your life opens up to exotic experiences, travel and an opportunity to meet people of diverse roots and backgrounds. You have the freedom to go places and do things for which many admire you. The final phases emphasize living in harmony with the divine laws of life.

6 in the Triune Cycles

The lessons of the first phase of the cycles find you in a position of responsibility to others that is not of your making. Perhaps you have to take care of an invalid parent or someone not able to keep up with life. Tension between your parents can cause a distorted view of relationships that puts you into a codependent spin, and your early relationships will be intense and challenging. You may seek outlets such as art or other creative activities. Your early career positions could end up being service oriented.

The focus during the second and third phases is more upon improved relationships, relationships that bring contentment and harmony. If you end up in a position of serving others, it will likely be from dharmic choice rather than karmic necessity. You may be drawn into education or media work, where you can get your message to more people.

7 in the Triune Cycles

The early years of this phase find you cut off from others and with a lot of time to reflect and review. Perhaps you choose this lifestyle like a monk, or perhaps events in your life place you into such a setting. You turn inward to search for spiritual roots and connection to your internal source of true wisdom. During this period, you may be inclined toward positions of research and investigation. Be careful that you are not using this phase as time spent in mental escape from repressed feelings and hidden fears.

During the second and third phases, the 7 still indicates quiet time and a reflective state of mind, and you may want to use this time in life to ponder and record truth that comes from the higher expression of the mind. You could choose a field of research that challenges your curiosity and thirst for accumulated important facts and documents.

8 in the Triune Cycles

The early years of phase 1 are characterized by confrontations with authority figures and possible abuse or misuse of power. Probably one of your parents in particular chooses to dominate the family environment with the gospel according to him (her). Money can be used as a tool for manipulation, which leaves you with a bad taste for money and success. You crave authority but find it slipping through your fingers in the early years. The use of money is important during this time, as there are many lessons associated with it for you to ponder.

During the second and third phases, the presence of this number can indicate a time to assume a greater role of leadership and authority. As you learn to trust inner authority and live by its guidance, you will find yourself wanting to empower others by educating them in the ways of discovering their own Source. This can be a time of prosperity and success.

9 in the Triune Cycles

The early years of the first phase can be trying and discouraging, because your hopes and wishes are thwarted at every turn and you go through the highs and lows of emotional mood swings. There are likely some deep secrets hidden in the closet of your dark side, which haunt you ceaselessly on an unconsciousness level. As you journey into the search for well-being, you can root these out and regain conscious domain.

During the second and third phases, the 9 can still indicate delay and self-searching, but it usually takes on a milder side of this process and directs you toward the realization of inner hopes and dreams. Your higher creative abilities flourish and expand. You are learning to let go of ego aspiration and let the inspirations from higher self enter more easily.

11 in the Triune Cycles

The 11 in the triune cycles is similar to the 2; please review that section at this time.

In the early years, the 11 can bring strange dreams, visitations from other dimensions (that you may not remember) and precocious abilities of thought or artistic expression. If these capacities exist, it may be difficult for you to develop them, because you may have a fearful family or a repressive social influence. The presence of 11 often means public recognition, which may come at an early age, though it is less likely that this will happen in the first phase.

Eleven in the second and third phases favors the manifestation of higher intuitive abilities and psychic talents. You have a charismatic flair of presentation, and you are articulate and inspirational as a motivational spokesperson. When 11 is in this position, the likelihood of public attention is heightened.

22 in the Triune Cycles

The 22 in the triune cycles is similar to the 4; please review that section at this time.

Twenty-two in this position brings a longing for mystical knowledge and proof of spiritual and mystical realities. You may feel there is something important to get done. Training during this time can later prove to be most significant to your destiny, but you may wonder why you take on a number of seemingly insignificant types of work and labor.

In the second and third phases, the 22 suggests the discipline and attunement necessary to get the work of the soul accomplished. You find yourself attracted to important people who are intent on getting revealed requests of Spirit completed. You are drawn to large institutions and organizations whose aims are well motivated and inspirational in their efforts.

Pinnacles

The meaning of the pinnacles comes from an old observation that there are four peaks of attainment during the life cycle. The prominent age around which the calculations are made is the thirty-sixth year (4 is the number of formation x 9, which is the number of completion). The pinnacles give an indication of opportunity and circumstances life offers along our path of self-awareness.

The first pinnacle is self-oriented and related to the start of life and the formative events that shape and influence our fate. The second pinnacle is related to group service as well as the obligations to society and the world in which we live. The third pinnacle is a combination of the entire birth date, and if your life is in order, this is a prime period of accomplishment and personal achievement. The fourth pinnacle presents a time for appreciation and reflection of life's experiences. If you have missed steps, this can be a time of some regret and remorse, but there is also the implication of a second chance to get things more aligned with heart and soul.

The pinnacles play an important role in the interpretation of life events. You will want to note particularly when the pinnacle is the same as other major numbers in your chart, such as the soul number or life number, for example.

To calculate the duration for each pinnacle, start with the number 36. Subtract your life number, and you get the length of the first pinnacle. To determine the length of the second pinnacle, add nine years to this number; add another 9 years for the third, and yet another nine years for the fourth pinnacle, which then continues until the end of your life.

To determine the number for the first pinnacle, add the month and day of your birth. To determine the number for the second pinnacle, add the day and year of your birth. To determine the number for the third pinnacle, add the first and second pinnacles. And to determine the number for the fourth pinnacle, add the month and year of your birth.

For the following example, the birth date is December 11, 1934, which results in the 22 (4) life number.

Duration	
First pinnacle	32 years (36 - 4, the life number, or until 1966)
Second pinnacle	1966 to 1975 (1966 + 9)
Third pinnacle	1975 to 1984 (1984 + 9)
Fourth pinnacle	1984 to end of life
Numbers	
First pinnacle	$1 + 2 + 11 = 14 = 1 + 4 = 5$
Second pinnacle	$11 + 1 + 9 + 3 + 4 = 28 = 2 + 8 = 10 = 1 + 0 = 1$
Third pinnacle	$5 + 1 = 6$
Fourth pinnacle	$1 + 2 + 1 + 9 + 3 + 4 = 20 = 2 + 0 = 2$ Note: You can find a potential master number here, if you reduce the 12 to 3 and add to the total o 1934, which is 8 $(1 + 9 + 3 + 4)$, so you get the $8 + 3 = 11$. See the explanation in the life number sescription that destribes locating potential master numbers.

1 in the Pinnacles

Develop independent style without rebellion, inspire and lead, innovate and invent, bring freedom to self and others, fight oppression and intimidation.

First Pinnacle

In your early years, you likely lived with a strong-willed parent (or parents) and encountered confrontations with authority figures and aggressive personalities. You were challenged, threatened and possibly abused. You struggled to assert your own identity and likely rebelled often against those who you felt oppressed you. You have developed a strong identity and believe that you have much to prove to the world about what you can do. There are, however, many obstacles in your way.

Second Pinnacle

You have been placed in situations where you have had to learn to be assertive and strong in the expression of your personality. It has not been easy, and you carry much anger with you. You are learning to recognize the proper use of will, and you can see that it is important to honor the individuality in others as much as you honor your own. It will be easier now to accomplish what you want, and others will respond to you favorably as you demonstrate a mature and direct manner of assertiveness.

Third Pinnacle

You have become more confident and content within yourself. As you learn to resolve ego needs and grow into an understanding of true inner needs, you find that life flows with more rhythm and ease. You may be called upon now to take the initiative not only for yourself but also in a way that will have impact upon the lives of many people.

Fourth Pinnacle

You have come to realize the importance of developing your individuality and being true to yourself in life's interactions, and you have come to appreciate the individuality of all children in creation. You seek to align your personal will with the higher will of divine guidance and have the opportunity to find the real purpose for your life.

2 in the Pinnacles

Learn tact and negotiation skills, develop healthy self-image, fight gossip and negative criticism, pay attention to details, advance through diplomacy.

First Pinnacle

Your early years can find you mired in details and frustrated by what seems like an infinite amount of trivial social mores creating petty actions by those around you. You are criticized and made to feel that you do not conform to the social norms of the day. Gossip, pettiness and unnecessary misunderstandings disrupt your life.

Second Pinnacle

You are beginning to recognize the dysfunctional behavior that is a part of the daily social interaction of the time. You are becoming more aware of people's insensitivities and petty nature and see these qualities more readily within yourself. With recognition comes the possibility of releasing them from your life, helping to identify dysfunctional patterns and then starting to bring a more healthy social interaction into manifestation.

Third Pinnacle

You are more comfortable in social situations and can participate in the trivial and banal protocols that are part of the daily fabric of social interaction. You have faced the skeletons in your own closet that have prevented you from becoming more vocal and active in bringing positive change to social cancers. Your openness and honesty are key ingredients that give others the courage to freely share the same.

Fourth Pinnacle

With experience, self-growth and maturity, you have come to a point in your life where you are free to shed the false persona that is so necessary for ego functioning in social discourse. You are able and willing to let your inner self be revealed, giving others a glimpse of your core eternal identity, which intimidates many and confuses more. With time you attract similar souls and start to build a base of cultural behavior mirroring the expression of eternal wisdom and higher truth.

3 in the Pinnacles

Develop creative potentials; overcome fear of feelings; speak and articulate issues; spread joy and cheer; sing, dance and be merry.

First Pinnacle

You were likely born into a family environment where feelings were repressed and inhibited, so it was not easy to be spontaneous or show creative splurges. The likelihood of sexual repression and even abuse is strongly suggested with this combination. Access may have been denied to modes or apparatus of creativity; for example, you may have exhibited great flair for music, but your family could not afford to provide the instrument.

Second Pinnacle

You are more able to develop and explore feelings and emotions, perhaps uncovering bitterness and despair from early years. You may well find yourself becoming actively involved with artistic expression, entertainment or some form of participation in the media. Singing, dancing, writing and other forms of communication are emphasized.

Third Pinnacle

Highly refined and subtle feelings of the soul come to the surface as you take time to clear out the debris of negative emotions stored in your experience for years and years. You may choose to become a performer of some kind and share your gifts of artistic flourish with the public. Imagination is more active and inspirations come more frequently during this influence.

Fourth Pinnacle

Late in life, you may find yourself becoming very active as an artist in some form of creative endeavor. You listen to the music of the spheres and communicate with other realms of existence. This is a wonderful time with friends and family and brings self-expression to a very highly developed degree.

4 in the Pinnacles

Build solid loyalties, overcome laziness and procrastination, establish a solid work ethic, build solid foundation for the future, overcome workaholic pattern.

First Pinnacle

You were likely born into a family where one or both of your parents were workaholics or obsessive-compulsive about what they were doing, and you probably experienced the loss of a parent who was absent a lot because of his/her job or career. Proportionate to the amount of time the parent was absent is the amount of confusion, pain and anger that resides inside the inner child who misses Dad or Mom. There is still a lot of pain and the tendency to sabotage your own work efforts because of the unconscious residue left over from that time. As a result, you may find yourself struggling with your work or career through this pinnacle.

Second Pinnacle

You are struggling to find your own separate purpose and life work, because you realize that it is not going to make you happy to please your parents or someone else by doing what you think they want you to do. You are overcoming your tendency toward procrastination and find something that you really want to do in your life.

Third Pinnacle

Things go better for you in your chosen life work. You have settled into a career routine that gives you satisfaction and a fulfilled sense of accomplishment, and you now have the additional time to give to your loved ones around you. Because you have found more of yourself and have grown in confidence and self-esteem, you have more to share and give to those closest to you.

Fourth Pinnacle

You are a rare person who has taken the time and effort to weave your way through the trials and tribulations of self-growth. You have sought a spiritual path in an effort to follow the higher will and have searched throughout most of your life to find the inner work of your life. This period finds you discovering that path and purpose, and once you have done that, you feel the integrative power of doing divine work on a mundane level.

5 in the Pinnacles

Introduction to varied cultures, travel, unusual inner and outer experiences, overcome addictions, sexual and sensual lessons, fun and humor.

First Pinnacle

It is very likely that you grew up in a family struggling with the issues of alcoholism, drug addiction and/or sexual addiction and abuse, even though the opposite might seem true in that your family did not appear to manifest any of these addictive patterns but did everything to look right and act properly social. Most likely your family behaved this way because they were trying to get out of the addictive pattern of the previous generation. This period will be rich in travel and numerous opportunities for you to be introduced to many choices of life experience and indulgences.

Second Pinnacle

You are learning to gain control of your senses, so to say. This is a time of recognizing the difference between addictive behaviors and healthy, life-supporting experiences. Your travel schedule will most likely pick up during this time, and you will circulate among a varied selection of human interests and cultures. From experience comes recognizing your own identity and what it is that best contributes to the ongoing evolution of your soul experience.

Third Pinnacle

You have traveled far and wide both on Earth and in other worlds. Your spiritual self is integrating with your material personality, and you relish life to its fullest. Unconscious excesses and past indulgences come into the light for scrutiny and resolution. You can look at your dark side as well as at the shining star of divinity within you and learn to live by inner guidance rather than external whim.

Fourth Pinnacle

You have seen the light and are learning to live in the light. Although your direction is decidedly spiritual, that does not mean you must exclude the joys of flesh and existence upon the material Earth plane. You have found the balance between learning and indulging. Now you absorb life experience and move readily into the next level of education.

6 in the Pinnacles

Many lessons of love, home responsibilities, caring for others (and most importantly, caring for yourself); develop artistic interests; overcome codependent issues.

First Pinnacle

Your early life was most likely made uneasy by the tension in your parents' relationship, and as a result, you struggle with issues of trust and intimacy and have difficulty differentiating boundaries in your personal relationships. Rather than trying to determine how others want you to respond, you are learning to honor your own inner feelings. This is a learning cycle for relationships, and you will likely deal with issues of divorce and separation at some time during this cycle.

Second Pinnacle

This is a time of sorting through your insecurities and issues of trust, commitment and boundaries. You have begun to learn that the most important relationship is the one with yourself. As you go through the self-healing cycle, you start to develop more healthy relationships in all matters of life.

Third Pinnacle

Your learning curve of self-healing and mending emotional scars has progressed well. Having attained a level where you are feeling good about yourself and your growth, you want to give more of what you have learned to others. This is a time of giving, sharing and reaping the rewards of balanced and rewarding relationships.

Fourth Pinnacle

You are blessed with the time and maturity to give of the accumulated wisdom accrued over the years of your life. More of your time is spent cultivating a relationship with Spirit, or God, in whatever manner you connect with Source. Your calm and melodious manner is a healing machine in itself. You have gained much from life and have much to give back to it.

7 in the Pinnacles

Religious and spiritual experiences, study and research, introspection and meditation, overcome arrogance, balance the spiritual and the material.

First Pinnacle

In the early years of your life, you may feel isolated and internally withdrawn. You relish quiet time and trying to sort through the troubles and mysteries of your life experience, which is why others may see you as detached and inaccessible. You play out many melodramatic scenarios in your head, and moments of perceptive thought into abstract realms of intuitive brilliance can be included.

Second Pinnacle

This is a time of introspection, research and putting ideas into a tangible form of expression. You are glad to have quiet moments to delve into the issues that are puzzling you. There seems to be so much to learn, and there seem to be so many ways of looking at things. You are now interested in zeroing in on what belief system works best for you and how you can apply it in your daily world of mundane experience. Deep religious and spiritual impulses spur you on to look for a more mystical side of your personality.

Third Pinnacle

The third-pinnacle influence is very similar to that of the second. Emphasis during this pinnacle is upon the spiritual and mystical experiences, and this can also be a time of extended thinking into etheric realms of the higher mind.

Fourth Pinnacle

The influence of this period is reflection upon the meaning of your life and putting things into perspective as you attain a level of maturity and wisdom that comes only from many years of life experience. You may choose now to be more open and vocal about sharing what were once taboo or sacred thoughts kept only to yourself.

8 in the Pinnacles

Promotion and advancement, assume authority and leadership, financial gains, trusting inner authority, success and recognition, triumph over misuse of power.

First Pinnacle

This time is characterized by lessons concerning authority figures and issues of power. You will likely find yourself in a situation where severe religious or perhaps rigid social rules are imposed upon your life at the expense of living. The imposition of authority thwarts your self-learning and the development of your own trust of inner authority. You may well experience abuse from the hands of someone in a position of authority. There are some tough lessons to be learned about the relationship between money and power.

Second Pinnacle

You struggle with issues of authority and with rules that were imposed upon you in early years and now conflict with your higher aspirations. You are learning to set boundaries and separate from Mom's and Dad's dysfunctional doctrines. As you find your spiritual and personal parameters, you can become more focused upon assuming roles of leadership, responsibility and influence. You are learning to handle and acquire money in a more successful manner.

Third Pinnacle

You are gaining more confidence trusting and following your own inner authority. The guidance and the healthy source of spiritual philosophy that you have found give you added reference and back up your soul guidance. You are finding financial stability and share your successful approach to income with others.

Fourth Pinnacle

This is a time of empowerment, a time for the peace of mind that comes from having learned to trust and obey your inner authority. You are confident as to what is right or wrong or best for you in the given moment, and your spiritual connection is stable and strong. You share with others the path that has taken you into this realm of success and fulfillment.

9 in the Pinnacles

Reach altruism and universal brotherhood, develop intuitive and creative talents, work toward realistic dreams, grow in awareness from self to higher self.

First Pinnacle

This can be a time of much struggle, frustration, delay and emotional swings. You may feel like life is continually placing roadblocks in your way. You will repeatedly be placed into situations that make you look at your own weaknesses and dysfunctional patterns. When you find reoccurring negative patterns, you have a chance to recognize and focus upon resolving them. The 9 is the number of dreams and wishes, so this can be a time when the foundation is laid for future plans, although delays are likely during this pinnacle.

Second Pinnacle

The description for the second pinnacle is similar to that of the first. However, if you are taking conscious responsibility for personal growth, there is a considerably increased likelihood of working though the negative side and bringing true dreams into reality. This can be a time of discovering hidden talents, possibly leading to public performances. It can also be a time of exotic travel and introduction to extraordinary people.

Third Pinnacle

This is a time of working through your deepest fears and having some of your fondest wishes come true. You move among creative circles of awakening people who have also made a commitment to live a rich and healthy life. Your awareness is increasingly sensitive to more subtle realms of life and light.

Fourth Pinnacle

You can learn now to become less controlled by unconscious motives and more connected to your core of consciousness. This can be a fruitful time of fulfillment and contentment. You live in harmony with both those in your life and the world around you.

11 in the Pinnacles

Public recognition and esteem, developing self-image, increased psychic and spiritual experiences, work through nervous insecurity, social reform.

22 in the Pinnacles

Affiliation with benign organizations, research, enlightened administration, applied idealism, discover inner work, study sacred sciences.

33 in the Pinnacles

Universal service, alleviate the abuse and suffering of the masses, work with nature spirits and ecology, serve public welfare, alternative healing.

44 in the Pinnacles

Apply divine guidance to leadership, nature-oriented architecture, intuitive science, applied sacred geometry, divine laws of money and prosperity.

55 in the Pinnacles

Implement utopian ideas, integrate personal will with divine will, get self-help to the masses, inspire nutritional and exercise programs.

66 in the Pinnacles

Drama and theater that educates and heals, conscious work with angels, large-scale alternative programs, pollution reduction, inspired speaking.

77 in the Pinnacles

Applied metaphysical philosophies, arcane schools, research of outer space, study of addictions, inspired nutrition, overcoming learning disabilities.

Stress Challenges

The stress challenges are the flip side of the pinnacles, so they are signposts along your pathway that warn you of possible pitfalls. They show you where you are prone to stumble and get caught in a negative trap, which is even more true when they are the same number as your stress numbers (see chapter 9 for a description of stress numbers). Whenever stress challenge numbers are the same as your major numbers (life number, soul number, personality number and so on), you want to take special note so that you are prepared consciously to meet the implied test of character.

The duration of the challenges is exactly the same as that of the pinnacles. If you are not familiar with the pinnacles calculation, you should review it at this time. To determine the number governing each challenge, you use subtraction rather than addition. Please note that when subtracting, always reduce master numbers to their single-digit number.

1. The first stress challenge lasts for 36 years minus the life number.
2. The second stress challenge lasts 9 more years.
3. The third stress challenge also lasts 9 years.
4. The fourth stress challenge lasts until the end of life.

To determine the first stress challenge number, subtract the month and day numbers from each other.

Be sure to reduce the month, day and year to a single digit.

To determine the second stress challenge number, subtract the day and year numbers from each other.

To determine the third stress challenge number, subtract the first and second stress challenge numbers from each other.

To determine the fourth stress challenge number, subtract the month and year numbers from each other.

For the following example, let's use the same birth date we used for the pinnacles, December 11, 1934. Reduced to single digits, these numbers are 3, 2 and 8.

Duration	
First stress challenge	32 years (36 − 4, the life number, or until 1966)
Second stress challenge	1966 to 1975 (1966 + 9)
Third stress challenge	1975 to 1984 (1984 + 9)
Fourth stress challenge	1984 to end of life
Numbers	
First stress challenge	3 − 2 = 1
Second stress challenge	8 − 2 = 6
Third stress challenge	6 − 1 = 5
Fourth stress challenge	8 − 3 = 5

1 Stress Challenge Number

If 1 governs the first challenge, you likely experienced a domineering parent(s) and became rebellious and angry. As you grow older, the pattern continues. Actually, the pattern remains similar through any of the challenge phases. It can be changed, of course—with conscious effort.

You will be confronted with considerable interference and resistance to your efforts, running into opposition no matter what direction you turn. Other people and events seem to have control over the major aspects of your life. You struggle with indecision and hesitation when you would like to be busy and accountable. In the process of reaching out to find the approval you seek, you lose your own direction and identity. Under such pressure, it is easy to try even harder, which results in a pattern of self-insistence and flagrant self-promotion; confidence turns to boasting, and courage turns to pushiness.

2 Stress Challenge Number

When 2 is the number of the first challenge, the probability is high that your parents were excessively concerned with what neighbors and others (society) were saying and thinking about them. Perhaps they were obsessed that every detail of their lives (and yours) meet with approval under public scrutiny; it was more important to please the public than to be encouraged to be yourself. This can leave unconscious resentment toward that society that was so important—more important to your parents than you. The unresolved resentment can cause you to be uncomfortable when dealing with society or having to make public appearances.

In all stages of the challenges, there is an oversensitivity to others' criticism or scrutiny. You swim in a tenuous pool of your own subjective emotions and are overwhelmed by the details and rituals of performance. Small issues become insurmountable hurdles that make you feel vulnerable and frightened at every turn. Comments and criticism cause you to overreact, and you are afraid to get close to someone for fear of rejection. You cannot release the effect of a thoughtless comment or casual remark that may have injured you. Rather than reacting naturally to your environment, you imitate what you believe to be acceptable behavior.

3 Stress Challenge Number

When 3 is the number of the first challenge, there is a likelihood of emotional repression and possible abuse; there is also a likelihood of sexual inappropriateness that has left an impact in your life. You lived in a setting that was emotionally stilted and insecure.

In all stages of the challenges, you are afraid of spontaneously expressing your feelings and creative talents. You are restrained, self-effacing and experience an aversion to social contact. When interacting socially, you are affective and overreactive. Perhaps the avenue to develop your talents has not yet opened for you. You feel awkward and clumsy trying to articulate yourself, and these moments of unease can prevent you from making the favorable impression that can open the door to the opportunity you seek.

4 Stress Challenge Number

In the first stage particularly, you find yourself surrounded by constricting family members who are rigid and probably obsessive about control and safe behavior, and you try to conform to unrealistically severe standards of constrained behavior. You likely experienced a workaholic parent who was gone a lot because of career demands. You were squeezed, ignored and uptight.

Through all of the stages of the challenges, there is a struggle with internal monitors that inhibit and restrain. Some lurking secret from the past is being denied—a cover-up is going on in your life. You are trying to earn your worth rather than feel worthy. You alternate between putting enormous effort into your work (which brings disappointment proportionate to your perceived effort) and entering a passive cycle wherein you become angered that others don't give you the chance you believe you deserve. You are out of sync, wasting when you should conserve and being careless when neatness is essential.

5 Stress Challenge Number

The first stage of the stress challenge is fraught with mixed messages regarding permissible behavior, experience and sex. You likely had one addictive parent and one reactive latent addict, creating confusion between the rules of behavior and what you witnessed. The old saying "Do as I say, not as I do" usually fits in this situation—the repressed parent said one thing while the indulgent parent did another.

Through all stages, this is a struggle with the issues of addictive indulgence and proper restraint. You are attracted to toxic and indulgent sexuality. You overload your senses with experience and are not learning from each experience, so you do not know when to let go and move on to a healthy pattern. This can be a time of alcohol and drug abuse. You are out of control—impulsiveness, speed, recklessness and overdoing are the norm.

6 Stress Challenge Number

In the first stage of the stress challenges, the 6 indicates a childhood pattern where the parents' relationship was not clearly defined or given healthy parameters. Codependent demands, immature expectations and poor communication skills are very likely, and so you are confused and distrusting of commitment.

In all stages of the 6, there is searching for a true mate, stability and harmony, but your idealism and desperation can get in the way of realistic interaction. You place unrealistic demands upon the people and organizations in your life. When they do not meet an impossible standard, you discard them in disgust and move on to the next. It is the same with relationships. You become opinionated, self-righteous and conceited rather than loving and flexible, wanting your partner and others around you to do things your way without regard to their needs or self-expression.

7 Stress Challenge Number

If 7 is in the first stage of the stress challenges, your early years were likely spent in isolation and withdrawal. You are cautious, concerned and critical of life. You live in the world of mental projection. Because of the instability and uncertainty of your environment, you have become aloof and detached, and this can lead to arrogance and judgment that gets in the way of open communication with others.

In all stages, the presence of 7 indicates the need to deal with the real world of feeling and sensuality, not just mental analysis. It is easy to get yourself in a pattern of cynicism and dread where you cut yourself off from the fun and pleasure that life can offer. You become an intellectual rebel and rail at the adversities of life rather than resolving the adversity that's going on in your own soul. Your mind becomes your armor, protecting you from softness, tenderness and warmth.

8 Stress Challenge Number

When 8 is in the first stage of the stress challenges, you likely experienced the early childhood tyranny of a very domineering authority figure. Money may have been used as leverage in place of emotional nurturing. As a result, you struggle with authority figures and distrust those who are in power.

In all stages of the stress challenges, the 8 indicates a conflict with power and authority. You struggle with money issues and how to best direct your life with the resources you have. Perhaps you use money as a manipulative tool to buy and influence favors. You can become extravagant and wasteful trying to prove to the world that you are a success. However, you are not in touch with your inner self. Consequently, your actions are hollow gestures and your symbols empty of real content.

9 Stress Challenge Number

There is no 9 stress challenge, because in the process of subtraction, 9 cannot be left if anything is taken away.

0 Stress Challenge Number

When 0 occurs, it offers no direct clue as to the challenge at hand. In one sense, the absence of a designated challenge suggests a kind of psychological break from the pressures of life. More accurately, it might be said that the presence of the 0 suggests the opportunity for choice. You are left to determine a strategy based upon the circumstances at hand. For some that is more difficult than being pressured to perform by some hidden force. The subchallenges—the two numbers that compose the challenge number—can give some insight. The subtle message implied is this: Here is a time to be aware of all of the possible lessons, from 1 to 9. This interpretation is quite similar to the 0 karmic lessons. If you seek a little more elaboration upon this issue, go to Chapter 10, the on karmic lessons.

8

Destiny Number

The destiny number, which is determined by adding the sum of the full name at birth to the life number, signifies that which you strive most to accomplish and attain in this lifetime. The two components of the destiny number represent the full implementation of your innate abilities combined with the entire spectrum of life experiences that are presented to you. The true destiny is reached when the responsible person has taken the necessary steps and years of commitment needed to recognize and significantly resolve the dysfunctional patterns in his or her life.

Having accomplished that elaborate, ongoing process, the next step—which may have been going on simultaneously with the other—is to chart the spiritual path of your choice that brings you in touch with your soul and its purpose. As the soul works through the personality harmoniously, it becomes increasingly easier to connect with the higher self and its direction. Once in harmony with the inner self, you can chart your course with conscious command.

The sad reality is that most people within the mass consciousness rarely get beyond their dysfunctional tribal limitations. However, in times of accelerated consciousness upon the planet—such as this time—greater numbers of souls are able to move through tribal limitation and into soul- or higher awareness. Beyond that are those souls striving for completion of the karmic circle and ascension.

The destiny description is mostly positive in tone because the implication is that if one truly has reached that state of awareness, there will be few blocks and negatives. The risk of putting this into print in such a totally positive way is that those with disorders of delusion could see themselves at this stage of growth—those in total denial of dysfunctional reality could make the assumption, in their mind, that they are at this plateau even though it is not true. Therefore, one should use discernment when reading these interpretations. At the same time, though, you can glory in the hope and the possibility that you will reach the fulfillment of your fondest spiritual aspirations.

1 Destiny Number

You move through life with undaunted courage and a zest for living. Your bold and independent leadership inspires others to search for their own identity and independence from unhealthy entanglements. Although you are strong, you are considerate of others' opinions when challenged. You live your principles in humble dignity but are ardent and convincing when boldly taking yourself and compatriots through changes and innovative stages of growth.

You boldly go where others fear to tread and relish the idea of being the first to do something, create something, conquer something or start something. Things very seldom stay in a rut when you are around, because you will stir up activity where boredom or pointless status quo exists.

You dance gloriously in harmony with that whisper of divine will that guides and inspires you through each daily turn of events. You stand up proudly against tyranny of all kinds and speak out loudly when you recognize injustice and misuse of will. You fear no evil and stand side by side with those angels who assist with the implementation of divine will. Although you may have struggled against the imposing will of dominant souls, you are forgiving toward those who would misuse the strength of will.

2 Destiny Number

You are tender, sensitive and sympathetic with your brothers and sisters of the world. Your silver tongue and gentle voice enable you to soften even the toughest of hearts, which allows you to bring peace and resolution where you find those in conflict. You serve your community where you best fit and are among those who give utmost aid and support to capable leaders. When called upon to take the lead, you are able to listen to all parties involved and find an amicable solution. You love to get along with others and live side by side in harmony even where differences of life and philosophy exist. Your appreciation of all of God's children makes you a fair and fine negotiator among those who are in strife and confusion.

You are thoughtful, patient and considerate of others when facing difficult issues. Your attention to detail and appreciation of every little thing in life are particularly helpful when research or meticulous need for detail is a must, and this makes you an appreciated part of the team.

You live in constant companionship with sentient beings on other planes. Your trust of intuitive guidance makes you revered by many, and you share your methods of doing so when sincerely requested. Your feet are firmly planted upon Earth, and your spirit is finely attuned to the heavens above. Your finely tuned sensitivity to other worlds makes you a valued communicator among levels of consciousness.

3 Destiny Number

You are charming, vibrant and full of joyous celebration as you go about your daily affairs. Your keen sense of harmony and aesthetic appreciation enables you to bring beauty and refinement to any environment. Your openness and fluidity of expressing feelings enable those who are more repressed and shut-down to find a way to better communicate their pent-up emotions. Your richness of creative expression touches every corner of the world you inhabit.

You are colorful and confident, a contributor to the aesthetic beauty of this world. Your penetrating vision and refined sensitivity to light, sound and vibration give you the acumen to bring harmonious resonance into any activity you perform. You thrive on joy and are active wherever discord and repressed emotions inhibit and restrain others from fully expressing themselves.

You bring music, dance and artistic expression into everything you do. Your enthusiasm for life is contagious to all and encourages even the most repressed and shut-down souls to open up and discover their own life potential. Your powerful sexual nature lifts and glorifies the union of body and soul. You strive to help others discover the purity and power of the transformed sexual energy that flows within each child of light. You consciously work with the elementals and angels of color, light and rhythm.

4 Destiny Number

Your patience and strict adherence to the laws of physics, chemistry, structure and the orderliness of the universe are appreciated when discipline and exact adherence to the laws of engineering are required. You are in awe and appreciation of the manner in which God constructs a universe and are curious to better understand the dynamics of universal manifestation.

You are loyal, dedicated and determined to implement divine design on Earth. You serve the higher plan willingly in whatever capacity the inner direction dictates. Your mastery of the laws of structure, engineering and alchemy is used well to build sacred temples and buildings for humanity. You work with brilliant minds and extraordinary souls to maintain a safe infrastructure in times of disaster and change.

Your attention to the physics and chemistry of the body helps you sustain a lifestyle and exercise plan that maintains health and aids in building your consciousness toward higher dimensions. You understand well the diffusion of energy through the circuit board of creation. You relish the times when you can participate in sacred ritual with your spiritual brethren.

5 Destiny Number

You are playful, productive and brimming with life stories collected from your many travels around the globe. Your comfort with people of all races and creeds makes it possible for strangers to share with you the most intimate details of personal and higher wisdom. You travel among shamans and corporate executives, peasants, poets and princes. Your childlike capacity to play and to find every new experience a delight is an inspiration to all.

Your sexual experience ranges from exotic to tantric. You enjoy the body immensely and take care to honor the best systems of diet and exercise. You delight in work that adds to the sensual and sentient nature of both the human and divine attributes of humanity.

Your studies have taken you through religions, philosophies and a broad range of scientific thought—there is no topic that bores you, because you relish every facet of life that God has created. Those with whom you exchange information appreciate this extensive backlog of data. Your humor and boundless curiosity about life make you a most delightful friend and companion.

6 Destiny Number

Your role as servant and healer introduces you to all kinds of situations humans dream up to frustrate and confuse their personal and spiritual growth. You delight in the process of education and revelation that leads them out of these paths of suffering and disease. You have composed a huge mental and emotional catalog of the games people play in the world of illusion and ego defense. You are adroitly clever at finding new ways to help others see their blocks and games so they can release the ego attachments.

You firmly believe in the sanctity of any relationship and strive earnestly to bring about healthy and open communication among individuals and collective groups alike. You understand the laws of union and marriage among people, among elements, among humans and angels. This knowledge assists you in mending and correcting improper alignment with the cohesive forces of creation.

You are found in temples, churches, synagogues, hospitals and schools of learning where service to God and care of being are shared. You delight in exchange with healing angels and inner-plane beings, who reveal the latest and most effective methods for helping others to get well. Your fine perception of the relationship between the inner forces and outer manifestation makes you an excellent alchemical healer in whatever fields you operate.

7 Destiny Number

You love to explore, probe and delve into the deepest secrets of humanity and the universe. You have studied well and are able to give most appropriate insight when called upon by other seekers. Your academic and personal studies have been supplemented by the guidance of mentors from the inner realms. They have helped you to sharpen your subtlety of perception. Your ability to concentrate and focus is immense and takes you to the precipice of manifesting matter out of thought.

You are attuned to the universal mind and know what the wise ones mean when they say, "You are what you think." Your knowledge of the nature of the mind finds you attracted to studies of transformational energy and systems of belief. You are in your most joyous element among those who study the process of bringing material manifestation from a thought form.

Your time spent expanding intuition and the psychic dimensions of the mind has taken you into uncharted areas of human consciousness. You enjoy exchanges with colleagues from other disciplines of study, seeking to build the road map of human genealogy through the realms of creation.

8 Destiny Number

You have come a long way and have accomplished much in your life. You have demonstrated the ability to master the financial segment of your life, so materially you are free from burdens and demands. Your managerial abilities and academic training have put you in a position where you have substantial leverage and an impact upon the lives of many people. Your decisions are usually accurate. Those who work with you or for you admire and respect you.

Your innate sense of appreciation for higher authority gives you the utmost of appreciation for the laws of cohesiveness and structure. You are able to visualize how each component of a structure or group plays its role in the laws of dynamics that apply to a given unit. This gives you unique skills of leadership and influence.

Your command of many fields of knowledge applies itself to the work you do. You grasp the dynamics of conversion of dimensions, which gives you the ability to bring extradimensional fuzziness into the existential clarity of the moment. Your practical application of these conversion methods keeps you constantly challenged and learning yet more about all worlds.

9 Destiny Number

You have reached a rarefied state of refinement and awareness. Always known as a little "far out," your once seemingly remote viewpoint is now being sought after by many on the path of spiritual progress. Your enlightened artistic work captures images and wisps of ethereal realities overlapping into third-dimensional consciousness. Your journey through every strata of human experience has given you maturity and a faith that is unwavering where others' faith crumbles.

Your uncanny vision allows you to see the perfected image of a project in the making. You strive to keep others aligned and on course with the possibility and dream of perfection. You are refined, poetic, profound and polite in your delicate handling of the crudeness in humanity. Your ability to see what humans can be allows you to be patient with them just as they are.

Your elegance and cultivated manner demand respect and attention. You find yourself surrounded by equally talented associates, who work together to bring inspiration to a downtrodden world. You are excited about bringing futuristic trends to the present moment. Because most of your time is spent in other dimensions, your contemporaries often do not realize how grounded you actually are.

11 Destiny Number

You have found your inner identity and move about in the social world with comfort and ease. Because of your heightened insight and fairness to both parties, you are often called upon to be a negotiator and mediator among those who quarrel and have disagreements. The probability is quite high that you will be called into some form of public service. Whatever your calling, you will most likely reach a prominent position within society. Your knowledge of both worlds becomes a source of guidance and inspiration to the struggling souls of mass consciousness.

The 11 is similar to the 2. For years you have seen realities and been connected to beings unseen by the masses. You can step in and out of different states of consciousness and are no longer considered to be strange or weird; you are like a mediator between worlds. You use your extended abilities of perception in the marketplace with respect and ease. You pull in bits of information that fill in the blank spots unanswered by the reach of logic.

22 Destiny Number

For most of your life, you have felt that you had a special purpose or work to accomplish. Now you realize that you have become a powerhouse of accomplishment and achievement. You will likely find yourself among souls who are working on a large scale to build a better world, a world founded in the divine laws of materialization and development of wisdom-based organizations. Your thoroughness and steadiness are important in projects of research and development.

The 22 is similar to the 4. You have awakened and prepared your mastery of matter. You work to shape, mold and marry the etheric form into material reality. You have realized the purpose of inner ritual and dynamically work with the laws of alchemy and chemistry, blending science with spiritual laws of manifestation. You have found kindred souls with whom your powers are magnified by the infusion of group consciousness.

33 Destiny Number

You have spent a lot of time working through the pain within your own heart. Now you focus upon relieving the suffering you see in those around you. Your artistic sense of beauty and synergy is applied well in areas of healing and mending the consciousness of humanity. As an artist, you see designs in the tapestry of creation and are able to present them in a way that uplifts others and enables them to connect with universal archetypes.

The 33 is similar to the 6. You intermingle the laws of botany, biology and physiology with an infusion of higher-octave energies to bring natural healing remedies to many. You are active in movements where people work to inform the public about alternative methods of well-being for all. Your findings educate troubled families, helping to define and dissolve ongoing dysfunctional family systems.

44 Destiny Number

You have learned well the proper application of power and authority. Your inner knowledge of energy flow makes you a powerful figure and leader. You grasp the inner laws of order and their delegation down through the ranks. Your ability to empower others and bring out the best of their productivity is an asset in all endeavors. In art, science, industry or whatever field you choose, your knowledge based on alchemy and science lets you draw out the power in people and nature.

The 44 is similar to the 8. You are active as a fundraiser, bringing together generous souls who wish to invest in ennobling humankind. You blend the power of prayer with the power of mind to help create archetypal patterns of evolution that can be imprinted into the higher consciousness of the masses. You are a master builder and leader in institutions that create enlightened home environments that elevate the residents' awareness.

55 Destiny Number

You are confident and willful in your expression of self. You have tamed your rebellious nature and destructive anger. You are driven by the grace of God and strive to bring forth the most blessed gifts of God to humanity. Your willingness to go where no one else has traveled gives others the confidence to take their own steps of growth into higher consciousness. You know God's will and strive to engender that harmony of alliance in other souls.

The 55 is similar to the 1. Your love of humanity and God has taken you on several journeys into the many levels of light. You work with elementals, angels and other inner-world beings to inspire within many the growing desire to live in harmony with the One. You are vigilant and strong in your work to negate the power of those who work with the dark forces of the inner worlds. Your allegiance to the archangelic hosts adds to the effectiveness of your work.

66 Destiny Number

You experience a rich emotional life. You have been through a lot of pain and emotional suffering, and your mission is to help alleviate the suffering you see in the lives of those around you. You are methodical and appreciative of the crystalline structure that underlies life. You are clear and concise in your communication. Your deep wisdom adds to your skill in the realms of media and artistic expression. As a leader, your first concern is for the welfare of those over whom you have domain.

The 66 is similar to the 3. Your artistic expression radiates a healing and helping quality that reaches deeply into the depths of viewers' souls and encourages the development of the best within them. You speak with the tongue of angels and bring healing with tone, color and vibration. You sing with the choir of angels, and your collective voice unites humans and gods in the joyous celebration of life on all domains. You help to attract funding for artistic efforts that enliven and inspire.

77 Destiny Number

You are infinitely interested in life. That may be more meaningful than many realize, for your intuitive mind often reaches out to the furthest regions of creation. You seek to understand humanity's place in this universal scheme of things and strive to improve the conditions of living for all. You are inherently an investigator and love delving into the deepest mysteries of life.

The 77 is similar to the 5. You blend the esoteric philosophies with academic philosophies to integrate the higher mind with the intellectual mind. You are active wherever there is a genuine intent to improve the lifestyle of the masses. You are found where systems of education aspire to integrate esoteric wisdom into the mundane curriculum of students everywhere. You are found where humor, laughter and love are shared.

88 Destiny Number

The 88 is similar to the 7. You dynamically work the laws of manifestation to create new forms out of etheric patterns. You are interested in the laws of creation and work to educate others about implementation of natural laws rather than tampering with artificial methods. You are found teaching the laws of prosperity and working with the manifestation of divine supply. You are a general among an army of followers.

You love to assist others in the discovery of new abilities previously unknown to them. You inspire in others the curiosity to carve new paths through the challenges of life. Your far-reaching curiosity seeks to unravel universal laws and apply them to the most mundane tasks. You are active in rituals of the group that magnify the presence of the higher expression of power and light.

99 Destiny Number

The 99 is similar to the 9. You are learning to be open of heart and wise of mind. Your affiliation with the angels of love and light brings an inspiration and radiance to your life that all can see. You are found where humanitarian and creative manifestation is generated. You have come a long way learning to trust and open your heart fully to humanity. Many speak of unconditional love; few achieve it. It is within your heart to do so and be an example of living love.

You work to bring about the highest artistic expression of each culture and to share it with all other societies. You are found where there is effort to eradicate disease and disharmony in the hearts of humans. You will fight where there is oppression and the interruption of personal choice and growth. You are a guardian of the greater plan, revealing only the information that is allowed by higher determination.

Stress Numbers

I first introduced stress numbers to numerology in a previous publication. The stress number serves to accentuate differences between two numbers; it helps to define the tension between the vibrational qualities of the numbers being compared. It is like a point of tension or opposition that needs to be overcome before the two compared numbers can function harmoniously together.

As implied by the use of the term stress number, these numbers are more pronounced when we are under stress. Under such pressure, we tend to manifest more of our unconscious mannerism rather than our best behavior; most of us, of course, do not like to see that part of our behavior. These mannerisms are presented to help bring negative unconscious traits into light. Once you recognize them, you then have a choice to resolve them; gone unacknowledged, they keep you a victim of your negative existence.

Intrapersonal and Interpersonal Stress Numbers

Stress numbers are divided into two groupings: intrapersonal stress numbers and interpersonal stress nmbers.

The *intrapersonal* number is calculated by subtracting the smaller of two primary numbers from the larger one. In this instance, "primary number" refers to the personality, soul, integrated self or life number. When subtracting, the numbers should be reduced to a single digit. First compute the difference between your personality (P) and soul (S) numbers, then between your personality and integrated self (IS) numbers and finally between the numbers for your soul and integrated self. From this set of calculations, you will get three stress numbers, unless two of the primaries are the same.

Now compute the difference between your life number (LN) and your personality number, then between your life and soul numbers and lastly between your life and integrated-self numbers. This gives you a second set of calculations, composed of three additional stress numbers for a total of six stress numbers.

Here is an example: Let's say your integrated-self number (IS) is 8, your soul number (S) is 5, your personality number (P) is 3 and your life number (LN) is 6. The stress numbers would be computed as follows:

Difference Between	Stress Number
S and P	$5 - 3 = 2$
IS and P	$8 - 3 = 5$
IS and S	$8 - 5 = 3$
LN and P	$6 - 3 = 3$
LN and S	$6 - 5 = 1$
LN and IS	$8 - 6 = 2$

Note that the combinations providing the stress numbers are also purposely written out. Refer to each stress number by the appropriate combination (subtraction) in the intrapersonal stress number descriptions on the following pages. The combinations are arranged in numerical order purely for purposes of systematic arrangement.

Interpersonal stress numbers are computed by subtracting the primary numbers in each person's chart from each other. That is, when comparing charts, the stress numbers are obtained from the difference between the personality numbers in each chart, between the integrated-self numbers and the life numbers. An example is given below:

Chart A	Chart B	Stress Number
P = 4	P = 2	$4 - 2 = 2$
S = 7	S = 1	$7 - 1 = 6$
IS = 2 (11)	IS = 3	$3 - 2 = 1$

A further use for stress numbers when assessing compatibilities between charts is to compute the difference between the numbers on the planes of expression: physical, emotional, mental and intuitive. If you desire a further comparison, look at the difference between the personality number of one person's chart and the life or soul number in the other's chart. You can also devise your own effective ways of using these stress combinations.

Intrapersonal stress numbers provide a method of examining potential crosscurrents within an individual's psychological makeup. Stress numbers help to pinpoint likely subconscious tensions between the needs and actions of the personality, soul and higher self. By consciously recognizing these stress areas, the combination can then be transmuted into a cooperative dynamic flow between the threefold structure of consciousness: personality, soul and higher self.

Interpersonal stress numbers are indicative of the differences between the two charts that should be understood for reaching greater compatibility between the two people and a cooperative blending of the two vibrational qualities of the involved primary numbers. They point out where resistance will occur between two people, but they can also reveal the easiest avenue for working harmoniously. Thus interpersonal stress numbers are particularly useful for understanding marriage and parent-child, employee-employer or other relationships. Used wisely, they provide insight that helps overcome the differences between the people involved, which allows them to form a more complete union.

As mentioned earlier, the descriptive paragraphs that follow emphasize the subconscious and karmic traits. You will think of wholly new ways to apply the stress numbers, because this new area of interpretation will require much further investigation and application. My desire is to get subconscious conflicts recognized and resolved for more effective living. Therefore, the emphasis from now on is upon the negative side of the stress numbers.

You might ask what it means when two numbers are the same—for example, if both soul number and personality number are a 2 or if two people have the same life number in their charts. In either case, this would provide no stress number. We have already discussed that each number has an assertive, a passive and a harmonious quality. When two numbers that should be compared are the same, the possibility of stress arises from an increased likelihood of going to extremes.

When two people have a number in common, it is like having the same Sun sign or similar aspects in their astrology charts: They may fail to see the imbalance in their mutual lives and commit excesses or omissions blindly together. Another possibility is that when someone fails to recognize a negative within him- or herself, it is very easy to overemphasize and pick on that idiosyncrasy of the spouse or partner. On the other hand, an ideal situation would be when one partner moves too far out of balance in one direction, the other partner goes the opposite way, so the cycle works to teach both the lessons of harmony and mutual growth. When you read the descriptions pertaining to the interpersonal stress numbers, it may appear that in certain instances, the role described seems more applicable to the other individual involved. Just remember, we choose the opposite sometimes to learn balance, so roles can often seem reversed. Such a situation, then, could indicate where balance is necessary.

The descriptions for the interpersonal stress numbers are admittedly quite general. They are intended as guidelines to help you establish your own concepts. For instance, the dynamics of the stress in a 5–9 soul combination would differ from the dynamics coming out of a 5–9 personality combination or a 59 life-number combination. Please use intuitive wisdom and common sense when evaluating the stress numbers.

Intrapersonal Stress Numbers

Combinations with 1

1–2 Stress Number 1

There is conflict between assertiveness of will and fear of social criticism. You are struggling within yourself to find your own self-convictions. In competition or under stress, you are argumentative and critical. You must outfox, outwit or outperform others. A karmic pattern of working out a tendency toward gossip or scandalous accusations may return, directed toward you in this life. You want to dominate relationships, and you find conflict with an intensely self-willed spouse, relatives or friends.

You might find it difficult to establish direction and conviction, particularly until your early thirties. It is likely that you were raised in a dogmatic and critical, religious or socially active family, which left you caught between strong personal ambitions and indoctrinated conscience. Common addictions include socializing, entertainment, pets, relationships, drugs, collecting, chocolates and smoking among many others.

1–3 Stress Number 2

There is conflict between self-will and creative urges, which is why this combination makes it difficult to articulate inner feelings. Conflict is likely with the father or a dominant female. You are unable to convey or express artistic or creative insights. Because you are lacking in conviction, you will say what seems momentarily appropriate and can become a machine-gun chatterbox. This demonstrates a superficial friendliness.

You need to work toward reducing critical speech and resentment of talent in others. When others direct malicious gossip and harsh criticism toward you and your endeavors, you are hurt very deeply. If you nurture resentment, you can delay your own advancement. Common addictions include shopping, pets, gardening, sex, gambling, entertainment, speed and danger.

1–4 Stress Number 3

The tension here arises between self-indulgent desires and karmic obligation to accomplish the work at hand. You resent any interference with selfish ambitions and have difficulty finding creative avenues to resolve obligations. It is necessary for you to develop patience and a better understanding of the feminine energy. You have a false sense of self-worth and desire positions of prominence without going through the hard work necessary to earn deserved recognition.

You are misdirected and extravagant regarding practical endeavors, and you are selfish about your own needs. There is a haughty attitude and a desire for display. You brag and gloat tauntingly about supposed accomplishment. You are prone to an uncertainty in disposition, slow to make decisions and quite stubborn once they are made—for better or worse! Common addictions include gambling, speed and danger, fanatic groups, sugar, smoking, work and sex.

1–5 Stress Number 4

There is tension of will and of freedom. Unable to consistently face life responsibly, you need to work to discipline instinctive impulses toward carefree and selfish living. You compensate for frustration by overworking yourself on insignificant projects. You seem to provoke quarrels at home and with others close to you. It is difficult to admit being wrong, and there is a karmic carryover here of self-opinion and lack of tolerance. You are prone to criticize people who are doing the very things that you get away with. You rebel against rules and regulations imposed upon you by society.

You fluctuate between pride and self-dignity, between courage and timidity. Thus you find yourself wavering between silence and speaking out emphatically when you recognize injustice and wrong action. Your frustration can come out in unexpected bursts of rage and fingering others for what went wrong. It is not easy for you to express personal feelings. When you let your emotions out, they can be violent and explosive. You are at your best once you have found a wholesome and heartfelt direction toward your predominant life goal. Addictions common with this combination include work, smoking, alcohol, sugar, relationships, religious fanaticism, gambling, speed and danger.

1–6 Stress Number 5

There is strain between will and emotional needs. You must learn to find the proper expression of freedom. In the past, you tended to avoid responsibility; it was quite easy to turn and run. After all, it isn't easy to hit a moving target. Life will not allow you to pursue a free choice until you learn to recognize responsibility and fulfill obligations that arise. It is likely that there was separation or conflict between your parents when you were very young. Jealousy and possessiveness may have contributed to that divisiveness.

You attract a spouse who is alternately overbearing one moment and indifferent the next. There is a fear of change, but life will put you into a position that demands rearrangement of your attitude. You prefer a spouse who reflects your own opinions. Common addictions include relationships, gardening, pets, sugar, food, books, reading, institutions (a compulsive need to participate in an organization) and gambling.

1–7 Stress Number 6

Emotions are caught between the impulses of the will and a fixed tendency of the mind. Emotionally you are contradictory and retreat from emotional discomfort into self-justified intellectual excuses. This stress pattern is deeply touched by the suffering of the world and, at extremes, becomes unstable because of keen sensitivity to astral turbulence in the environment.

There is a likelihood that you had detached parents, particularly your mother. Did she put her needs ahead of yours noticeably and often? The conflict between these two emotionally restrictive numbers suggests difficulty in dealing with others at work or in the exchange of opinions and ideas that contradict your biases. You can cover your frustration and insecurity with a know-all, do-all bravado. Common addictions include power, alcohol, ritual, relationships, book reading, institutions (a compulsive need to participate in an organization), fanatical groups and religious fanaticism.

1–8 Stress Number 7

There are tremendous power needs here, with an almost unbearable desire for attainment and sense of pride. You need to learn wisdom as an antidote for selfishness. There is an irrational, seething venom of impulsiveness within that attracts hostility from contradictory people. It is likely that two strong-willed, intellectual parents had difficulty expressing emotions. They had to outdo each other and lied when they had no other recourse. Under pressure you will lie very easily. You possess an almost ruthless need for power and control. Your karmic tendency is toward misuse of power and will in past lives.

With this stress pattern, you are completely out of harmony with the feminine energy and prone to vastly overcompensate with powerful male ego. You can be completely inconsiderate of others when on the way to the top. Proper use of intellect to investigate deep feelings of inferiority is one means of dissipating tension. Common addictions include smoking, power, alcohol, sex, institutions (a compulsive need to participate in an organization), fanatical groups, gambling, speed and danger.

1–9 Stress Number 8

There is a pull between extreme, opposite polarities. Self-will is pitted against the altruistic need to serve mass consciousness. You seek attention to build ego. There is a likelihood of dissension with authority. You are cynical toward successful leaders and covet influence. You use self-deception and unscrupulous means, tricking the public. In personal relationships, you are opportunistic and exploitative. You take advantage of others' dreams and idealism to attain your own ends. You are indifferent to the plight of the poor and helpless.

Until a proper perspective is placed upon wealth, you will likely experience financial reversals. You can offset the negative here by altruistic application of your individuality to help others, but it will take rigorous effort. Common addictions include hobbies, pets, money, chocolate, sugar, food, institutions (a compulsive need to participate in an organization), religious fanaticism and entertainment.

Combinations with 2

2–3 Stress Number 1

With this stress pattern, you tend to be torn between self-criticism and creative potential. There is a fear that your ideas will not be accepted by the public. You need to strengthen your self-confidence and will. You likely express a false pride to mask the self-doubt indicated. You are plagued with sensitivity, apprehension and worry over minute details and inconsequential trivia. You lack the male drive to initiate positive action.

Your passive-aggressive nature is disguised beneath a confused, wishy-washy, easy-going persona. Do you receive much criticism from coworkers? You must use your own strength of will to discern what is significant to your life, then go after it, regardless of outside criticism. Common addictions include shopping, chocolate, alcohol, sugar, sex, relationships, food, entertainment and socializing.

2–4 Stress Number 2

You have conflict between your work and the expectation of others. You must learn to see both sides of issues clearly and objectively. Develop your intuition to solve indecision. It is easy for you to give excessive attention to material goods and achievement. Your tendency is to let details bog you down, preventing completion of your work. It is very easy for you to hide your lack of confidence behind self-created details and petty regulations. You can easily become a tattletale and exaggerate other people's minor problems.

You will adhere to the letter of the rules rather than using them constructively for achievement. You confuse goals, and confusion of values plagues your desire for accomplishment. When boxed in, you become loud, crude and explosively abusive of tongue. Common addictions include shopping, hobbies, work, chocolate, alcohol, sugar, collecting, institutions (a compulsive need to participate in an organization), fanatical groups and socializing.

2–5 Stress Number 3

Tension between impulsiveness and social restraint is found in this stress pattern. You speak out frivolously and disrespectfully, although you need to express yourself in a cheerful, positive manner. This suggests a past-life pattern of sexual indulgence and misspent creative talents. You are overly sensitive to public criticism: "Why can't people keep to their own affairs?" It is difficult for you to recognize how critical you are of others who are trying to express their own creative talents. You are likely to overindulge at the table when under pressure.

This combination indicates conflict between conscience and impulse regarding sexual needs. You are highly condemning toward others' transgressions, but deep down, you are envious because you would like to be in the same position. You must seek harmony in the proper expression of your own creativity and sexuality. Common addictions include smoking, shopping, pets, alcohol, sugar, sex, collecting, book reading and socializing.

2–6 Stress Number 4

There are crosscurrents of emotionalism. You are torn between what others demand and what feels proper to your own being. It is likely you were caught between a solicitous parent you did not respect and an emotionally inhibited parent whose love you wanted very deeply. You will have to work at establishing emotional equilibrium, which will not come easily, because it is easy for you to deceive yourself where emotions are concerned. You are hurt deeply when you discover that a loved one is manipulating your emotions for selfish needs. The flip side is that you can turn into a most unbefitting and caustic critic.

You should avoid psychic or occult studies until you get a grip on your own emotions. You have likely toyed with others' emotions in earlier lives and must learn to be forthright and honest in relations rather than trying to please or manipulate. Common addictions include work, power, money, alcohol, sugar, relationships, collecting, religious fanaticism and socializing.

2–7 Stress Number 5

A seething desire for self-gratification is caught between intellectual and social censors. Your mind and emotions tell you that it is no longer necessary to crave that which you know is not best, and yet you are tormented by sensual and sexual fantasies. In earlier lives, you may have attempted to ignore or prevent sensual and carnal desires for religious or social reasons. However unfortunate, damning a desire does not terminate it. Now a war rages between temptations of the flesh and your religious and intellectual upbringing, which taught purity and lust-free loving.

In a man's chart, this combination indicates an intellectual disrespect for women but a latent physical desire for them. In a woman's chart, it indicates dissatisfaction when sensual desire cannot be controlled. You must work out sexual conflicts by learning to identify within yourself the proper action for your own life stream. Common addictions include smoking, shopping, pets, alcohol, sugar, collecting, institutions (a compulsive need to participate in an organization), fanatical groups/religions and entertainment/movies.

2–8 Stress Number 6

Emotional tension arises from conflict between personal desire for recognition and public acceptance. There is a karmic suggestion of past misuse of wealth and power. Criticism by coworkers and associates brings disappointment when it comes from those you most want to please. Promotions and increased earnings will not come easily, and you are likely envious, even jealous, of people who seem to get ahead with little effort. When that takes over, you can become a smirking and cunning backstabber.

You are not easy to get along with if things are going against you, since you may take out your aggravation on the loved ones closest to you. You can become sullen and morose for long periods of time. Your masculinity suffers when you cannot live up to expectations in your career and profession. You must learn to let go of the need to prove how important you are to others. You will earn valid recognition from valid actions. Common addictions include smoking, pets, power, alcohol, ritual, relationships, collecting, institutions (a compulsive need to participate in an organization) and gambling.

2–9 Stress Number 7

There is mental confusion between your public image and your idealized concept of yourself. You have a rigidly defensive belief in what you are doing. You won't accept anything people say without challenging them to provide proof. Once under way, it is hard to persuade you to alter course. You may err in isolating yourself from what outsiders are thinking. You become awkward, verbally impulsive and nerdy. A fixed determination to follow your intellectual decisions can create emotional upheavals with employees and coworkers.

If your emotions were not confused, it would be easier for you to trust the more refined feelings of the heart and soul: your intuition. Until the higher intuitive mind is developed, this combination leaves you torn asunder by emotional demands and intellectual rigidity. Common addictions include pets, chocolate, alcohol, sugar, collecting, books, reading, institutions (a compulsive need to participate in an organization), fanatical groups/religions and movies/entertainment.

Combinations with 3

3–4 Stress Number 1

There is conflict between your creative talents and working environment. As a child, you may have shown talent that was stifled by parents or circumstances. You need to assert self-will to fulfill creative proclivities and would be best in crafts or an artistic career. A past-life neglect of talent is suggested when this combination occurs. Rather than assert yourself to make something of your creative skills, you are inclined to pursue pleasure and material security. Conflict with male energy prevents the development of courage to face the adversities of your endeavors. You are likely to develop phobias about losing your personal possessions and money. Be careful to avoid grudges.

When thwarted, you can be pugnacious and petty. You have a quick temper and can be resentful about destiny passing you by. This dominating laziness makes you vulnerable to the unscrupulous. Common addictions include gardening, work, chocolate, alcohol, sugar, sex, fanatical groups and religions, gambling, entertainment and movies as well as socializing.

3–5 Stress Number 2

There is desire for unconventional indulgences and a fear of family and social opinion. At extremes, licentious and exotic cravings for stimulation rule you. You easily confuse sex and love, and you can become involved in depleting relationships. Your physical eye dominates the inner eye when choosing a mate; passion may rule over discretion. Casual partners might mistreat you.

You can be impetuous and caustic when threatened. You are intense, angry and volatile inside. This intensity might be hidden under a veil of vacillation and indecisive gestures. You tend to attract antiestablishment and unconventional friends. This can be an excellent combination when working in communications. When transmuted, there is a strong indication of success in art, writing, communications or sales. Common addictions are shopping, sports, power, sugar, sex, relationships, food, entertainment and movies and socializing.

3–6 Stress Number 3

Responsibilities and emotional crises keep your life upset. Marriage and partnerships can be genuine hassles and sources of frustration. It is likely that emotional conflicts in your parents' marriage had an impact upon your early childhood. You are alternately indifferent or overly involved in others' emotional problems, but it would be best for you to get your own ship in port before attempting to steer others. It is difficult for you to deal cooperatively with your partner or spouse when the relationship becomes too emotionally entangled, particularly where possessiveness and jealousy are concerned.

You can turn within and ignore others when under pressure, preferring sulking to dialogue. The passive personality needs constant emotional attention and may find this through shopping or accumulating material items. Do you find it easier to build your security around a stable person near you than to find it in yourself? You must uncover and release emotional conflicts from early childhood. Common addictions are gardening, money, chocolate, sugar, sex, relationships, food, fanatical groups/religions and entertainment/movies.

3–7 Stress Number 4

You want to create and express profound ideas for the world, but the opportunity for working out your dreams comes belatedly or after much struggle. When mind and heart blend, this is an excellent combination for literature and writing, but the mind needs steadying or you are fickle and unstable. You can become fanatically conspiratorial and sarcastic about life. This stress-number combination suggests that one of your parents was intellectually biased and the other one emotionally dependent. You benefit from marriage and working with others but prefer your own ingenuity.

You feel you are worth more in your work than your job usually indicates. When intellectually threatened, you become autocratic and respond with an acerbic tongue. Love and desire for material acquisition can interfere with natural creative ability. Indecision can plague you when head and heart are at odds. Common addictions are gardening, work, alcohol, ritual, food, books, reading, institutions (a compulsive need to participate in an organization), gambling, speed and danger.

3–8 Stress Number 5

This is a struggle for freedom between creative potential and the strident restrictions imposed by self or others. You have a militant attitude toward restrictions and rules. You carry a chip on your shoulder and seek a target, looking for anyone to start an altercation with. You are prone to brusque and impulsive reaction. Although you enjoy telling others what to do, you are resentful of advice from others. You tend to blurt out accusations or contrary statements, and then you suffer in regret. Sexual desires are strong and can put you in compromising situations. Is sex a barometer of your success?

Your self-image suffers when you attempt to buy esteem. You do not respect conventions, and this disregard tends to be repulsive to those of finer taste and sensitivity. A healthy attitude toward constructive creativity can help greatly to make this a powerful combination for successful growth. Common addictions include speed and danger, alcohol, institutions (a compulsive need to participate in an organization), sex, sugar, food, power, gambling and socializing.

3–9 Stress Number 6

This stress-number combination indicates emotional suffering through marriage, romance and affections. You can become cold and detached in order to protect yourself. Expect considerable difficulty in your emotional relationships. In marriage you will constantly resent the burden and responsibility of seemingly unjustified demands. This can lead to love affairs in search of the ideal mate. But this unrealistic search will haunt you until you realize that you are incapable of being ideal to someone else and release your hang-ups.

The suggestion here is that you have had difficulty giving constant love in past-life patterns and must strive to earn love now by giving it ceaselessly. Be careful, however, not to become a false martyr. There is a tendency to be careless with little things like payments, appointments and birthdays/anniversaries. Common addictions are pets, chocolate, sugar, sex, relationships, food, fanaticism, entertainment/movies and socializing.

Combinations with 4

4–5 Stress Number 1

In this stress pattern, there is a very difficult tension between the desire for play and the need to work. You must seek constructive direction for will through adversity. This is not the best combination for business; you alternate between miserly restriction and impractical spending. You want to be recognized for great work and may take shortcuts or exaggerate credentials to get that recognition. You feel compelled to outperform all in your path.

You must work diligently to recognize the source of your insecurity; it is likely that there was a conflict with the father in your early years. In your efforts to advance, you are prone to attract dishonest or misleading characters who have quick and appealing solutions. Many reversals will force you to examine your motives and seek your true place in the scheme of things. Common addictions are speed and danger, gambling, fanatical groups, food, sex, ritual, alcohol, money, work and smoking.

4–6 Stress Number 2

There is emotional tension that comes from both work and home. You find yourself repeatedly beset by your spouse, your boss and your own self-criticism. You attract a possessive and envious spouse and friends. You try to pump yourself up by putting others down. You tend to acquire trite symbols to build up your self-image, such as trophies, awards and conversational

cause you to lash out verbally about neighbors' faults—let this be a clue that it is time to face up to your own. As you work out inner conflicts, you will have a chance to serve as a peacemaker and mediator. Common addictions are hobbies, pets, sports, sugar, ritual, books, reading, institutions (a compulsive need to participate in an organization), gambling, speed and danger as well as socializing.

5–8 Stress Number 3

The primary struggle here is to use creativity properly for constructive purposes. You fluctuate between superficiality and the demands of your profession. The suggestion is that in a past life, or lives, you squandered creative talent for sensuality and superficial living. You probably have difficulty finding the motivation and direction you want in life. Oddly, you may attempt to force situations that create discord for your ambitions rather than the attainment you are seeking.

This stress pattern produces a restrained emotional makeup. There often is a feeling of being unable to enjoy the spoils of social status and good living. You need to look deeper within to attune to the higher creative laws of the universe. Common addictions are speed and danger, gambling, food, sex, alcohol, power, pets, gardening and smoking.

5–9 Stress Number 4

A tension develops here between idealism, excessive habits and the desire to seriously discipline your life. You are capable of creating a very convincing image of your idealized self. The only person who does not see through it is you! Many traits and habits keep you short of your aspirations, and you will have to work hard all your life to reach most of them. Do not be discouraged; it will help to develop some common-sense idealism. You rotate from overindulgence to remorse for excesses, then to an idealized state that discounts the flaws erroneously.

Guilt associated subconsciously with past-life abuses makes you a target for chastisement and almost masochistic punishment. You have difficulty taking advantage of opportunities when they come your way. There is hesitation and uncertainty about what principles you stand for, because your value structure has a rocky foundation. You benefit from deep study of spiritual, philosophical, religious or metaphysical systems to build an inner foundation. Common addictions are gardening, sports, alcohol, sex, food, institutions (a compulsive need to participate in an organization), gambling, movies, speed and danger.

Combinations with 6

6–7 Stress Number 1

In this stress pattern, there is a classic struggle between head (intellect) and heart (conflicting emotions). The need is to find your own will through conflict. An individual with this combination must learn to control emotions and not be controlled by overreaction and moodiness. The disruption of emotions by subconscious turmoil has the effect of distorting reasoning. You tend to rationalize to justify your insecurity rather than applying reason to recognize its origins. Your friends and mates are most often also emotionally inhibited and intellectually unsure. You manipulate such friends with a kind of arrogant, know-it-all attitude.

Do you become intimidated easily? Not knowing exactly where you stand on the issue under debate causes indecision. Because you then feel humiliated, the next time it occurs, you become belligerent and unyielding on some petty point. Until you establish a solid sense of will and confidence, your consciousness will be split between the forces of mind and emotion. Common addictions are fanatical groups, institutions (a compulsive need to participate in an organization), books/reading, relationships, ritual, sugar, power and pets, to mention a few.

6–8 Stress Number 2

Sensitive emotions and a drive for power engulf you in everyone's wrath. A past-life pattern of selfishness and arrogance—with a caustic tongue for opposition—is suggested by this combination. Even now you can be very self-centered and trite. You like to prove others wrong just to prove yourself right. There is disdain for the world around you, and you create circumstances that justify your attitude toward yourself. You show very little ability to express genuine affection. Your rude manner and tactics disappoint and injure those desiring your friendship and love. In return, others disappoint you, and so the wheel turns.

Your pride and ego will be severely tested until you are willing to release your blocks and turn outward to assist the world in the attempt to shed all needless suffering. Common addictions are speed and danger, entertainment, gambling, food, sex, ritual, sugar, money and power, to name a few.

6–9 Stress Number 3

This is another emotional conglomerate of discord with a crosscurrent of emotions running in three directions at once. You will attain inner serenity only after surrendering the little self to the directives of the intuitive guidance of the soul. You have very likely been a martyr in a previous life and felt others turn against you. This has left you very caustic and reserved in your expression of inner feelings. It is hard for you to give of the heart completely; you fear that admirers will reject your affections. This fear works subconsciously to attract a demanding and unresponsive lover who brings that which you feared most into your house.

You can alternate from being an emotional icebox to being in a state of frantic delirium. Then in the next moment, your whole attitude can sink into pessimism and sorrow. Delays and frustrations seem to plague you at every turn.

Face this combination and work your way through the labyrinth of emotional dilemmas, and you will be very effective at assisting other souls out of their doldrums. Common addictions are socializing, entertainment/movies, fanatical groups, relationships, sex, chocolate, pets, gardening and smoking, to name a few.

Combinations with 7

7–8 Stress Number 1

This highly mental combination has difficulty finding satisfactory direction of self-will. Mental quandary and gloominess follow you. A hollow feeling toward the values of the world pervades your life. An intellectual isolation from others leaves you somewhat cynical toward trust and friendship. There is suggestion of an attitude of intellectual oppression over others in an early life. It put you in a vacuum this time to learn the imbalance of willful mentality without compassion and sympathy for others. This gives a strong sense of accomplishment and the possibility for responsible leadership.

You have a good mind but have difficulty expressing your ideas clearly. You tend to resist new ideas and projects, wanting absolute proof of feasibility. However, once started, you can organize and capably finish. Common addictions are smoking, gardening, pets, alcohol, ritual, food, books, reading and fanatical religions/groups.

7–9 Stress Number 2

Feelings are torn between mind, idealism and the demands of society. This pattern indicates that when you were young, you found yourself under much pressure to live by some vague ideal your parents had decided was their dream. The thing is, you just happened to come for another purpose. You have an excellent intellectual capacity and intuitive and inventive potential. Your nervous sensitivity and lack of emotional refinement create difficulty working with others despite your originality and ability.

You can be harshly critical of yourself and others because you are intensely aware of the misspent energy in your life and in the lives of those around you. You can create antagonism in people who could be helpful by letting your sarcasm go too far. By learning acceptance of others and overcoming your inner arrogance, you can be innovative and attain considerable success. Common addictions are entertainment/movies, religious and group fanaticism, institutions (a compulsive need to participate in an organization), books, reading, ritual, alcohol, money, power and hobbies.

Combinations with 8

8–9 Stress Number 1

Past misuse of will puts you in a position of choosing between selfish aspirations to power and an opportunity for selfless service to humankind. There is much self-control and desire to lead and influence people. It is very easy for you to arrange other people's lives and tell them what is best for them. You did it in other lives, and maybe you will let go this time and do a better job with your own life. You could be a great savior to humankind or a megalomaniac dictator. You feed your low self-esteem by ridiculing others. Use your originality and determination to build a better you. The world will automatically benefit from your contribution.

You have a reserved and gruff exterior and an excellent mind. Beneath this is a stubborn determination that helps you overcome obstacles and attain your goal. Just be careful not to trample others on your way. Common addictions are speed and danger, movies, gambling, sex, alcohol, money, power, sports and work.

Interpersonal Stress Numbers

Combinations with 1

1–2 Stress Number 1

The stress here is of willfulness. The 1 wants independence and is careless about the 2's cautions or criticisms. The 2 needs to respect the individuality of the 1 and overcome a nitpicking attitude. The 2 needs the 1 for security; the 1 dislikes the 2's dependence. The 1 enjoys the way the 2 takes care of little matters, but the 2 dislikes the 1's lack of appreciation. Because of the 1's attitude, the 2 learns to be more independent, and the 1 learns to be more cooperative. Until then, arguments and petty bickering will prevail. When working together, the 2 gives support to the initiative of the 1, and both set up a dynamic duo of cooperative wills.

1–3 Stress Number 2

Sarcasm and bickering will likely occur until harmony is established. The 1 sees the 3 as emotionally weak and superficial. The 3 sees the 1 as arrogant and unfeeling. The 1 is critical of little things the 3 does, and the 3 retaliates by criticizing the 1 and undermining his/her initiative. Threes like to socialize and go out; 1s may prefer an occasional visit with good friends. Threes worry often and inhibit the 1 from making changes. The 1 criticizes the 3 for being unable to give up sentimental attachments and move on in experience. At worst, this breeds an environment of criticism, indecision and disagreement over trivial issues. When in harmony, each provides valuable clues for the other in establishing an ability to see issues clearly and become more cooperative in daily relationships with others.

1–4 Stress Number 3

This is likely to create considerable stress upon emotions and the ability to communicate feelings and personal concepts. The 4 is serious, structured and unyielding; the 1 seeks freedom from structure. The 1 dislikes the 4's restrictions, and the 4 becomes upset with the 1's careless disregard for convention. Strong emotions will flare up and explode as temper. The 1 is likely to subconsciously undermine the 4's confidence toward work, while the 4 withholds cooperation with the 1's new interests. Sexuality might be used as a tool for manipulation; for instance, hang-ups could develop in sexual expression when these two are out of harmony. Each partner involved will struggle to express words and feelings in an articulate and comfortable manner. When in harmony, there is potential for innovative and creative work together. One or both parties involved most likely had a domineering parent or parents who worked hard and probably gave the child needed warmth and emotional support.

1–5 Stress Number 4

With this combination, both parties will have to work hard at finding mutual balance between impulsiveness and the desire for total freedom. This is an on-and-off type of relationship where things go well at one moment then become totally uncooperative the next. If both share interests, flexibility could be helpful. A strong sexual drive directed mutually toward a constructive goal could produce tremendous accomplishment. The 1 expects the 5 to take care of his/her needs, while the 5 becomes irritated by the 1's constant opinions about his/her new interests. The 5 wants to be left to free action but becomes upset with the 1's indifference. One or both parties likely had parents who left them pretty much alone to decide their own life means and course; neither likes to be tied down to a job and responsibility.

1–6 Stress Number 5

A struggle for freedom is the primary stress in this combination. The 6 clings to the 1 for security within self. The 1 dislikes and is resentful of being tied down to responsibility but needs the 6 in order to learn more concern for others. The 6 becomes upset with the 1's lack of interest in domestic issues. The 1 dislikes the 6's worrying; conversely, the 6 cannot understand why the 1 is so sure things are going to work out all right. Each is learning the true law of freedom, but it will come at considerable cost. The 1's need to learn freedom truly comes to fruition when responsibility has been met; the 6 finds freedom only after letting go of others to trust in self-confidence. One or both of these parties lived with a parent who on some levels rebelled against home, family or social restrictions.

1–7 Stress Number 6

Considerable tension hinders the building of mutual trust and responsibility with this combination. The analytical 7 cannot deal with the impulsiveness of the 1, and the 1 becomes impatient with the indecision of the 7. There will be very noticeable differences in philosophy and life attitudes, which can become pronounced when childraising is an issue. The 7 has all sorts of theories about life but can be emotionally out of touch with the needs of the 1. The 1 also has trouble handling emotional responsibilities and can become impatient and inconsiderate. There will be much shifting of blame when the relationship goes awry. Domestic and emotional harmony will be a struggle. One or both of the parties involved likely comes from a home where a divorce occurred or the parents perpetuated a conflictual relationship.

1–8 Stress Number 7

In this combination, 8s want authority and try to dominate. The 1 prefers individuality and does not want anyone telling him/her what to do. The 8 needs the 1 in order to learn to recognize the authority in everyone. The 1 needs the 8 in order to learn to balance will and power. There will likely be a constant intellectual struggle, each trying to outscore the other in arguments, each using quotes and facts to support his/her position. If the 7 energy is used wisely, it will force both to look more deeply into life studies to find mutual respect through the development of deeper insights into mind and soul. One or both parties involved most likely had a detached and cerebral parent or parents who had difficulty expressing emotions.

1–9 Stress Number 8

This is a tough combination, because 1 is selfish and 9 is selfless. The difference here creates a struggle for authority. The 9 expects the 1 to live up to the 9's ideals, and the 1 wants to be free. There is a constant pull between idealism and realism. The 1 may attempt to dominate the 9, forcing the 9 to look deeper into the principles of practical idealism. The 9 needs to learn acceptance of the 1's individuality, and the 1 must learn more selfless concern for others. There will be subtle little—or sometimes big and not so subtle!—power games played by each in an attempt to prove his/her own position. This can create completely different attitudes toward money and finance, creating dissension. One or both parties likely experienced parents who were constantly struggling for power in the home and over each other's lives.

Combinations with 2

2–3 Stress Number 1

Another conflict of wills, but this time the competitive nature is not as obvious as when a number 1 occurs also as part of the combination. Communication will be erratic, contrary and confused. There is constant misunderstanding, and lack of clarity in communication will plague the desire to get along. The 2 looks at topics from more than one angle and believes the 3 is superficial and shallow. The 3 knows from the heart and becomes irritated by the vacillation and indecisiveness of the 2. There can be a problem with this combination in determining who will take the initiative and leadership. Either of these parties, or both, probably comes from a highly emotional environment. This could be a very creative and articulate combination when the two numbers work together.

2–4 Stress Number 2

This is a very likely combination for petty bickering. The 2 is seldom content with the way the 4 does his/her work. The 4 works very hard to please society and spouse but is likely to be unhappy pleasing him-or her-self. The 4 wants to set the rules, and the 2 upsets the 4 by dreaming up so many alternatives. At the crux, the 2 is very hard to please and constantly measures success by the standards of others rather than by inner awareness. The 4 dislikes the 2's constant fluctuation in taste and values. The 2 does not like the 4's lack of imagination and serious attitude; the 4 cannot understand the 2's flighty moods and whims. The combination working harmoniously balances the 4's steadiness with the 2's ability for cooperation and assistance.

2–5 Stress Number 3

A superficial level of communication is suggested by this stress combination. The 2 dislikes the 5's impulsiveness and lack of regard for convention. A 5 becomes irritated by the 2's social conventions, suspecting shallow thinking. The 2 shudders at the 5's generalizing and carelessness; the 5 is uncomfortable with the 2's unreasonable attention to detail and protocol. The 5 seeks change and activity, and the 2 is slower to make friends and try new outlets. The various activities of the 2 and 5 make it difficult to establish a deep understanding and communication. They can be mutually extravagant; do you both get behind in payments? The 2 is likely to become possessive and jealous of the meandering nature of the 5. The 5 becomes aggravated by the 2's insecurities and distrust. Both parties must establish an open and honest dialogue and exchange affection to overcome shallowness and petty pretense.

2–6 Stress Number 4

This combination easily gets into a rut of stubborn resistance instead of accommodating mutual needs. The 2 can wallow in self-pity, making the 6 feel guilty, and the 6 thus becomes overly indulgent to the 2's whims. The 6 then becomes a martyr, believing that he/she must suffer torment and pain. The 2 dislikes divorce; because of conventionality, he/she will bear the aggravation in silence. Both parties in this combination are prone to nag the partner about his/her work and profession: The 2 likes more status, and the 6 prefers greater security through increased earnings. Both must let go of emotional and social hang-ups and work to establish mutual stability. An excellent opportunity might come from working together in a group or organization (charitable or professional) that works to assist others.

2–7 Stress Number 5

There is a struggle for freedom from intellectual pride and socially ingrained consciousness. The 7 is infuriated by the 2's constant nitpicking at his/her opinions and intellectual pride. The 2 dislikes the 7's aloofness but can learn from the depth and wisdom of the 7. The 7 wants nothing to do with the 2's sentiment and emotionalism while failing to recognize that this is exactly what he/she is seeking to develop. Neither likes being pinned to the other, yet each clings tenaciously. Each overplays and overdramatizes his/her condition. Each is plagued by a vague restlessness and search for something or someone different. With this combination, both are learning to let the other be free; with freedom each can grow closer to the other because of a greater range of experience shared.

2–8 Stress Number 6

Holding this relationship together will require much attention. Competition develops between outside pressures and interests versus the attempt to hold on to a caring relationship. The 8 is absorbed in career and job demands, leaving the 2 feeling neglected. At the same time, the 2 wants the social trappings that indicate success. The 2 seeks outlets in various causes and pretends not to appreciate the achievement of the 8. The 8 often overlooks the home and family on the way to bigger things in career, while the 2 learns about money and commercial responsibility. This often necessitates overcoming fear and emotional insecurities. The 2 works subconsciously to undermine authoritarianism with subtle sparring and devious little tactics to show disregard. Both parties will have to avoid negligence toward partnership and strive to maintain their union.

2–9 Stress Number 7

With this combination, the parties involved will strive to find more significance in life. This will involve a difficult search for truth and self-understanding. Both parties in this combination are prone to the impracticality of idealism. The 9 resents the 2 putting the blame on him/her, while the 2 cannot understand the 9's blind faith and flighty reality. Both can exhibit wide mood fluctuations and need to develop intellectual detachment as a balance to broadly fluctuating emotions. Each party can be impractical and at times irrational, blaming the other for setbacks and circumstances. For example, the 9 is worried about world problems and war in the Middle East, while the 2 worries about the leak in the bathroom faucet. Both parties need to dig deeper into spiritual or philosophical wisdom to adequately understand their mental and divine wisdom within.

Combinations with 3

3–4 Stress Number 1

A distinctly different lifestyle and attitude challenge the "will" aspect in both parties of this combination. The 3 misconstrues the 4's seriousness, and the 4 is irritated by the whimsical 3. The 3 may depend upon the 4 for support, but the 4 takes work so seriously that he/she fails to give emotional strength. The 4 needs to learn to loosen up and enjoy life more spontaneously, but he/she cannot grasp the spontaneous and illogical whims of the 3. A significant difference in goals is likely. The 4 seeks a boost to will, but the 3 has so many distractions that it is difficult to sustain support. The 3 seeks strength of will, but the 4's discipline and serious outlook are difficult to accept. Both parties must be willing to recognize the fundamental individuality and will in the other. Together, this combination blends spontaneity with discipline.

3–5 Stress Number 2

This combination breeds mutual superficiality and disregard for regulations. The fun-loving qualities in each chart create a surface-level relationship with little cooperation or mutual purpose. The 3 is intolerant of the 5's excesses but displays his/her own extravagance other ways. The 5 is self-indulgent and tasteless, which chafes at the artistic and refined qualities of the 3. Daily bickering and constant hassles over small issues become routine until regeneration occurs. The 5 can learn from the refinement of the 3; the 3 can learn spontaneity from the 5. This combination can create a mutual lack of interest in social dicta, leaving both parties out of touch with current customs. Both must rise above the pain criticism causes to unite the potentially dynamic combination of creativity and originality latent here.

3–6 Stress Number 3

This is another emotionally difficult combination that can become entangled in inhibited feelings and restricted communication. The 6 demands attention and dislikes the 3's varied interests and time-consuming outlets. The 3 has trouble handling the 6's domestic needs and dictates of personal attention. The 3 means well but manages to say just the thing to trigger the 6's sullen and morose withdrawal. The 6 means well but dampens the 3's enthusiasm by playing upon the theme. The mood cycles run almost in counterrhythm, making it difficult to get together even when both desperately desire understanding. At worst, poor communication exists and very likely separation and divorce occurs. This combination must learn to articulate feelings clearly and to carefully understand the deeper need of the partner.

3–7 Stress Number 4

This is a difficult combination for working to merge mind and emotions. Expect constant struggle due to divergent philosophies and attitudes toward life. The 7 does not understand the optimism and sense of knowing experienced by the 3. The 7's cynicism and doubt alienate the finer sensitivity of the emotional 3. Both hold stubbornly to old ways and outwardly reject the other's viewpoint. The 3 prefers more attentiveness; the 7 prefers to be left alone to pursue self-interests. The 3 can benefit from learning to think deeply and analytically, like the 7; the 7 can learn to accept feelings and inner impressions. Neither will easily accept an opportunity to balance these two dichotomous approaches. It is probable that one comes from a warm home environment and the other experienced an intellectually detached parental influence.

3–8 Stress Number 5

An intense struggle for freedom is suggested with this combination. The 8 constantly dominates the situation, causing the 3 to hold in emotional resentment. The 3 follows intuition and comes up with insights that undermine the authoritative attitude of the 8, upsetting the 8's ego. The 8 cannot learn to let the 3 free to follow the job of heart. The 3 has difficulty letting the 8 be free to pursue his/her ambitions for success and attainment. The 3 becomes possessive and jealous, and the 8 tries to fulfill the 3's emotional needs by providing material tokens of security. The 3 helps the 8 to appreciate the joys of the humane side of life; the 8 helps the 3 to be more practical and ambitious toward life realities.

3–9 Stress Number 6

This emotionally fluctuating combination must seek a realistic attitude toward responsibility. The 3 relies upon the 9's idealism and faith, while the 9 expects the 3 to take care of business. The 3's worry tendency upsets the natural idealism and optimism of the 9; the 9's detachment creates an emotional frustration for the 3. The 3's varied interests and diversions antagonize the 9, who would like more personal attention. On the other hand, the 9 can get caught up in ideals and causes, becoming quite indifferent to the personal needs of the 3. Both parties must strive for mature solutions in areas of responsibility and support. Each tends to place often totally unrealistic demands upon the other for security and domestic tranquillity.

Combinations with 4

4–5 Stress Number 1

The numbers 4 and 5 are like polar opposites, so this combination will undergo considerable strain in accepting the individuality and will of each one involved. The 5 can abuse the privilege of freedom and individuality, and he/she resents the possessive and plodding 4. The 4 clings stubbornly to habit and custom and becomes annoyed with the 5's total disregard for rules and accepted norms of behavior. Their struggle will likely persist: the expansive tendencies of the 5 against the restrictive nature of the 4. The 4 works hard to make things comfortable and cozy, but the 5 is seldom home to appreciate the work. The 5 has no tolerance for the confinement imposed by the 4. There will be many arguments that flare up intensely and are over quickly. The 5 can learn patience and discipline from the 4, and the 4 can learn to be more independent and spontaneous from the 5.

4–6 Stress Number 2

The old nemesis of nagging and criticism can plague this combination until an attitude of cooperation is established. The 6 nags the 4 about working so hard and neglecting the 6 in doing so. The 4 then becomes busy with other projects to get away from the 6's complaining. The 4 expects the 6 to take care of responsibilities and family needs, resenting the 6's interference. The 4 will harass the 6 about minute procedures or daily routines. The 6 fights back by criticizing the 4 about work and personal habits. The 4 does not understand why the 6 fails to appreciate how hard he/she has worked to provide security; the 6 responds by resenting that the 4 has been spending so much time at the job and cannot express emotional support openly. The 4 can learn to feel from the 6, and the 6 can learn to discipline emotion from the 4.

4–7 Stress Number 3

We see a dead heat when the fixed 4 meets with the opinionated 7. The 4 hides emotions, and the 7 secludes feelings behind a strong intellectual facade. Both have trouble with emotions, and this creates a climate of stifled feelings, which inhibits communication and flow of expression. Stubbornness will characterize the texture of this relationship. The 7 chastises and belittles the 4's lack of intellectual depth; the 4 dislikes the pompous insinuations of the 7. The climate of communication is strained, and disagreements are laced with pent-up emotions and unexpressed feelings, which color and intensify the tension. Each has attracted the other to learn the importance of recognizing personal feelings and clearly expressing self.

4–8 Stress Number 4

Disagreements over methodology, habits and financial attitudes are suggested by this combination. The 4 works hard and diligently for gains and resents the 8's flippant attitude toward money and success. The 4 likes to hold on to every penny; however, the 8 wants the good things in life. Both are inordinately stubborn at their worst. The 8 can prosper from learning discipline from the 4; the 4 needs to learn to be more innovative about work from the 8. Controlled emotions in both parties make it difficult for them to recognize their partner's needs. One—or both—likely comes from a home where a parent or both parents spent long hours pursuing work, which left the child emotionally starved. When united on a project, this could be an unbeatable team.

4–9 Stress Number 5

With this combination, there is a struggle of identity and individual purpose. This partnership fluctuates between the 9's idealism and the 4's practicality. The 4's rigidity irritates the 9's desire to live in dream worlds of the neverlands; on the other hand, the 9's lack of common sense develops within this prone 4. Sexual guilt could very well develop within this relationship because of the blend of the conventional 4 and the possibly unconventional 9. The 9 learns true freedom only from discipline; an excellent example being the 4. The 4 needs to break from the rigid and preestablished attitudes to soar to greater heights, like the 9. Each will attempt to flee from the lessons he/she can gain from this combination. Yet, as with any pair, there is a tremendous opportunity for learning and growth.

Combinations with 5

5–6 Stress Number 1

This is yet another dynamic combination. The channeling of will and the expression of individualism are two of the significant lessons indicated. The 5 craves freedom and resents the 6's constant need for emotional support and domestic cooperation. The 6's serious attitudes are unsettled by the 5's casual behavior. The 5 feels inhibition of will, and the 6 feels that the 5 neglects consideration for his/her identity and needs. The 5 can learn that freedom comes from fulfilling obligations, and the 6 can learn to let go of overattachment to security and to family support. One—or both—likely comes from a home where the parents were constantly at odds about philosophy and each other's expected roles.

5–7 Stress Number 2

Verbal sparring and disagreement over small issues can plague this relationship. The 7 sits among intellectual clouds and pontificates about the 5's superficial lifestyle. The 5's zest and exuberance are diminished by the 7's lack of participation in experiential life processes. A nagging and constantly petty interplay can develop between the high and the flighty. The 7 can learn to disengage pompous intellectuality and enjoy life as the 5 does. The 5 can learn to see things with more depth and insight as demonstrated by the analytical 7. One—or both—of the partners likely comes from a home where intellectual detachment by one or both of the parents contributed to emotional discomfort.

5–8 Stress Number 3

Detachment and trivial behavior toward the feeling nature can become a stumbling block with this combination. The 8's formality toward emotions is not stimulating to the curious and expansive 5. The 8 finds the 5's enthusiasm and unpredictable temperament too threatening, causing even more inhibition and controlled behavior. The 8 inhibits the 5's self-expression but can teach the 5 to become more articulate and definitive. The 8 learns to loosen up more and becomes more expressive rather than tight and restrained. There is a strong likelihood that one—or both—partners comes from a family where prestige and attainment were put ahead of personal warmth. When in harmony, this is an excellent combination for successful communication.

5–9 Stress Number 4

Both partners may have had a hard time keeping their efforts grounded and functional. The 9 drifts into dreams of neverworlds, and the 5 takes this world very superficially. Because neither is apt to take the lead in bringing organization to the relationship, they could drift through life aimlessly. As situations crumble, both will have to learn discipline and the need to work conscientiously together to build a foundation for any mutual success. Both, however, dislike the 4 vibration, so a struggle will exist in establishing practical realism. The scattered 5 will have to work at understanding the sensitivity of the 9. The idealism of the 9 is confounded by the blatant indulgence and worldly ways of the 5. An artistic and creative temperament pervades the actions of this combination.

Combinations with 6

6–7 Stress Number 1

Herein is the combination for building an identity from the struggle between mind and emotion. The 7's intellectual detachment forces the 6 to look back within self in order to resolve inner emotional insecurities. The 6's constant referral to feelings perplexes the 7, and the resulting heart activity undermines the best efforts of the 7. The 6's will is strengthened by self-survival, and the 7 learns to be more emotionally compassionate toward the will in others from being around the 6. A fundamental difference between approaches to life will bring these two into heated debate and constant sparring. The 7 relies upon logic; the 6 works from feeling and intuition. Both will benefit from learning to ap preciate the other. One—or both—of the parties probably comes from a home environment with a similar emotional/ intellectual split between the parents.

6–8 Stress Number 2

This combination breeds bickering, unless each works to complement and understand the other. The 6 enjoys the material comforts of home but dislikes the inability of the 8 to express warmth and emotional tenderness. The 8 puts time and energy into work and attainment, thereby resenting that the 6 does not appreciate his/her efforts to provide security. The 6 worries about money and family, putting pressure upon the 8's earning capacity. The 8's drive for money and success offends the 6's sensitive feelings. Arguments may ensue regarding the most socially acceptable etiquette and procedure. The brusque manner of the 8 is annoying to the 6; therefore, the 8 becomes intolerant of the constantly whining 6. Through cooperation and sharing, the two can balance this conflict between the drive for success and tender consideration for others.

6–9 Stress Number 3

This is perhaps one of the more difficult combinations for establishing communication and harmonious flow of emotions. Each party seeks emotional support from the other and is often unprepared to give in order to receive. Unrealistic goals and demands lead to bonds and proposed pacts that often prove to be pure fabrication. The 6 has no capacity to understand the 9's impersonal idealism, and the 9 feels the 6 holds consciousness back by trying to tie the 9 down to mundane trivia. Both parties suffer from a feeling of inadequacy, trying to alleviate each other's wildly fluctuating moods. Each tends to discuss frustration lightly with the other, and both will benefit from learning to articulate feelings more specifically. This is a potentially creative and highly artistic combination.

Combinations with 7

7–8 Stress Number 1

Intellectual authority and personal pride are factors that bring the conflict of will into sharp focus. The 7 will use facts and figures to support a position of attack and parry. The 8 intensely dislikes being put down and thrusts at emotional doubts and weaknesses to maintain leverage. Each can be very stubborn and unyielding, and the lack of emotional balance in this combination makes for a subtle power play. The 7 tries to reason with the 8; the 8 uses past experience as a basis for making decisions. This combination naturally breeds a competitive rather than a cooperative climate. A good combination of reason and power can emerge when the two are united comfortably.

7–9 Stress Number 2

This combination of mental realism and emotional idealism creates a climate of mixed philosophy and confused goals. The 7 chides the philosophical and intellectual weakness of the 9 and cannot understand the vague mystical leanings that motivate the 9. The 9 detests the constant intellectual doubting of the 7 and yearns for someone to share his/her deep-seated idealism. The quarrelsome atmosphere strains emotional harmony, creating an atmosphere of nagging and petty criticism. The 7 could learn much from the emotional and idealistic 9, and the 9 can become more organized and articulate about ideas by being around the 7. One—or both—of the parties likely comes from a home where parents were at odds between heart and head.

Combinations with 8

8–9 Stress Number 1

The difference in direction of the wills with this combination arises from the 8's desire to accumulate the goods of this world and the 9's deep-seated need to let go. The 8 interprets the 9's philosophy as undermining and unrealistic. The 9 becomes bored with the 8's constant materialistic appraisal of life values. The 8 needs ego support of the will to accomplish something. The 9 could care less about some of the 8's ambitions. The 9 seeks an ideal mate and finds the 8 lacking in areas of emotional sensitivity and humanitarian idealism. This is a very opportunistic combination for growth when the partners recognize the potential of the two numbers together.

10

Karma and Numerology

T he doctrine of karma is quite complex, and it would take up considerable space to discuss it completely. I intend for this chapter to specifically outline some principal themes to clarify karma, particularly as it relates
to numerological interpretation.

Karma is very intimately interwoven with the doctrine of reincarnation. The
soul seeks to evolve by learning from the variety of experiences available on this
material Earth plane. In successive cycles—or simultaneously, according to
some doctrines—the soul incarnates into a personality structure, learns about
life, adds to its wisdom and finally withdraws for introspection upon the inner
planes. The personality (physical, emotional and mental bodies) provides vehicles through which the soul interacts with the lower planes. This cycle repeats
itself until the soul finally reaches a point of mastery over the lower vehicles. At
that point, it no longer incarnates into the physical realm but takes on a more
subtle and refined body on a higher plane of manifestation.

Through the personality, the soul accumulates and eventually masters the
various challenges, experiences and lessons of life. One symbolical method
of describing these life lessons is through numerology. This does not imply
that there are nine simple lessons to learn. The interaction between the numbers creates shades and subtle mixtures of life experiences. However, for purposes of clarity and definition, we concentrate on the primary phases of
growth through study of the nine basic numbers.

One fundamental law of karma is force, which impels consciousness—be
it in a one-celled microbe, an animal, a human or an angel—to progress

toward the next phase of cosmic, universal, planetary, social, human, animal or biological growth. In humanity, this law expresses itself through human will. It is the will factor that urges and compels expansion and unfoldment through life's experiences.

A second fundamental law of karma is that of cause and effect. "As you sow, so also shall you reap" is a pertinent allusion to this law. In the process of learning, we often overdo or avoid the lesson at hand, which creates imbalance and perpetuates karma. Finally, through study, higher guidance and attunement to the soul, we reach a point of balance wherein the lesson is mastered and we reach a state of balance and harmony. Once we reach this dharmic balance, the lesson is completed. We are then free to move on to new experiences. There eventually comes a time when the soul has accumulated and balanced out all of the Earth-plane lessons. Then the soul is free from the wheel of karma and enters a new cycle of experience, in a higher realm or level of consciousness.

Almost every number in the chart has karmic implication in a sense. Each number shows potential skills and deficiencies. If that lesson were not important to our growth, we would have chosen otherwise. The very fact that we are embodied at this time indicates that we are still working on karma.

Missing Numbers

The primary indicators of karma in numerology are the numbers that are missing in the name given at birth. They define where specific imbalance exists. The absence of a number reveals an area of a person's life that will require extra attention to balance the lesson indicated. Some believe that an individual with no numbers missing has no karma. Such thinking is incorrect. Later in this chapter, a special description and explanation will discuss this condition in a chart.

Each missing number represents a karmic lesson that was not learned. This lifetime, then, is your opportunity to correct the situation or balance the condition. The absence of a number—or numbers—merely indicates that in a previous life or lives, you have gone to excess or failed to master the lesson at issue. (There are several references in this book to the theme of balance and lack of balance, to excess or deficiency.) Numerology gives us guidelines regarding our experiential progress. As previously stated, every number in the chart has a karmic implication. The missing numbers help define which karmic lessons need the most attention in this life cycle. The interpretations for missing numbers will help you understand how they reveal very important insights into the nature of your character and behavior.

❋ ❋ ❋

Each karmic lesson is described separately using assertive and passive descriptions, to help you recognize more accurately the lessons that have been out of balance and now need harmonizing. The passive description suggests that the meaning of the lesson was likely avoided in a previous life or lives; the assertive paragraph suggests that the lesson of the number was overdone. By reading both, your own inner guidance should help you recognize which is applicable.

The Karmic Accumulation Number

An entirely new approach to delineating the karmic impact is also detailed following the individual descriptions of the karmic lessons. This new interpretation is the karmic accumulation number. To determine it, add all the missing numbers into one total. For example, if the numbers 8, 4 and 3 are missing from the name at birth, the karmic accumulation number is 15 (8 + 4 + 3 = 15). If the total is between 1 and 21, or if it is 22 or 33, do not reduce it.

The karmic accumulation number gives perspective on an individual's overall reaction to the weight of the necessary lessons. It should be emphasized that the dynamics of karmic numbers are mostly expressed subconsciously through our lives. Only a few are obviously conscious traits.

The karmic accumulation number hints at a lot of tendencies acquired through previous personalities. Some of these may still remain in the subconscious and reveal themselves through the current personality. By recognizing these traits consciously, you can transmute the negative and integrate the positive into the present life. This provides a better opportunity for attaining a more accomplished and fulfilled life. If you do not accomplish this, then you can become bogged down by the weight of the past and never really accomplish desired intentions of this life cycle.

Remember that these traits and karmic tendencies manifest through the personality and will reveal themselves with differing hues and nuances, depending upon the personality number. They will become particularly pronounced when assessing stress patterns or during the personal year or month whose number corresponds to the karmic number that is missing. I hope the descriptions in this chapter will be of particular value, helping you to understand and more harmoniously cope with the conditions individually chosen in this lifetime.

I realize that the descriptions in this chapter are potentially upsetting and possibly depressing. We need to be reminded that karma is self-imposed illusion, and seeing the illusion is the prelude to enlightenment! The first law of karma brings us to a discomforting awareness, and the soul finally breaks through with truth. Use your imbalance as a springboard to accelerated growth.

The descriptions for the karmic lessons are not intended to be an indictment, and not every statement in each description need apply. Perhaps just one minor aspect needs resolution. Discretion is needed when using these to evaluate another person's chart. When studying them for your own personal edification, read the descriptions and watch the reactions in your own emotions or intellect. If you are honest with yourself, those that apply will cause a reaction. If you want to ignore or deny certain ones, those may very well be especially applicable to your life. The crux of your self-examination lies in establishing an honest appraisal of your emotional and intellectual response.

The Karmic Lessons

1 Karmic Lesson

Assertive: There has been a tendency in past lives to dominate or control the will of another person or many people. Too much individuality has been a problem in the past, indicating a lack of concern for others. You have had difficulty trusting others and difficulty working cooperatively to finish the job.

Passive: There has been inability to trust your self-confidence. You have relied upon others to make decisions and have not been willing to face decisions or take advantage of opportunities that were presented to you. You have been jealous of others who were decisive and successful. There has been an attitude of over-conservatism and fear of taking a chance.

Current Opportunity for Harmony: Life will bring strong-willed people into your experience with whom you will have to struggle to find your own self-confidence and beliefs. You will be given many tests to strengthen your own individuality. If you take advantage of this, you will find yourself becoming increasingly more respectful toward the will and individuality of others. This is the first step toward cooperation of wills.

2 Karmic Lesson

Assertive: A past-life pattern of criticism, a caustic tongue and impatience is the indication with this lesson. You have lacked the ability to work harmoniously with others and have been divisive and isolated in your attitude. Too much attention to detail and lack of patience are also suggested.

Passive: There has been a tendency in your past to avoid details and become slack in attitude. There was a carelessness when settling matters like agreements and a decided lack of concern for others. You lost your own identity through attempts to please others, thereby losing awareness of your opinions and beliefs.

Current Opportunity for Harmony: Life will bring to you people who are highly critical and petty. You will have to carry the brunt of seemingly unjust gossip and rumors. Negativity will follow you at home and at work. Learn to give more attention to detail and small personal considerations. It will be hard learning to watch your tongue and thereby overcoming negativity, criticism and judgment toward others.

3 Karmic Lesson

Assertive: You are dealing with a past-life tendency toward superficiality, wasted talent and carelessness. You sold out your creativity for fame, fortune or to live the good life. It is likely that you have used your creative energy for gratification and indulgence. You were prone to exaggeration, jealousy and criticism of people's talents. There probably is past sexual abuse.

Passive: This past-life pattern shows unwillingness to develop or express creative abilities, with a tendency to spread talent too thin. You have had difficulty communicating your feelings or thoughts to others. You possessed minimal faith in your own potential and developed a low opinion of yourself.

Current Opportunity for Harmony: Life will bring challenges to your self-expression and to your creative skills. You will be forced into situations requiring you to overcome encumbrances to your self-expression. You may have a lisp or other speech impediment or poor posture as a result of bending under others' opinions. It will be difficult to get into the theater, orchestra or creative opportunity of your choice. This time you must learn to appreciate your artistry and work for its fullest expression.

4 Karmic Lesson

Assertive: You have worked so hard in the past that it narrowed your vision and perspective. You became very fixed, opinionated, dogmatic and unwilling to try new ideas or ways of doing things. Your convictions prevented you from understanding others, causing you to be stern and overbearing with those with whom you worked. You stayed attached to a stubborn and unyielding disposition.

Passive: There has been a decided distaste for hard work and methodical labor. You preferred ease and comfort without earning your share. This indicates laziness and a search for the easy way out. You suffer personal hang-ups about accepting your own self-worth.

Current Opportunity for Harmony: Success and accomplishment will not come easily, and you will have to work hard to earn your rewards. Whatever your achievements, you will likely experience several types of work before settling down into one that feels right. Any attempts at shortcuts will end in disappointment, or worse, outright failure. You must build success block by block, on a solid foundation.

5 Karmic Lesson

Assertive: This is a past-life pattern of irresponsible and carefree living, with a kind of cavalier "love 'em and leave 'em" attitude. You had difficulty establishing responsibility in personal relations. Inability to stay in one place or at one job is indicated. There is a strong likelihood of sexual indulgence and promiscuity. It is also likely that there has been abuse of the senses and emotions through excessive gambling, drinking or use of drugs. A disregard for the law is also suggested.

Passive: A past-life fear of new experience, change and progress is related to this lesson. You were uncomfortable dealing with human interaction. You possessed little understanding or tolerance for others. Fear of sex or rejection of sexuality has created confusion in that aspect of your life. Disappointments or setbacks may have driven you to sensual self-indulgence.

Current Opportunity for Harmony: Life will bring constant change. People with backgrounds and philosophies very different from your own will appear in your path. You will mix and mingle with diverse personalities and attract extremely wide-ranging experiences and situations. Although this can be confusing, there are many chances for learning. Once you learn to accept people for who they are, you will be able to seek and define your own comfortable standard of conduct based upon inner law, not social norm. You must persevere in situations long enough to absorb their lessons. Also, know when to let go. There is a need to work out sexual guilt.

6 Karmic Lesson

Assertive: You have been quite a difficult person to live and share responsibilities with. There has been a tendency to make everyone's business your own. You have meddled in others' lives and manipulated emotions for your own personal security. As a spouse and a parent, your disposition has been cranky, cantankerous and contentious. You have not learned the importance of sharing trust and building relationships on mutual responsibility.

Passive: A past-life pattern of refusing to face responsibility to self, home, family and others is indicated. You were careless with and unsupportive of loved ones. You resented having to provide for them rather than pursuing a career or opportunity of your own. You may have done many things but seldom carried them through to finish your obligation. You have given little attention to the care and nurturing of those for whom you were responsible. Emotional instability and misunderstanding are indicated.

Current Opportunity for Harmony: Life has likely put you into a family where there is dissension and friction between your parents. The possibility of more than one marriage in your life is high if you are unable to learn this lesson now. Your emotions will be tested and strained until you are willing to face and forgive the subconscious blocks deep inside. Family, friends and neighbors will constantly demand your time, energy or counseling ability. Marriage and home will bring many unexpected burdens and adjustments. You will experience considerable tribulation in adjusting to spouse and home. As you learn to cooperate and share the responsibilities of life, things will fall into place.

7 Karmic Lesson

Assertive: There has been too much past-life emphasis upon intellectual effort and academic knowledge. You became specialized in certain areas of study. As a scholar, you enjoyed the awe and prestige associated with your position. As a result, you became narrow, opinionated and severely sarcastic toward opponents or people you deemed to be below your level of intelligence. You subsequently lost touch with the human equation and day-to-day understanding. There was a preference for living behind high-toned theory, but with little of the layman's common sense. You have cut off feelings with excessive reasoning and become skeptical and cynical of mundane human events.

Passive: There has been a past-life pattern of shallow thinking and superficial living. An unwillingness to take things seriously or to investigate life deeply has left a need for deeper searching. You have resisted disciplining the mind to be thorough and scientific in your reasoning. Another possibility is of past disillusionment in a former religious incarnation, perhaps as a nun, monk or ascetic. Lack of deeper wisdom has perhaps led to superstition and a belief in false doctrines.

Current Opportunity for Harmony: Life will bring you circumstances requiring you to overcome these doubts and superstitions by building a solid faith based upon intellectual knowledge and spiritual wisdom. You must work to integrate reason with intuition. Seek the deeper teachings of spirituality, science, metaphysics, psychology and the cosmos. Along the way, many adversities may befall you, forcing you to examine truth more completely. True faith will be yours once you begin to acquire a fundamental grasp of esoteric wisdom teachings. Meditation, introspection and techniques of self-exploration that open inner doors will benefit your search for answers to cosmic riddles.

8 Karmic Lesson

Assertive: This suggests a former misapplication of power and wealth. You have dominated and manipulated others through force or intimidation. Wealth may have been squandered or employed for domination of others. This is a strong indicator of overbearing pride and personal ambition. Your way has been the only way, and you sternly forbade deviation. There has been overemphasis upon your personal influence in leadership and social circles. Former greed is also a possibility with this indicator.

Passive: There has been a past-life tendency to disregard material aspiration. You have not been willing to use your abilities to lead others and assist society. A decided distaste for money and a lack of courage to take financial risks are suggested; ineptitude and inefficiency in commercial enterprise is another possibility. You have not wanted to take responsibility for anyone but yourself. Thus you've missed opportunities for promotion or advancement. There has been difficulty breaking free from an authoritarian parent or some deeply inbred doctrine that has dominated your consciousness.

Current Opportunity for Harmony: Life will put you into situations that constantly test your authority. You will work under intolerable authority and see misuse of power and ineptitude at every turn. You must learn to take responsibility for your own financial and business affairs. You may very well earn a great deal of money and suddenly lose it; its absence will cause great pain. In the same light, if you strain for money, it will remain elusive. However, if you value it properly and use it wisely, you could easily become financially successful. There is an obvious need to balance between leadership and bossiness. As your leadership abilities mature, you will find many people willing to respond.

9 Karmic Lesson

Assertive: You have been an impractical idealist and dreamer, roaming in your personal, misty world without being able to produce a tangible contribution. Eccentricity has predominated over good taste, and your generosity usually bordered on squandering. Artistic potential was dissipated by nervous tension and lack of direction. You have been overly sentimental and romantic in personal relationships, which allowed you to be used by others. You thought you were loved for your golden heart, only to become depressed and disillusioned when your pockets were fleeced.

Passive: This indicates difficulty handling personal emotions and relating emotionally to others. Your selfless, impersonal routine smugly disguised an inability to sustain any personal commitment or share in affection and love. You have meant well but left little to those whose lives you touched. Overly concerned with your own suffering and loss, you have been less than sympathetic toward the suffering of others. You have been unwilling to face and deal with the harshness and cynicism of life.

Current Opportunity for Harmony: Life will bring you one difficulty after another in the form of emotionally traumatic situations. These will put your personality under stress until it finally reaches out to your soul for relief and instruction. Marital, job and health setbacks will cause grief. Eventually this opens the heart center, bringing you the chance to understand and sympathize with the suffering of others in life. You will benefit from working with groups or organizations that foster new avenues of research as well as metaphysical or educational instruction. This is a difficult turning point for letting go of the personality so that it may blend with the aspirations of the soul.

0 (Zero) Karmic Lesson

Does the fact that no numbers are missing from the name indicate there is no karma? Don't count on it! (No pun intended.) We are all here to work toward balance in our lives. Generally, 0 for karmic lessons in the chart represents a turning point in consciousness where you have come to a relatively harmonious point in your growth. You have an opportunity to choose from within just how to proceed, having no specific push from the pressure of missing karmic numbers. If this freedom of choice is not handled well, you may create greater imbalance, returning next time to deal anew with missing numbers.

On the other hand, you may use the information wisely, thus becoming able to leave the wheel of karma and proceed along the evolutionary spiral. When you are approaching the completion of karma, having no missing numbers can indicate that all of the lessons need to be learned and understood in relation to one another. When such an understanding is consciously sought, the sincere seeker enters into the subtle and more esoteric study of numbers.

I will say more about how the absence of missing numbers influences our consciousness at the end of the following discussions on karmic accumulation.

Putting Karma into Perspective

Warning: Sometimes students just starting to learn about reincarnation and karma read evaluations like these describing karmic patterns and become overwrought, anxious and uncomfortable because they interpret this to mean they are guilty of doing everything listed in the karmic descriptions, or perhaps they mistakenly believe that this is all the karma they will need to deal with in this lifetime. Some authors of numerology books have stated that we live nine lives and learn one lesson in each lifetime. I have seen nothing in literature or personal experience to support that notion.

From my study of the works of the great akashic readers such as Edgar Cayce and more recent channels, I learned that almost all suggest that we live many more than nine lives. I have many friends who are quite competent channels and intuitive consultants, and from their knowledge I conclude that there appears to be no exact rule as to how many lives we spend on Earth. It seems to be an individual matter of determination. Although there are many exceptions, the average for most mortals seems to range from 150 to 250 lives. Therefore, we may just be working on imbalance from a recent incarnation. Or we may be trying to complete a cycle where an issue has been embedded in the subconscious for many, many lifetimes and is only now coming into focus.

This information is rendered to assist your understanding, not to upset it. If you are troubled by something written herein, seek your own inner guidance for clarification. It probably stirs a strong reaction because there is truth in the description. It is very possible that some aspect may have been overlooked herein, and your own intuitive insight can add other valuable perspectives.

1 Karmic Accumulation

You are intent upon doing things your way. This can make you aggressive, at times almost militant. Your keen independence and self-reliance make it difficult for you to accept advice, and you are prone to disagree with superiors. Normally enthusiastic and impulsive, your inspiration is of short duration. When things do not work out immediately, you become discouraged and allow negativity and procrastination to undermine your efforts. Part of the reason for your short concentration span is that you have been too reliant upon others or allowed them to dominate. Now you struggle with the sustained effort necessary to accomplish your goals. Until you overcome these tendencies, you will find yourself lacking in the ability to concentrate and think logically.

You are naturally popular and will be placed in a position of notoriety, where you will exercise authority and leadership over a number of people. This could even lead you into a position of considerable prominence and give you an opportunity to make a lasting contribution to society. It is not easy for you to sit still because of your abundant energy. Once you have learned to direct this nervous dynamism constructively, there will be little to stop you from attaining success and recognition.

You can succeed in commercial enterprises if you use your originality, ingenuity and resourcefulness. However, you can also turn right around and become rash and impulsive, causing you to lose a profitable transaction or to offend someone who could be of help. Your dislike of supervision makes you seek self-employment. Business breakthroughs will come after many setbacks and at considerable expense to your vitality.

In friendship your individuality cannot be concealed. You do your own thing, and those who have similar interests stay around to enjoy your fellowship. If they have differing interests, you shrug it off and move on to new acquaintances. Once you do establish a bond, trust is vital; your word is valued and respected. You appreciate the chance to meet new people and can be socially dynamic and entertaining. You have strong convictions as to what is right and wrong, and you cannot easily be dissuaded.

In love and romance, you can be fickle. Are you constantly seeking a new mate? Once you think you have the right partner, you want to dominate the relationship. Thus, you'll probably be best off selecting a mate who is willing to go along with things and is not overly assertive. Your emotions can get away from you in love affairs, and you rush headlong into them with little thought to possible consequences. You can be intense and passionate but lose interest quickly.

In marriage you will work hard to make the partnership satisfying. Peace and harmony will not come easily, however, and you most likely will end up with an equally strong-willed spouse who is a constant challenge. You are demanding and strict as a parent but want to see your children have the best possible opportunities in life.

2 Karmic Accumulation

You are doggedly determined to resolve life conflicts and find peace and harmony. You seek to give and receive kindness and consideration, and you are willing to assist another unselfishly. At your best, you are discreet and tactful in speech. You handle situations with diplomatic aplomb. Because of your sensitivity, you respond readily to kindness and consideration from others. On the other hand, your need to help others sets you up for being used by those who rely upon your aid rather than performing their own tasks. When injured, you turn your attention to your employment and immerse yourself in work as a substitute for emotional fulfillment.

With this combination, consciousness can be split, and you may at times have trouble knowing which way to turn. Your outer personality is agreeable and willing to give and take; however, your attitudes run deep. So it takes an act of parliament to change your mind. A strain of seriousness runs through your sense of humor, often overwhelming it. You are conscious of human weakness and frailty and exhibit great sympathy. You will take the opposite side of an argument, just to keep conversation lively.

Where business is concerned, you are not one to make bold and pioneering decisions, preferring to evaluate and take a more conservative path. You are not overly ambitious for material gain; however, you do have a kind of material luck that keeps you going. If you are weighted down with responsibility and decisions, you will juggle for time and seek opinions, thus missing the boat. You prefer working with labor and personnel problems to working with the commercial aspect. Memory of dominance by others and heavy responsibilities early in your life triggers a subconscious rebellion toward heavy pressure. This makes it difficult for you to make up your mind.

You retain friendships by playing the follower rather than the leader. Your willingness to lend an ear causes friends to seek you out to discuss personal problems. There is a decided dislike of dissension, so you will go out of your way to avoid antagonizing someone. When conflicts arise, you solve them by diplomacy rather than force.

In romance and love, you are loyal. Mating games are not a sport to you! You are conservative toward love affairs, even prudish. It is easier to stick with a relationship that's going fairly well than to break up and try to establish a new union, risking hurt and rejection. You seek a strong and dependable spouse you can turn to for strength and security. You work best with a more aggressive mate who takes charge of domestic decisions. Your approach is persuasive yet tactful, maintaining peace through reasonable debate. You enjoy children but will have many quarrels and disagreements with them when they try your patience.

3 Karmic Accumulation

Deep in your heart, you want to create and bring beauty and joy into the world. Your early years will involve frustration, repression and/or inhibition of the talents you want so much to share. You have a high degree of personal magnetism that attracts artists, freethinkers, malcontents and generally creative types of people. Your moods swing quickly but seldom go up or down to extremes, and the fluctuations do not last very long. This lack of emotional control can be crucial, preventing you from sustaining a creative drive long enough to gain success and recognition. You have an extraordinary imagination and know how to dramatize events with flair; capitalize upon this by entering the field of writing to catch public attention.

You would do well in creative or artistic enterprises, but you are not cut out for the purely commercial and technological side of business. Most likely you will hold many different positions until you settle into a suitable one. Your personal affairs and moods keep your mind drifting away from the routine of your job. When this happens, you appear distant and detached from coworkers, and your supervisor is inclined to reprimand you because you are not paying attention to your responsibilities.

You are fond of company and socializing, and friendships are very central to your life. Because you are swayed and influenced so much by their opinions, you will find that destiny brings many opportunities through your acquaintances. You are flattered by and responsive to friendly overtures and respond warmly, with a refined affection for those who awaken warmth within your heart. However, when out of harmony, you can become careless and unconventional regarding your affections and personal love. There is a strong attraction to sensuality, but when boredom sets in, you may experience rapid change in lovers, with much hurt and disappointment. You are unable to give completely, and then you are surprised when your lovers terminate affection. You can be secretive and flirtatious and at the same time desire a loyal and loving mate of your dreams. Once hurt, you can pass through a phase of total disinterest in sexual needs, preferring to express your drive in hobbies or work.

You would be most comfortable with a patient, comprehending mate who is willing to boost a dubious self-image. You are prone to feel that everyone recognizes your flaws while overlooking the many commendable strengths and talents you possess. A happy marriage will be long in coming, but once found, it gives you the chance to be a colorful and inspirational spouse and parent.

4 Karmic Accumulation

You are a fixed, determined and hard-working individual. Life allows you very little time to enjoy the luxuries of fun and amusement. Without some restraints, you can become a workaholic, which could be detrimental to your health. Your childhood was likely burdened with some form of heavy work that caused you to feel resentful. You have respect for authority and would like to be an authority figure yourself. You deal with emotions similar to how you deal with life. When challenged, you may react with stubbornness, anger and seething resentment. You like to be one of the crowd and are very much aware of people's motives. When you experience or witness injustice, you can become moody and develop a deep, simmering dislike, maybe even hatred. Because you think you have everything working well, you do not handle opposition well. You can become outraged and indignant because you do not feel that anyone has the right to change the precision machine you operate.

Although you are inclined to be somewhat obstinate, you are fundamentally practical, organized and particularly good at maintaining the daily routine of a business or office. The subconscious tendency is for you to become restless and try to change the routine to suit yourself; however, you have learned to discipline yourself and work for the good of the organization. Because of your loyalty to the organization, you may be called upon to take a supervisory role, which you can handle well. Your preference is to be left in a job where you know the routine and do not have to deal with greater responsibilities and the personal problems of the employees. A tendency toward moderation and conservatism runs deep in your consciousness, and you may almost reach the top of your field, although you lack the intense, self-sustained drive necessary to reach the top of the competitive totem pole.

In love, romance and marriage, you are loyal and intense. You are faithful to your partner as a rule. When your work is not going well and your mate is not supportive or encouraging, you are vulnerable to the charms of another admirer who is willing to build up your pride and sense of worth. Once attached, you are a potent and conscientious partner. You take pride in home, family and possessions, and you work hard to be a good provider.

5 Karmic Accumulation

You are extremely active and independent in mind and body. You do not like to stick with anything for very long and jump quickly to new projects so you are often involved in two or more things at once. You will probably make many trips and have many strange experiences before your life is complete. In fact, you often go out of your way to seek thrills and dangerous stunts. There is a need to use discretion where stimulants are concerned (smoking, drugs, alcohol) because your body could suffer considerably and because the likelihood of being heavily involved in overindulgence is extremely high. You are caught in excruciating dilemmas between desire and a fear of sexual and sensual habits. This uncertainty will attract numerous opportunities for you to learn to control and master these fears and cravings. You act on impulse at the moment and react childishly to any kind of restraint upon your free-flowing nature in action or thinking. You may react with a temper that is of short duration and is gone as quickly as it appears.

Your career and business endeavors are likely to be multiple and varied because of your restless nature and lack of regard for monotonous routine. Sales and positions with variety and action are your forte. Your curiosity and inventive potential could produce a new product or method of merchandising. You prefer not to work hard for a living and would like to make easy money.

This indicates an individual who will be popular and lively in society. You are not prone to develop many deep friendships, preferring to stay on the move in order to meet someone new. Personal magnetism works favorably in your friendships, but your emotions can create sorrow.

In love and romance, you have a kind of carefree spirit others find appealing. You are a natural at flirtation and prefer not to be tied down. You live each moment fully with a devil-may-care attitude about tomorrow and enjoy the sport and intrigue of new love affairs. Unfortunately, you confuse sexual and emotional needs. You are aware of your sexual charm and do not hesitate to use it. Your emotional variability can reveal a hardness that can create unpleasant surprises for your lovers. You are not likely to enjoy the restraint of marriage. Even though you envision yourself as a model of loyalty and devotion, you may very well be flirting at the office or next door. You prefer a mate who gives you a great deal of room and freedom, but most likely you will choose one who would prefer it if you were a homebody.

6 Karmic Accumulation

You are concerned with ways to make life easier for the human race, which can put you into a position where you can be used. You are apt to deceive yourself into thinking you have done much, especially if the missing numbers are 2 and 4. However, overall you are effective in roles of service and support. At times the altruism of your motive is dubious and you overplay the role of helpmate, trying hard to express your concern, particularly if 1 and 5 are the missing numbers. Your charitable nature and concern for others often cause you to overlook the needs of those closest to you, and you may even overlook your own misfortunes because of your absorption in other people's needs.

This generosity in your blood excludes as a livelihood highly competitive business and commercial enterprises that would require you to make hard-nosed, impersonal business decisions. There may also be little aggressiveness toward acquisition of power or wealth. If involved in business, you are able to accomplish transactions without stepping on toes or hurting feelings. This enables you to make close friends among associates.

Friendships are compulsory to your well-being, and you are blessed with a few very endearing friends for most of your life. You adopt many of your opinions from those close to you, and you feel their joys and misfortunes. It is true that you have been imposed upon too often, but this should not leave you distrustful toward everyone. At times you have been known to push another's goodwill a little bit too far yourself.

Tenderness and concerned understanding permeate your attitude toward love and romance. You prefer one emotionally rewarding relationship to passing affairs. This emotional need can be your source of aggravation when your partner falls short of the same sincerity. You long for a happy marriage and will work hard to make a go of it. There is a strong attachment to the home, and even though you may travel, you look forward to returning to domestic surroundings. You work well with a spouse who is willing to take charge of domestic decisions, and you probably have opinions on home management yourself. Loyalty is uppermost, and you are loyal to the union even after your mate has lost interest. You would rather stay in a poor marriage than go through the legal/emotional hassle of getting out of it. There may be anxiety and difficulty with children and subconscious blocks preventing a complete bond of trust. Part of your discomfort may stem from your childhood, where emotional confusion arose from detached or unsympathetic treatment from one or both parents.

7 Karmic Accumulation

There is a deep philosophical and secretive aura surrounding you that piques the curiosity and interest of people you meet. You pursue new studies with intensity and leave very few stones unturned in your search for the essence of a matter. You are quite set in your judgments and opinions, so anyone wishing to change your mind had better beware. Your wry wit and pointed sarcasm are appreciated by some people and feared by others. Your outer appearance of intellectual prowess hides a turbulent emotional sea whose tides you fear may be so extreme that you keep them behind a mental dam.

The 7 karmic accumulation number is a very intuitive indicator, and in your periods of introspection, you will learn to trust the message from within. Your analytical mind explores every angle of behavior and prepares a logical course for each event. However, when emotions become involved, all of your logical preparation falls apart and you act impishly on impulse.

Your business drive is fettered by a fundamentally religious and philosophical nature. It is difficult for you to worship Mammon, and the value system of economics is alien to your inner being. If you do enter business, your analytical ability and suspicious nature allow you to make cautious, if not dramatic, decisions that may get you close to the top of the ladder because of consistency. You would enjoy any kind of investigative research or analytical employment.

This is not the most compatible indicator for friendships. People find you somewhat haughty and intellectually aloof, which can make it difficult to be close to your feelings. Once a friendship is established, you are intensely loyal, and many turn to you for insight from your reserve of wisdom and mundane comprehension. You are threatened by the fact that others may learn about your emotional insecurity; therefore, you put up a mental defense. Once they have accepted you, you allow deep feelings of loyalty and concern to be expressed. So the benefit is ultimately both yours and theirs.

In love and romance, you need a mate you can intellectually respect. Mental rapport is important for inspiring excitement in the rest of your system. You are possessive and fervent once attached. It might be best to choose a lighthearted mate to offset your seriousness, but if your spouse does not reach certain intellectual standards, you can become disinterested. You may, in fact, have more of an intellectual companionship than a strong emotional and physical relationship. You enjoy the debate of minds and thrive on verbal entanglements. This karmic accumulation number may leave you a little uncomfortable with children, their noises and problems, especially if it is the numbers 2 and 5 that are missing.

8 Karmic Accumulation

You are constantly seeking ways to bolster your ego and image. An aspect of pride makes you believe you deserve to be in a position of authority; however, at the same time, you are unwilling to put forth the effort that makes you worthy of the rank. At negative extremes, you can become ruthless, to the point of inflicting pain upon others. You put on an air of bravado and confidence that masks a very deep-rooted fear that you may not, in fact, be able to handle the situation. There is an enormous drive for success, and most likely you will end up with a significant position and sizable earnings, unless greed enters your heart. You become uneasy and dissatisfied readily with the way things are progressing and then doubt the abilities or motives of those with whom you are associated. This indicator suggests one who is constantly on the move, teaching business or engaging in charitable or civic affairs. The early years of your life presented numerous adversities and impediments, forming a subconscious attitude of defiant belief that you can meet any challenge.

Most of the previous statements apply to your business as well as general life attitudes. You have difficulty with bosses and managers and need much leeway to make decisions. You will not be in the lower echelon for long, no matter what kind of organization you have chosen. You have a knack for contributing ideas for better technical production and more effective utilization of personnel, and you exercise sound judgment in the expenditure and investment of money. Unfortunately, your personal financial decisions may not be as fruitful.

You play a convincing charade about friendships, acting as if you can take 'em or leave 'em, especially if it is the 3 and the 5 that are missing.

Underneath this act, you want to be liked by all, and secretly you need acceptance from others to have peace of mind. Because of your need to have supportive friendships, you develop loyalty and will offer helpful advice about any impersonal topics. When friends get too close to your emotional framework, you become uneasy and temperamental. A strong competitive drive makes it difficult for you to accept friends and social acquaintances for what they are instead of for what they have.

Oddly enough, this business-like attitude also permeates your romantic life. Your detached emotional nature generates a sort of indifferent attitude. You would do best with a strong-willed mate who is ambitious but able to give you constant boosting. If your goals are too similar, competition rather than compatibility will no doubt prevail. When support is not given or the marriage falters, you easily justify outside love affairs or indulgent habits.

9 Karmic Accumulation

This is a most challenging indicator, because you must learn to recognize and let go of restraining insecurities, possessive attitudes and relationships that are no longer moving in a direction compatible with your evolution. There is a deep yearning for emotional contentment, especially with 6 and 3 missing. However, emotional fears are lodged deep within the subconscious, and it will take some traumatic encounters with life circumstances to bring them to surface awareness. You seek a comfortable home and stable marriage (especially with the 6-and-3 combination), yet something inside does not let you become personally attached to either of these. You are besieged by feelings of loneliness and isolation even when among others, especially when 7 and 2 are missing. Your idealism does not always have the impact you would like it to have upon the mass consciousness.

This is not the most aggressive indicator for business. You prefer to let others handle the responsibility and leadership while you provide the inspiration and support. You would be good in fields of motivation, public relations or personnel work rather than on the competitive battlefield. No matter what your business, the work you enjoy most will have to do with some aspect of religion, consciousness development, advanced science, metaphysics, social reform or related fields.

You are capable of establishing friendships with people who have interests that are totally paradoxical to yours. You hope to maintain closer relationships with all your friends, but life brings you new friends rapidly, and even they will move on to new things. You are apt to be emotionally affected by negativity from other people. In fact, your generosity and desire to help often attract people who trample over your feelings, treating you with indifference or even maliciousness (especially if it is the 1 and the 8 that are missing). You are almost always in disagreement with people who live by conventional social norms, so you spend much time speculating about more modern or even futuristic forms of government and society. Universal causes and thinking are important to you. You will fit well into an impersonal role, working to bring about global expansion in human consciousness.

You are highly idealistic and sentimental about romance. You will probably experience occasional spiritual and platonic love affairs. You work best with a mate who is tolerant of your unconventional ideas and shares a general concern for the world and humanity. You seek an ideal union and impose almost impossible expectations upon your loved one. This is not a favorable influence for marriage; perhaps you will experience more than one before finding the right mate.

10 Karmic Accumulation

You almost inevitably succeed, but that doesn't prevent you from having a horrible fear of disaster every time a new project looms near. Indication of significant failure in a previous lifetime makes you hesitate to initiate new endeavors or unwilling to sustain the confidence and effort needed for success. (I recently worked with one chart with 4, 7, 8 and 9 all missing, which adds up to 28, and 2 + 8 equals 10. The above description for this combination could hardly seem more appropriate.)

You have great ideas and initial enthusiasm; however, subconscious fears can prevent you from completing many of your schemes. There is a curious fluctuation in your temperament, ranging from excessive confidence to overwhelming insecurity about your abilities. One moment you are inspired about great projects to help humankind, and the next you are completely self-centered. You can become easily convinced that your opinions just happen to be exactly correct, which then makes it difficult for you to alter a course of action, be it for better or worse. You will encounter intense resistance when attempting to push your opinions forcibly upon those around you (especially when 2 and 8 are missing).

Your cycles in business also fluctuate from near success to the brink of failure until you learn to resolve the underlying fear of failure. Your enormous talents can go to waste because you lack the confidence to develop them thoroughly. You are best working cooperatively with others and are often indecisive and discouraged. Once you have been told how to do a job, you are capable of much achievement if left alone to work independently. Even though you desire a role of leadership, it does not come easily. You are excellent in work that inspires others. However, once things are under way, you prefer to move on to new territory.

You need many supportive friends around you and attract individuals who also have considerable unexpressed abilities. Your choice of friends is very important, because some could easily prey upon your weakness and self-doubt. You would benefit from being around people who use metaphysical, self-help and growth techniques with maturity and wisdom.

Your behavior in love and romance is changeable and insecure. You seek a partner who recognizes your needs and gives you the confidence to push a little harder. You may seek love affairs to bolster a sagging self-image. You work best in marriage with a mate who is flexible and supportive. You are not particularly domestic and prefer not to be tied down to all the demands of family life. You have an abundant vitality and recover easily from illness. (See also the 1 karmic accumulation number.)

11 Karmic Accumulation

This indicator suggests someone who is highly idealistic and intuitive. You possess a comprehensive awareness of the needs in society and therefore work to cultivate a favorable public image. Your destiny will probably at one time put you before many people. There is a natural inclination toward religion, the occult or metaphysical studies—will you follow it? The suggestion is that in an earlier lifetime, you may have misused psychic or intuitive abilities: if 3 and 8 are missing, for political expediency or manipulation of others; if 2 and 9 are missing, because of misplaced idealism. If 4 and 7 are missing, you may have let intellect dominate over intuitive development; if 5 and 6 are missing, you may have unwittingly misled others because of your own opinions and hang-ups. You enjoy inspirational and advanced thinking but at the same time cling to old and tried ways. Once you have taken a stand on an issue, you will go to an unprecedented sacrifice to defend it. Once you have established the law, you expect everyone to fall in line and abide by it; you fail to see that they may not share either your opinions or your zeal.

Business success and attainment can come to you if you use patience and tact rather than force. Generally, this combination is not conducive to business pursuits. You are better advised to seek a career in religion, social reform, education, government or consciousness instruction. Your heightened powers encourage leadership. There is a natural inclination toward awakened, modern thinking and farsighted ideas, but you can doggedly persist in defending some cherished personal belief. It is not easy for you to admit mistakes. Just do it, and be free to move on in truth and confidence.

When this indicator appears, the individual will attract friends from diverse and seemingly incongruous backgrounds. Your intensity and magnetism will draw or repel new associates with equal strength. You innately want to reveal the glory of higher wisdom and universal truths, but you must guard carefully against twisting and coloring truth to support your personal rendition. You may unwittingly attract eccentric personalities and consciousness leaders of dubious motive who could be sources of considerable trouble.

Unchecked, the vibrations of this combination can breed excessive eccentricity and unstable proclivities.

A similar idealism influences your attitudes in love, romance and marriage. You expect your level of awareness to be returned immediately. You seek an ideal union and see yourself as nearly perfect. In fact, you can become quite an undesirable partner because of moodiness, lack of patience, emotional volatility and the constant push to have your mate live by your standards. You are constantly dreaming about the perfect soul mate. (See also the 2 karmic accumulation.)

12 Karmic Accumulation

Life will bring you numerous occasions that will require you to make a sacrifice. These occasions must be consciously recognized and dealt with accordingly, or they can become a subconscious pattern. The latter might not be as easily understood because of its deeper content. You live in a kind of constant anticipation that the things near you may be gone tomorrow. This constant emotional anguish creates suffering, real or imagined, and the discontent leads you to sources of self-discovery or emotional outlets. You possess a natural flair for drama and are like an actor or actress on the stage bemoaning his or her torments, especially if it is the 3 and the 9 that are missing.

You may have to take care of an invalid relative, go into military service or take over for a coworker right at a moment in life when you most desire free time to further a personal ambition. Who knows why you are constantly being called upon to take care of someone else's needs! Just remember: As you sow, so shall you reap. Your natural, creative and artistic inclinations may at some time be utilized as a means of conveying to others what you have learned. You could very well end up writing or lecturing about the lessons you have learned from your struggle with life.

In business and employment, you are placed in positions where you do a great deal of extra work, often behind the scenes, while someone else gets the applause and promotion. You have difficulty staying in one career because of your restless and creative nature. Success and professional recognition will most likely come later in life and after considerable struggle and sacrifice. You seek friendships and enjoy social events and being popular. You tend to dramatize your experiences and respond impulsively to the excitement of the moment. Friends enjoy your spontaneity and flexibility. Your desire to please places you in positions where you are unable to say no. Then you readily discover that you have become somewhat of a sacrificial martyr, spending much time taking care of others' lives.

Working out the knots in love, marriage and romance will be constantly trying. Your lovers, spouse and children will require an inordinate amount of attention. You sometimes wonder if you will ever get away from the demands of kids, activities, illnesses, wives' club activities, husband's job demands and in-laws' interference. You can easily feel discouraged and unappreciated—with good reason.

13 Karmic Accumulation

Probably no other combination directs as much attention to the work ethic as this vibration. During other lifetimes, you have not worked to your best ability, or you may have worked just toward your own selfish ends, especially with 5 and 8 missing. This indicator suggests a time to consider others and to enter work with others in mind.

You must learn to complete the work you have come to do. You have the capability but often give up or avoid the responsibility of the job at hand. This is an indicator of learning to enjoy work for the sake of work and nurturing healthy respect for discipline and accomplishment. Your role may not seem of significance to society, but you are now learning to serve as one becoming attuned to the divine plan for Earth. There is a tendency to hold yourself back. It is as if you possess a lack of ambition, a kind of humility that prevents you from attaining the limelight. It is not that you lack capability or opportunity, but just that you seek to do your job well and may lack glamour or imagination in the process.

In commercial and business endeavors, you may find it emotionally hard just working to make a living. You may face several setbacks, even failure, before finding the meaning of work and a truly meaningful job. You push yourself harder and longer than your coworkers. When serving in a supervisory position, you expect the same from your subordinates.

Much sadness and unexpected disappointment through friendships are likely. Most friendships that develop will be intense and loyal; however, they will be relatively short in duration. They do not end with animosity or hard feelings, but destiny simply spins a different web of fate. You leave saddened, pondering the circumstances that separated your mutuality. You are considered stubborn; oftentimes misunderstandings occur because of your set code of conduct. Despite a fixed attitude, friends can count upon you and respect you for solidity.

The romantic and marital details of your life bring periodic cycles of frustration. You are loyal and ardent in love but may experience an unfortunate love affair while seeking attention after reversals in your career. You suffer a great deal through your love life because of an innate discipline of emotions, preventing you from giving and accepting love fully. There may be weird estrangements from spouse or family resulting from incompatibility, even though there is still love.

14 Karmic Accumulation

This combination brings a major turning point in consciousness. It is one of regeneration and growth through much tribulation and rearrangement of character. You have resisted learning from past-life experiences and have a difficult time growing out of the illusion and enticement of the senses. You are ambitious but clever about the political approach you use to gain prominence. Your subconscious karmic pattern is to seek freedom, intrigue and personal kicks. Your present desire is to fit into social conventions and expectations. This leaves you with a very formal but outgoing manner that constantly has to monitor the surging quest for freedom and indulgence.

You must learn to accept past mistakes and move on to new experiences. No amount of mental or emotional reexamination can alter the past; however, you need to review it long enough to discover and eliminate the underlying cause for self-inflicted errors. You seem to constantly fluctuate between the desire for complete freedom and the need for security. This constant strain can disrupt your health if you are not careful. You are curious about life and hate to miss any experience.

The possibility of success in career and business is quite high. You would do best to work with people because of your extensive interests and adaptability. You are ambitious; however, there is likelihood that you will change goals just before you reach success. If things get out of hand, your aspirations may cause you to become involved in underhanded or dubious circumstances. This combination indicates the probability that you may earn a great deal of money. It could just as easily be lost, unless you purposely concentrate on financial planning.

Your exuberance and vitality make you a popular and sought-after friend and social acquaintance. You do not like to be tied down and move confidently among people from diverse backgrounds and social standing. Your peppy style brings cheer to others. On the other hand, you can be inconsiderate and hurt others, unknowingly perhaps, by your actions and impulsive statements. You are not so much malicious; you're just insensitive to undercurrents and must guard your tongue to prevent tactless and revealing slips of speech.

You constantly search for the essence of love. This keeps you flitting from one romance to another, seeking that nebulous happiness. You can confuse sex and love and get yourself into ambiguous situations regarding your affections, loving more than one person at a time—one near and one alluringly distant. You disdain the thought of public attention being given to your personal love affairs. Happiness in love and marriage will be elusive, so you do well playing the field. Keep it that way until you are certain a partner is totally right for you. Only time brings proof.

15 Karmic Accumulation

An aura of ignominious humility looms around you and you work to appease a subconscious guilt associated with past-life mistakes. An unfettered ego and insolent treatment of those disagreeing with your ambitions are to blame. Your public manner suggests consideration and sympathy, and you work hard to truly cultivate these qualities. Your emotions are greatly unsettled, and you become overly upset and embarrassed about the most inconsequential incidents. You will encounter people with powerful egos on many occasions; from these experiences, you will learn much about people's problems and need for identity.

Of course, in most cases you are witnessing the type of attitude you have held in a previous life or lives; now you are acquiring firsthand insight as to the negative impact it can have upon others, especially if it is the 2, 5 and 8 that are missing. When you let pride or ambition get out of hand, something or someone will come along to put you right back in your place in a hurry. This can include being fired from a job or perhaps coming down with an illness. Then you will have time to reflect and recognize unbecoming ego needs within your character.

You work hard to establish stability, consideration for others and a down-to-earth attitude about life and people. You dislike the disruptive nature of disagreements and work quickly but patiently to dissolve hostility. There is a need to help others, but you have a meddlesome practice of trying too hard. Stay out of the way unless asked to help.

Your preference in business or career is not in the more competitive sectors. You are at your best when working with people in a manner that enables them to accommodate life more easily. You work long hours with unmatched diligence and are willing to take on responsibilities—even if they aren't yours—with patience, diplomacy and the desire to serve. Again, beware of overdoing it.

You enjoy making new friends and are often called upon to counsel and cheer others. Your considerate attitude and desire to get things together in your life are appealing factors. Sometimes you become blind to the way others manipulate your trusting nature. You are learning to be a good friend— but to be a good friend, you should not have to try so hard.

In love, romance and marriage, you seek a happy and harmonious relationship but are likely to attract a jealous, possessive and domineering mate. You are strongly attracted to your mate and the thought of domestic harmony. Many obstacles may delay your harmonious relationship: parental disapproval, insufficient funds or interference from a job. There could be more than one marriage. You must learn not to nurture grudges but seek to overcome the strain of disagreements.

16 Karmic Accumulation

You are constantly looking over your shoulder, expecting a catastrophe or unexpected disruption in your marriage, work or personal life. There is a need to build a stronger faith through deeper investigation of universal laws. You think often about emotional matters but are prone to making hasty and erratic decisions where emotions are concerned. A predominantly intellectual attitude motivates your impulsiveness more than physical restlessness does. You will learn to deal with your emotions after unexpected and sudden mishaps in life.

You enjoy intellectual debates and derive great satisfaction from coming up with some point or fact with an unexpected thrust. You benefit from learning to concentrate your interests on one thing at a time. You can make impulsive decisions that surprise even yourself and, once made, you may stick by them even though you suspect the results will be disastrous. You will very likely encounter complications in obtaining a higher education. At some point in life, you will experience disappointment because you have not completed the proper degrees or scored well on some standardized test. Even though you may not have obtained a complete formal education, you must trust the wisdom within yourself.

You are conscientious and hard working in business and career. You desire recognition more than money, yet you possess reluctance toward aggressiveness and have some timidity in accepting your worth. You can, therefore, fail to reach full job potential. This fear can stem from a past-life pattern of overdoing your role and falling into disgrace of some kind. Once overcome, you may very well attract public recognition and success—deservedly.

An intellectual detachment characterizes your friendships. You enjoy people around you who are also deep thinkers and/or constantly searching for further understanding of their psychological and spiritual nature. You enjoy close friends but would rather be alone than with a noisy group. You aren't much of a conversationalist because your mind is made up on most matters. You are generally a considerate friend, often witty, sometimes sharp tongued and usually stimulating.

In love and romance, you first seek an intellectual rapport; on other levels, you can be somewhat impersonal. Your constant search for the perfect combination may lead to a variety of love affairs before settling down. You are idealistic about love and explore different ideas about sex and love relationships; this can complicate the personal experience with your mate. Your desires for a perfect union can put unrealistic demands upon your spouse that can hardly be fulfilled. Once you have overcome the emotional complications and learn to unite head with heart, there is a chance for harmony and security in love.

17 Karmic Accumulation

It may take you some time in life to replace an innate sense of pessimism and despair with an awakened sense of optimism and faith in your future and the world condition. You have the drive and energy upon which to build your confidence and inner strength. If your plans and actions are not built on an honest and legitimate foundation, you could tumble from a position of great authority. This is a plateau of learning where power should be used constructively.

There will be disagreement with people in positions of authority who misuse their power or who fear to alter the prescribed ways to progress. Interestingly enough, you are subject to the same resistance within. You do not like to be told what to do by another and have difficulty working comfortably as a subordinate. Your ambition is powerful, and you will persist with hard work, sometimes beyond endurance of the physical body, to achieve your goals. Part of your drive for attainment is compensation for subconscious fear of losing your identity— by getting lost in the crowd, by becoming another automaton in our technological society or by failing to leave your mark in the world.

Your career and commercial talents are marked. You have a capable mentality and a good sense of organization. You have the foresight to visualize a project and then anticipate the needs and outcome of the directive you have set in motion. You are persistent and can be tactful enough to obtain the cooperation necessary to complete the requirements of the job. Be careful that impulsiveness and pettiness of ego do not interfere with your work.

This is a curious combination for friendship. You want friends, but you want them on your terms. You alternate between a come-on and a put-off. Your blend of outward optimism and latent pessimism affects the way you deal with friends. You like friends but do not go after them; rather, they seem to find you. You work hard to make things work and just as quickly become indifferent, expecting things to fall apart. One moment you may demand too much; the next you may turn around and avoid any feedback, making friends feel unneeded. Those who persevere find you a loyal friend and enjoy your buoyant, boisterous and practical side.

Your lively nature is unsettled and fickle, and you seek love affairs as an outlet when the breaks do not go your way and you are down on life. You could very well marry for social or political reasons rather than follow your heart, creating a cold or unfulfilling union. You are likely to marry more than once or engage in an attachment to someone below your social or intellectual level. When the finer emotions rule and you find a strong, independent mate, you are a loyal and dynamic partner.

18 Karmic Accumulation

You are hard pressed distinguishing between practical idealism and naive gullibility and deception. You see life through rose-colored glasses, which causes you to overlook gross flaws in yourself and others. An innate generosity can put you into a position where you give too much of yourself, which is not always to your best advantage. Watch out that this generosity does not become obsessive, causing you to blame yourself for everything that goes wrong. The suggestion is that you have deceived others in a past-life pattern and now must conquer deception and deceit in self and by others. This will be difficult because you easily become confused when strong empathetic emotions are aroused. Turmoil within keeps the body tense and emotions on a raw edge. You will benefit from a system of multiple-consciousness discipline applied every day. Your intellect is expansive and very logical; however, at times you show complete disregard for convention, becoming argumentative and negatively eccentric.

As you may suspect by now, this is something less than a stellar indicator for business. You can handle routine and technical work, but emotional inadequacies and insecurities may prevent your intellectual concepts from clearly reaching the heart of those you wish to enlighten. You would derive a much broader satisfaction from providing humanitarianism, creativity and assistance for those in need. You may possibly one day work with an organization that is involved in psychic, occult or metaphysical teaching and investigation. It may take some time to start this association, because you may be afraid to join a meaningful organization for fear of some unknown hindrance to your growth. This makes you feel guilty about failing to learn a subject that can be helpful in preparing you to do beneficial work. Be rid of the guilt and get on with it!

Your attitude toward friendship is precariously balanced between an ambivalent need for friends and outward reserve. You often associate with eccentric and individualistic friends and often fail to recognize glaring flaws. You can appear very distant, which does not make it easy to become your friend. Your feelings run deep, but you are afraid to let them show. Excessive control over your feelings causes misunderstandings.

Your romantic needs and sensual desires are all related to your sexual enjoyment. Your ability to respond sexually is linked blatantly to emotions that have both positive and negative influence. You depend a great deal on others for contentment and may suffer when they fail to live up to your trust and expectations. There is a likelihood of considerable melodrama and hidden intrigue in your love life. Marriage relations will have hidden circumstances that need to be resolved for mutual harmony. Desired harmony will not come easily; there is a strong likelihood of more than one marriage.

19 Karmic Accumulation

This indicator suggests the misapplication of will in a previous life pattern—the will was directed in a forceful and domineering manner to control others. Consequently, when this number occurs, you can expect to meet many willful people in home and work who constantly challenge, doubt or defy you. One or both parents will be domineering or authoritative to an almost unbearable degree. Your behavior can fluctuate from acquiescence to brash aggressiveness. Life should teach you to respect individual will and to work cooperatively with the will in others. You are driven by a desire for complete freedom on the one hand and security through another person on the other.

You sometimes feel you know it all and become very impatient with the dull or unexciting beliefs of others. When you turn to others for advice, things usually do not work out. Little by little, you have learned to make up your own mind and follow your own decisions. You will have the opportunity to overcome selfish concerns and underlying eccentricity through a refinement of emotions and a more magnanimous attitude toward humankind. When it appears, grab it and hang on.

Your capable and forceful nature is quite suited for the demands of business and a challenging career. You will be best in work with diversity and much activity. You are more likely to be an employer than an employee. You have developed a genuine concern for those working for or with you and will work to advance them once you have overcome ego threats in self. You can climb to the highest peaks but may collapse to the depths when ambition or pride thwarts your personality. You will constantly run up against conservative business supervisors or associates who are stuck on the treadmill of tradition and do not have your imagination.

The hasty vibration of this number makes you one who changes friends often and moves on before establishing much depth. There is little art or style of accommodating new acquaintances, and your caution makes it hard for others to move toward you. You easily use friends to further your own goals and get along best with those who make the least demands upon you as a friend.

Your love life may be just as changeable as other friendships. You are direct in relationships and are not prone to much preparation for lovemaking. You can give of yourself in the mood of the moment but lack patience to maintain long-term relationships. Learn that it is more difficult to give love than to receive it. As a marriage partner, you can be difficult to understand because of rapid changes in moods, ideas and beliefs. You may become excited about something one day and forget about it the next. You will likely attract a strong-willed and contradictory mate.

20 Karmic Accumulation

You are at a point of developing a greater social awareness and consciousness. Sensitivity within self needs to become directed to an awareness of the needs in society or community. The suggestion is that you have experienced public embarrassment in a previous life because of personal mistakes or overdone ambition that created injustice for others; this is especially so if it is the 3, 8 and 9 that are missing. Another karmic pattern suggested here is that of a person who held a position of prominence and used it to attack and chastise opponents. Somewhere along the way you misused authority.

With this indicator, there are subconscious proclivities to lose consideration and patience toward others. You must guard against a careless tongue and root out your judgmental criticism of differing lifestyles and beliefs. Your personal and moral convictions are well defined, but you sometimes twist your opinions to justify questionable actions. The hypersensitivity and nervousness of your temperament can be unhealthy if care is not exercised.

Your business nature is not as much aggressive as it is persuasive; your actions are political rather than directly forceful. This indicator suggests serving in a public role at some time in your career. The fields of philanthropic or social reform ministry, government or large corporate operations are most appropriate venues. You work at being humble and can be self-effacing. You are cautious and discreet with an almost morbid fear of being caught off guard by the public. Loosen up—this is a tension you don't need.

Your manner of expression with friends is warm, direct and can become demanding when ego gets in the way. You enjoy hobnobbing with a variety of personages and have a fondness for people in general. Beware of becoming so involved with yourself in conversation that others are merely a source of feedback to your personal opinions. You can be stimulating and witty in relaxed moments, but when you try to come off as clever and witty, the results may appear contrived.

You are less aggressive and more romantic in matters of love than many. You prefer an established emotional background as part of the prelude to interplay. You enjoy the romantic, elegant and sentimental trappings of love. In fact, these are essential in stimulating your continued interest in a partner. You seek refinement in your mate, and social standing can be a factor in your choice of spouse. You are repulsed by crude or routine attitudes toward the relationship. At best you are a concerned, sympathetic and tender lover and partner.

21 Karmic Accumulation

Despite the many tribulations that befall you, there is a recurring awareness within that you are approaching the end of long study in the classroom of life. There is at the same time an urgency to complete tasks and some indifference about where to go. This is a number of synthesis of body, mind and soul. You are approaching a turning point in evolution but have some major hurdles to overcome. Life will call upon you to share and describe your wisdom, but it will not be easy to convey the ideas or words you want so deeply to share. Your ability to evaluate life from so many levels and perspectives causes you to change your mind often about the same subject.

A kind of vague guilt complex haunts your life. Do you have a feeling that you should be accomplishing more inner growth and development? At the same time, life will put demands upon you that seemingly make it impossible to pursue those goals. You often overlook the fact that the most important growth comes in the situation at hand when you learn to apply esoteric law to apparently mundane tribulations. You are extremely impressionable about your environment, and you are psychic and mystical in your attitude toward life.

Business interests will be varied, and you are likely to make many changes in your career direction. You tend to prefer work of a humanitarian nature. You will likely encounter hidden resistance and secret antagonists in the pursuit of career goals and ambitions. You are at best working in areas that deal with ideas rather than physical effort.

Friendship brings mixed experiences. You enjoy the merriment and good times of friendship because of your gregarious nature. On the other hand, friendship will likely bring many behind-the-scenes upsets. It is not easy for you to establish really deep friendships, and you hold back part of yourself while professing to pour out your heart. You struggle to balance your extroverted needs with the worries, disagreements and emotional upsets that are attracted to you. In particular, you enjoy people from fields or professions such as the arts, communications, writing, theater and education.

In love and romance, your moods fluctuate considerably; however, emotional equanimity is important to romantic interests. Without it, your sexual and emotional cycles alternate between intense activity and disinterest. You prefer a mate whose refinement of feelings enables the tender and delicate facets of love to emerge. In truth, your inner being craves the spiritual union of the male and female aspects of your being into the full realization and marriage of cosmic consciousness.

22 Karmic Accumulation

You are entering a cycle of self-mastery and expansion of soul. When this number results from the total missing numbers in the name, it is time to get your life in shape; be careful not to fall into a pattern of growth slippage. The indication is that you have a very important role of mastery (through application of higher law) in this lifetime. In earlier years, you were troubled, because public recognition for your work did not seem to be of the same magnitude as your opinion of yourself. A kind of overinflated outer confidence hides a subconscious feeling of inferiority and lack of recognition. Once the soul consciousness is more fully awakened, you will begin to more fully understand your inner work and dissolve this covert insecurity. This is especially true for those who also have a 22 soul number, a 22 personality number or a 22 life number.

You possess a natural ability to meet obstacles head-on and deal with problems before they grow to insurmountable proportion. Your fixed determination to achieve a goal makes you alternately open and accessible, then rigid and unbending in your reaction to opposition.

The aspect is high for career. Your persistence and tenacity make you a valuable asset to an organization. You are flexible enough to recognize new procedures or products that improve business. Your integrity and balanced sense of individuality, perseverance and organizational skills enable you to be effective in virtually any commercial endeavor. You will be most satisfied once you are performing the inner work that your soul has come to fulfill. Expect difficulty in learning the spiritual laws of prosperity and use of money.

Your interaction with friends is rather clouded while subconscious motives mix with your conscious desires to create somewhat ambivalent associations. Although you enjoy and desire friends, oftentimes the obligation to them prevents you from accomplishing what seem to be more important interests. Your greatest happiness comes once you have begun to attain soul awareness. Can your friends share this aspiration of spiritual expansion and growth? You are highly judgmental; once this is controlled and directed in a tactful and considerate manner, you can effectively show your friends deep insights about themselves.

Your attitude in love and romance might be called "enlightened detachment." Your spiritual drive causes you to be less romantic and rather distant in the day-to-day expression of affection. You seek a mate who balances with you on the emotional, mental and soul level. However, your tendency to impose certain spiritual expectations upon the loved one may prevent your partner from progressing into his/her own desired pattern. At your best, you are a patient soul capable of giving deep love to your mate.

33 Karmic Accumulation

Emotionally you are very sensitive to the injustice and suffering you see in the world. It is like a burden around your neck, and you want to solve every problem and help every person. This is sometimes your biggest problem; because of this intensity, you overdo, and in some ways, it blocks your effectiveness. Can you recall a specific instance of this situation? You may waste time and effort persuading people that they need your help. Let the natural capacity to heal be summoned spontaneously.

Your subconscious feelings of guilt and emotional turmoil surface and occupy a tremendous amount of your conscious time. It will take equal time and turmoil to bring these hang-ups into harmony. These conflicts have a similarly distressing impact upon your business attitudes, friendships and family life. You are a very emotional being with highly fluctuating moods. This makes you difficult to be with; one cannot be sure when your ups and downs will occur. Once your life becomes centered, you will be effective in work with organizations of healing and service.

0 (Zero) Karmic Accumulation

What does it mean when no numbers are missing in the name at birth? Is there no karma at all? This question frequently arises. The answer is yes, there can still be karma. None of us would likely have chosen to incarnate presently if there was not some karmic imbalance in our evolution. As a general rule, a name with no missing numbers suggests a dharmic lifetime rather than one that is heavily karmic.

What is a dharmic lifetime? It means, roughly, that rather than having to spend so much time straightening out past imbalance, the individual will be able to concentrate more upon the furtherance of evolution and soul growth by opening new avenues of unfoldment and work.

This is a plateau period of one's evolution. You have to make a choice as to how you wish to progress in consciousness. This is not as easy as it appears, because there is little push from within and there are fewer specific needs to fulfill. You do not have the missing numbers to provide a focus or impetus for specific action. Unknowingly you could begin to drift and lose control of destiny. If no effect is directed purposefully to your growth, then, in subsequent lifetimes, new missing numbers could occur and your wheel of karma would spin along through new cycles. The 0 indicates that you have the chance to decide and accomplish what you feel from the soul to be most significant for accelerating growth. Use it fruitfully.

As we approach accelerated cycles where many of the Earth's humans will be completing the need to incarnate, this indicator in the chart may have particular significance. When no numbers are missing and all other patterns are balanced, there is a suggestion that if this life is handled well, it may be the last incarnation. However, this is a condition that depends on your handling of life and is not fully dependent upon the implications of the chart—just because a number or numbers are missing, it does not eliminate the possibility of completing the karmic wheel in this lifetime.

Based on my experience, when this condition exists in the chart, the individual should learn to handle, master and balance out the qualities of each number. It will require first mastering the numbers separately and then understanding the relationship of each number to the others. Of course, this means the numerical qualities must be learned and applied in life with other people and situations. Just learning the qualities from reading books and studying in the classroom is not enough. With this concept in mind, one way to evaluate the karmic accumulation is to add all of the numbers together: $1 + 2 + 3 + 4 + 5 + 6 + 7 + 8 + 9 = 45$, or 9. The remainder of this section applies to the chart with no missing numbers.

This is a life pattern where personality shortcomings must truly be brought into conscious focus and harmonized. You have a tremendous depth of awareness and view life events with an eye to purposeful responsibility. A distinct sort of detachment and impersonal feeling pervades your attitude toward life; it is literally as if you have been through it all before and have begun to tire of earthly routine. It is difficult for you to sustain a prolonged interest or enthusiasm for mundane activities because your soul cries out to be free of this dimension; it is restless to move along in its destiny. All of a sudden, the sobering thought may overwhelm you: What a task it is to finish up the demands of this earthly plane!

You can be suspicious, critical and moody. These qualities must now be transmuted into those of optimism, hope and a trusting faith in higher guidance. Your logical procedure is to generalize by bringing the overview of wholeness down to each small part. When an adversary starts to pick at the details of your structure, you become uneasy and at times defenseless. Because of your expansive outlook and understanding of so many viewpoints toward life, it is easy for you to switch views or to succumb to another's viewpoint for the sake of harmony even though you still disagree. Let this ambiguity work for you in a dynamic way rather than through passive omission.

Motivation is an ingredient that often haunts you, for there seem to be many things you could do, and yet it is hard to decide. Be careful that your desire for release from this plane does not lead you into escapist behavior. If you have not discovered your heart's desire, the deeper teachings of metaphysical and related studies will be of great guidance and comfort. Learn to give thanks for all that comes to you and visualize the possibilities in yourself, others and each situation that arises in your life. You are closer than ever to the possibility of attaining that aspired goal of completing your sojourns on Earth.

Symbology of Letters

A t the heart of numerological interpretation are the letters in the name. In the first portion of the book, the numerical equivalents were given for each letter; in this chapter, attention will be directed to the specific symbolic meaning of each letter and its meaning for the natal and progressed charts.

To better understand the symbolic meaning of letters, it is helpful to consider the basic symbols of consciousness that underscore their meaning: The full circle represents the superconscious of inclusive, embracing awareness. The half circle represents the subconscious, or soul. Straight lines represent the consciousness; the vertical is usually male and the horizontal is female. When angled lines occur in a letter, they represent progress and an exchange of awareness; They may be assertive or responsive, depending upon the origin and direction of flows.

As a further aid to the delineation of the letters, think of a letter as operating on three levels: The top represents the spiritual aspect, the middle the mental-emotional, and the bottom is symbolic of the physical plane where Spirit is planted on Earth. Let's use the letter A as an example:

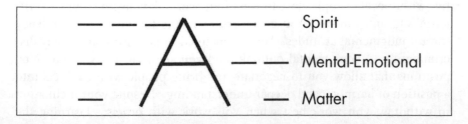

Following are individual interpretations for the twenty-six letters of our alphabet. The initials Wl, Ws, and L are abbreviations for will, wisdom and love, respectively. For further clarification as to the origin of these combinations, see the reference chart in Chapter 3 on page 15, where you will find the primary and secondary arrangements of the numbers. For information on progressed charts, go to chapter twelve.

A (1) Wl-Wl

The A symbolically originates on a higher plane, and its thrust is down and outward to the planes below. The horizontal bar represents an intuitive link on the mental level that forms a balanced triangle and then plunges to Earth with direct force. When A appears in your name, there is an indication of independence, aspiration and ambition. The direct impact from the A creates rapid thinking and inspired ideas. You are original in action and more often start new projects than finish them. The value 1 of A makes your actions direct and to the point once your mind is clear. You possess a strong sense of self-reliance and independence and do not like to have others impose or interfere. Yours is a carefree and courageous attitude. You can be blunt to a fault and need to weigh ideas carefully before presenting them. However, you enjoy debates and friendly intellectual sparring with friends and coworkers. When inharmonious, you can become self-centered, opinionated and fiercely independent.

Many As in the name stimulate impulsive actions, adventurous longings and a need to work at completing projects in motion. A as the first letter in the name emphasizes assertiveness, leadership qualities and willfulness. An A at the end of the name indicates a tendency to initiate good ideas or projects too late.

Progressed Chart

Impulse toward major new undertakings, change in job or residence, breakthroughs in consciousness, spiritual illumination, new friends or opportunities, promotion, overcome lethargy and indifference, can indicate setbacks or reversals when negative, near-death experience at the extreme.

B (2) Ws-L

The B draws spiritual and physical awareness into the emotional-mental level for evaluation. This enclosed pattern reveals shyness and introspective withdrawal. People close to you often overlook your sensitivity to criticism and antagonism. You go to great lengths to avoid your tendency toward judgmental attitudes. You are inclined to be critical and finely discriminating in your mental outlook, and you see it as a flaw. You enjoy positions that allow you to negotiate and bring people with conflicts into a position of harmony and deeper understanding. Despite your inclination to withdraw, you work best when you work with others. Learning the axioms of cooperation will prove valuable to your future. There is an inclination to carry out projects to the tiniest detail; sometimes this angers more impulsive types. Your negative tendencies are self-criticism, indecision and overzealous opinions of what is right or wrong.

When many Bs appear in the name, the above negative tendencies may be pronounced. As the first letter in a name, the B stimulates emotions and brings success through constructive cooperation with others. As the last letter, the tendency is to criticize self for recognizing proper behavior only after the mistake is made. Remember that looking back is valuable only as a guide for future behavior.

Progressed Chart

Examine false survival image, build new image from inner self; nervous strain; build upon intuition, need to rest, seek harmony with others, make improvement in career or work, take time to cooperate, do not force issues, make improvements in the home, seek the cause of emotional disharmony.

C (3) L-Wl

Symbolically, the C starts to form the circle, but it leaves an opening to communicate that which has been accumulated through eons of time and experience. A natural sense of joy and freedom flows from the possession of the C. You have noticeable originality in thought and speech and should strive to cultivate these creative abilities. You are a natural, gregarious host and enjoy the company of artistic friends. You often see only the good in things, yet are sensitive and susceptible to disillusionment or injured feelings. You benefit from partnerships, and your outward personality attracts creative coworkers. When in disharmony, you may suffer from throat afflictions and tend to scatter your creative abilities too thin.

Many Cs in the name suggest a special destiny; through sheer perseverance, you will reach goals and lessons after much resistance. C as the first letter accentuates the voice and likelihood of exposure to the public. As the last letter, it indicates that creative inspiration comes late and often from another source rather than from one's own fund of originality.

Progressed Chart

Expression of talents and creative gifts brings new adventure and friends, inspired creative thinking, a time to enjoy life; heightened intuition and psychic experiences; work through emotional blocks; new business endeavors; marital differences come to surface; follow your own guidance.

D (4) Wl-L

This letter is enclosed, so consciousness is centered and directed. The soul awareness flows along all levels and brings the essence of 4 into mundane fruition. Those of you with D in the name will work hard to overcome set-backs and mundane obstacles. With self-discipline and frugal habits, you will be able to acquire the security and personal comforts you desire. Once given a task, you work diligently until it is completed exactly as ordered. You eas-ily become set in your ways, critical and temperamental. Your fixed attitudes in love and home can be difficult for loved ones to reconcile. Control a sim-mering temper. A practical, business-like manner underlies your actions.

Many Ds in the name emphasize that determined, narrow and tenacious attitude. There can be a tendency to overestimate your capacity to provide for others. Be careful not to promise more than you can produce. When D is the first letter in the name, you take your work seriously but will move to greener pastures if everything looks favorable. When D is the last letter, you may seek new opportunities after the best situation has passed.

Progressed Chart

Stresses health; be careful with nutrition and diet; business trips, strained love relations, activity with residence or property; work through your stub-bornness and repressed emotions, pay attention to organization; a time to build a solid foundation in home, career, love or personal consciousness.

E (5) Ws-Wl

The E expresses on all levels; it will have you reaching for experience in all sectors of life. Those with the E in their names are curious adventurers who seek experience for its own sake. The E in your name encourages experience and absorption in active life events. You may hesitate often, but in the end, you learn much from the new people and events the E attracts. This stimulates mental activity and self-expression. You exude much energy in daily living. You may find yourself being very fidgety, intellectu-ally curious and with a knack for altering situations to suit yourself. You have a keen perception of events; however, you may lack a depth and con-centration of thought. Oftentimes this includes a casual interest in reli-gion, philosophy and the occult.

You are adaptable, restless and always on the go, especially when there are several Es. E as a first letter suggests an active mind and much attention to communications and dealing with the public. It gives a decided ability to use words well for the ministry, sales, entertainment or whatever your calling may be. When E is the last letter of your name, you often reach conclusions too late or are unable to solve intricate parts of a life puzzle.

Progressed Chart

Accelerated activities, possible change in residence or job, many short trav-els, active love life, overindulgence in sex and senses, chaotic happenings with unexpected twists, fluctuations in job and business; awakened interest in religion, philosophy and occultism; new (and sometimes eccentric) acquaintances, new job direction, desire for freedom, tension at home.

F (6) L-Ws

The thrust of the F is outward on the spiritual and mental-emotional level—the consciousness is directed to spiritual and mental levels to best deal with responsibilities in life. You will attract many opportunities to protect and take care of others, although you withdraw into emotional and mental realms when you are upset and ill at ease amid discord and tension. Your firm sense of right and wrong leaves you quite upset at injustice around you. Because of your sensitive receptive personality, you respond readily to consideration and affection. You suffer from the weight of your own burdens, at the same time taking upon yourself the problems of others close to you. You will face many sacrifices in life.

Many Fs suggest a sort of higher protection, despite the numerous setbacks and responsibilities that befall you. F as the first letter suggests somewhat subdued and withdrawn behavior; you will be faced with many added responsibilities and can mature from facing them fully. As the last letter, F indicates that it is difficult for you to get started; you put off even the necessary until later.

Progressed Chart

Adds to home and personal responsibilities; needs to make emotional adjustments, learn to accept duties with willing attitude and complete them efficiently, learn to release stress; spiritual peace from fulfilling personal burdens; seek quiet of mind, community service; accentuates discord or harmony in the home; be careful of martyr complex.

G (7) Ws-Ws

The G is almost a circle but turns in on the mental-emotional level to dwell upon the accumulated wisdom within. Your thrust in consciousness is toward deep thought, philosophical speculation and analysis of life issues. Your aloof and detached attitude can cause misunderstanding in people close to you. You are somewhat self-contained, perhaps not readily responding to warmth or attention. Your reserved, somewhat self-deprecating and anxious nature can cause you to wear yourself out through negative thinking.

More than one G indicates that you possess keen analytical ability with pronounced insight into the subtle motives behind people's outer actions. G as the first letter indicates a strong desire to delve into the mysteries of life; you will work hard but are acutely aware of your value and balk at selling yourself short. G at the end of your name suggests that you can become bogged down by the weight of all the accumulated knowledge and concerns you carry.

Progressed Chart

Can bring expansion in business or work; examine possibilities for financial gain, guard health, scrutinize possible changes thoroughly; can bring advancement, emotional impulsiveness; search for deeper happiness; overcome inward brooding and direct abilities outward.

H (8) Wl-Ws

The H possesses two parallel vertical lines representing movement, that is, elevation in consciousness. The horizontal line represents a building block on each plane. When this letter appears, there is opportunity to climb the heights of consciousness. Remember that climbing brings the danger of falling. You have an innate executive capacity and seek out the struggle for accomplishment and success. You enjoy people, possess a refined intellectual outlook, are active and get your point across convincingly. You are impressed by pioneering people who you believe have outstanding personalities. You attempt to emulate productive qualities you see in them. You are uncomfortable when conditions become disturbing, to the point that you lose confidence and feel out of control.

H as the first letter enhances leadership and an ability to attract success. As the last letter, it indicates a tendency to demonstrate your best abilities and talents too late. Many Hs in your name can suggest an overbearing and self-centered arrogance.

Progressed Chart

Likelihood of promotion and advancement; implement ideas for gains and success; selfish and greedy goals can undermine enlightened judgment; time to distinguish healthy feelings from toxic personal needs; promotes establishment of a new self-identity; seek love and attention, work out internal conflicts and misunderstandings with others.

I (9) L-L

The letter I is a straight line, symbolizing the vertical thrust between two planes of consciousness; it is direct, intense and dynamic. Because it is the last single-digit letter, it brings one cycle to a close, resolving individuality and building toward universality. This leaves its beholder sensitive and fluctuating in temperament. You are often susceptible to hurt feelings because of your tendency toward idealism. When out of balance, you can suffer deeply through sacrifice and disappointment in personal relationships. Let your innate humanitarianism and impersonal inner guidance become the focal point in your inspired musical, literary or creative endeavors. The 9 lets go and accumulates cosmic rewards.

I as the first letter in the name enhances quickness of thought, psychic sensitivity and awareness of mass consciousness. As the last letter, it can bring misunderstandings, hurt feelings and poorly defined relationships. The intensity and directness of the I can bring emotional fluctuations in the form of mood swings, depression and discouragement.

Progressed Chart

Seek the source of mood swings; increased intuition and psychic inspiration; seek ways to assist others; nervous strain and health problems; worry and nervousness increase; abrupt and unexpected changes in job, family and relationships; realistic idealism, realistic dreams fulfilled, highest attainment.

J (10 or 1) Wl-Ws

J is the only letter that looks back with its cup (u) holding on to the wisdom the soul has accumulated, using that as a foundation for progress. You are somewhat more hesitant to start than the other letters with the 1 value. However, once your mind is set, you show strong leadership, innovative thinking and orderly skills for achievement. If cautious and prudent, your abilities can bring considerable gain and reward, particularly if the J is the first letter in your name. The J adds sparkle and dash to the personality, which helps in your dealings with the public. There is a strong moral and ethical fiber running through your personal and business dealings.

J as the last letter suggests you may miss the point of business or conversation—and be embarrassed later. Trust is important to you, and much suffering can come through affections. Your buoyant optimism and good nature usually allow you to rebound from adversity and enjoy life.

Progressed Chart

Helping others get started; added responsibility and opportunity to increase earnings; new direction in business or personal affairs, change in residence; brings strain and alterations in personal relations; avoid shortcuts and irresponsible projects; increases initiative, establish foundation for expanding awareness.

K (11 or 2) Ws-Ws

The arms of the letter K move to and from the higher and lower planes through the mental-emotional. As the eleventh letter, the K has higher potency and potential. You are someone with a highly kinetic imagination and exciting personality. You are powerful and forceful once your mind is set, but you must understand others' needs and attain your position through cooperation and diplomacy rather than domination. Your extreme nature and immediate sense of values can get you into tight situations. No problem, though—you resolve them with an easy flair. You flourish emotionally in an environment of harmony and tenderness.

K as the first letter gives dramatic coloration to your expression, a gay and cheerful disposition, as well as a tendency to want to help others with any problems. As the last letter, K suggests that you can be resentful when others fail to carry out their roles in a cooperative manner. Those who have K in their names have a keen eye for detail and work to bring peace over each little area of disagreement.

Progressed Chart

Brilliant, original thinking; fixation on details can cause you to miss the greater point; brings unusual and strange experiences, confused emotions; time to deal with self-doubt and lack of self-image; brings psychic and spiritual breakthroughs, can bring financial gains; watch for dishonesty and exaggeration.

L (12 or 3) L-Ws

L receives a direct thrust from the higher consciousness and softly expresses itself in the material form of word or expression. You have a comfortable but colorful style when presenting yourself and your ideas. Your understanding of what motivates others is quite perceptive and useful. Your inquisitive nature is constantly in search of greater learning and self-expression. You are prone to excessive worry when friends and acquaintances disagree with you or each other.

As the first letter, L helps with public recognition, social popularity and creative use of words and ideas, often placing you in a leadership role. As the last letter, L indicates that you can waste much time and energy pursuing a less-than-worthy course of action. The L vibration is romantic, intuitive and uplifting in nature. When in harmony, your sensitivity enables you to size up people quickly and accurately.

Progressed Chart

Speaking, publishing, meeting new friends and love; stimulates arts and entertainment; travels can bring happiness and popularity; favorable for marriage and home; relaxation and study bring spiritual gain; work through toxic thoughts, emotions and actions.

M (13 or 4) Wl-Wl

M grasps concepts on the mental-emotional level and then secures them to a firm sense of reality. You are a natural builder and seek solid ground upon which to build your life and principles. You have a natural technical and organizational ability that serves you well in the practical world. Your controlled emotional nature makes you appear aloof and difficult to know completely. You keep yourself under strict discipline; personal control is always an issue to you.

M as the first letter in the name gives qualities of integrity, concentration and service to humankind. Many Ms can indicate hard-headedness and narrow attitudes. M as the last letter in your name suggests resistance to building a proper foundation and credentials for your efforts. M in the name stresses reasoning capability, but you can experience difficulty expressing your ideas clearly to others. Your work is to build higher ideals into form.

Progressed Chart

Financial gains with proper foundation, financial lessons; watch for strain on health; future planning; deal with added demands from work and career; travel, secret affairs; review spiritual values and goals; caution with contracts and business; try to avoid needless quarrels, overcome opposition by facing solutions squarely.

N (14 or 5) Ws-Ws

The flow of the letter N is one of rapid inspiration from above, tempered with evaluation of experience below. The N seeks experience and knowledge of the world and then places the lessons before the higher self for appraisal prior to new growth. You are energetic, adventurous and constantly turning over new stones in your quest. A constant search for new knowledge can make your belief structure inconsistent, yet your restless pursuit of knowledge leans toward a deep faith and optimism about life. Your need for change and excitement gives you an openness and appeal that summons other intriguing personalities. You enjoy luxury and sensual comfort and are prone to indulgence.

N as the first letter enhances social contact and recognition. N as the last letter in the name indicates a tendency to perform services of giving as a means to get something in return at a later date. You are at your best in positions dealing with people on a daily basis.

Progressed Chart

Exercise talents and expand horizons; fluctuations in career and finances; brings sensual intrigue; confusion deciphering proper spiritual path; unique and adventurous experiences; brings new friends and important social contacts; work on underlying friction in family; restless search for love and fulfillment; physical exercise important.

O (15 or 6) L-L

The O is our ringpassnot and can embrace universal wisdom, or it can become woefully restricted and egocentric. The nature of the O is to embrace the world's problems openly, and those with O must guard against taking on more burdens and responsibilities than they can handle. Your embracing attitude places you in roles of service in the home and the public market. You respond to the demands of domestic responsibility and find deep satisfaction in that role. You collect experience, both trivial and neces-

234 ☞ *Forever Numerology*

sary. You must learn when to turn loose from those people or concepts with which you have lived too long.

O as a first letter or as the first vowel makes one vulnerable to depletion of energy as the result of openness to other's problems; beware of being used by others. O as the last letter causes prolonged worry and concern over previous relationships or actions that did not work well.

Progressed Chart

Activates money matters in the home and business; opportunity to assume responsibility and leadership; emphasizes marriage, its problems and joys; define boundaries and recognize codependency; interest in the occult or religious studies; discord upsets health; resolve conflicts in home and family relations.

P (16 or 7) Ws-L

The preponderance of the P's influence is intuitive and intellectual. Its nature is to store wisdom and disperse it prudently upon need. The P provides impetus to the study of deeper philosophies and spiritual sciences. You are aloof and distant, with your head in unknown spheres. Do some people consider you difficult to know? You are a lovely person with a great sense of drive and purpose once your sights are set. Your drive should best be balanced with a humanitarian consideration or your personal ambition can become unchecked. You want very much to establish yourself to leave an impression despite unfavorable circumstances and a lack of recognition.

As the first letter, P suggests an intensity of drive with clarity of mind. As the last letter, it indicates frustrated ambition for control and power. The power will either come late or remain elusive. Higher wisdom should be sought to direct this energy to more fruitful use.

Progressed Chart

Disappointment through love and affection; study mental sciences and deeper metaphysical studies; confuses sexual need and love; emotional repression and confusion; avoid prolonged withdrawal and depression, make it a point to open up and enjoy others, use inward wisdom wisely in outer world; brings recognition for specific skills; use discretion in major decisions.

Q (17 or 8) Wl-L

The Q is like an O with a way out, and it is a dynamic shot of energy into one's life endeavors and aspiration. The qualities of the awakened Q are a volatile additive to your success quotient. This vibration can create so many eccentricities that many people will find you indefinable. When greed is overcome, this can be a strong indicator of financial accumulation. You have the vision to dream and the potential leadership to put your dreams into action, directing and inspiring others. You repeatedly defy social restriction and opposition from those you consider inferior while taking a fiercely independent position in your self-expression.

As the first letter, Q is highly inspired (or can become purely eccentric), depending upon the consciousness. You do not like to become dependent upon others and enjoy people who are equally creative, artistic and progressive.

Progressed Chart

Sales and promotion of unique item; carefully seek application for unusual ideas; brings bizarre traits into light, conflicts in home and marriage; attracts eccentric and colorful acquaintances; significant change in work and finances; activities upset emotional equilibrium; need for recognition and power; can fall for get-rich-quick schemes.

R (18 or 9) L-WI

The R has the stored-up potential of the P, but R goes through emotional anguish to bring wisdom into Earth-plane expression. The R has tremendous potential, but it brings many trials and tribulations for emotional growth. Your artistic and poetic temperament finds it difficult to deal with harsh realities. You are a natural leader when inspired and are responsive to advanced concepts of social thinking and action. You set idealistic yet sometimes impractical goals that can lead to disappointment and cause you to become cynical and mistrusting.

The power of the R can be used many ways; however, it usually is best expressed when channeled into selfless humanitarian aspirations rather than purely selfish ambitions. This is true especially when R is the first letter. When R is the last letter, unaccountable diversions can prevent completion of desired goals. Many Rs in the name can stimulate nervous excesses and concern that can deplete the health if not corrected.

Progressed Chart

Religious and spiritual revelations; exercise caution in major decisions; brings delays and disappointment; plan and do not plunge; emotional trials; consider motives for marriage carefully; great spiritual growth through trials and tribulations; expand in compassion and tolerance, use creative mind; deeds without work may collapse; time for self-growth.

S (19 or 1) WI-L

The S is symbolic of the progress of the soul on Earth and in heaven. It is much like the divider of the universal yin-yang symbol. The S weaves its tapestry of consciousness, bringing unity and breakthrough. The S in the name gives an intense creative drive and brings flashes of insight and innovation. You are drawn to religious and philosophical research but usually follow your own brand of unorthodox and individual belief. A distinct need for self-expression and individuality pervades your nature. You desire to make a favorable impression and to be recognized for your unique personality. When out of balance, you attract needless accidents and minor setbacks.

As the first letter, S suggests that you are quick to spot a deal and handle opportunities shrewdly. However, when it is the last letter, there is a likelihood of seeing clearly through situations only after it is too late to cover up misjudgments. The presence of S helps to stimulate the noblest spiritual aspirations.

Progressed Chart

Seek application for new invention, overcome passivity; sudden changes in family, job and/or consciousness; may bring change of location, unexpected events, with beneficial results in the end; unnecessary arguments and emotional bickering, spiritual and mystical revelation; enhances urges for creative thinking; extraordinary events in love affairs, confrontation with strong-willed adversaries.

T (20 or 2) Ws-Wl

The T seeks out wisdom on the higher plane and brings it down in flashes of intuitive inspiration. If you have a T in your name, you are very exacting in your expectation of others but can also be very patient. You exude a warmth that enhances the maternal domestic qualities, and you are skilled in tact, diplomacy and cooperation. You seek congenial interaction with others and become anxious when relationships deteriorate and cooperation is impeded. You are at a point where it is time to release old ideas and negative traits; let them be hung upon the cross. Now you are free to pursue nobler service.

T as the first letter suggests a tendency to carry out others' ideas well and instruct rather than take bold initiative. When T is the last letter, you can easily get yourself into confused states, and then you lack certainty and will not take advice. You should guard against the tendency to become critical and trite.

Progressed Chart

Emphasis on partnerships and business, desire to travel and see the world; enhance earnings; brings important lessons in growth through trials; need for security; brings significant relationships; correct impulsiveness and overemotionalism for better health, stress self-discipline; others may interfere in your work; benefit from periods of solitude and meditation.

U (21 or 3) L-Wl

The U represents the fully receptive nature of the soul along with a multitude of gifts possessed by the inner self. The soul expresses itself through feelings, making them central to your makeup. You experience a wide range of emotional reactions to life. Usually you rise from depression and despair to turn your nurturing qualities into assistance for others. Your natural dignity brings traits of charm, effervescence and persuading confidence into expression when you are in harmony with self. On the negative side, you can be enraptured with so many issues or projects that you scatter your talents, preventing goal attainment. U in the name enhances writing, academic studies and artistic potential. There is a curious fluctuation between optimistic aspirations for achievement and periodic pessimism.

When U is the first letter or vowel in the name, it emphasizes travel and communication. In fact, it can bring an almost divine aura of protection. As the last letter, it scatters native abilities and brings more risks than benefits to unplanned endeavors.

Progressed Chart

Mixed time of opportunity and inner fears; may have to force self in order to awaken creative talents; evaluate situation thoroughly before making major moves; unconventional and broken love affairs; brings out underlying emotional troubles; relatives and family can become difficult; take advantage of good opportunities in business and work; a time to release emotional blocks in order to awaken inner qualities of the soul.

V (22 or 4) Wl-Ws

V is the twenty-second letter (keep this in mind when working with V), and its symbolical pattern is to draw directly from spiritual sources and plant the inspiration with firm direction into the material life stream. When awakened, this gives qualities for enlightened business savvy along with inspired leadership for interjecting higher wisdom into established social patterns of human endeavor. You are quite capable, determined. Once you are dedicated to a person or cause, your loyalty is the greatest. You will have to work hard for success, but an unlimited opportunity exists for those who live by the higher precepts working in the new laws of manifestation. You can envision a project, inspire others and bring things into fruition.

When V is the first letter, you will take on difficult plans and bring together the people necessary for most efficient execution. When V is the last letter, you are likely to talk more about dreams that might have been—or perhaps plunge carelessly into something without full knowledge of the consequences. You should work to awaken the latent potential of this master number.

Progressed Chart

Discovering work of the soul; discipline yourself, get project under control, apply religious or metaphysical principles to your daily endeavors; wise investment can bring prosperous returns, compatible relationships bring special personal satisfaction, celestial ideas bear fruit; termination of old debts; hard work results in great rewards.

W (23 or 5) Ws-L

The W draws inspiration from Spirit, validates it on the material plane, consults the higher self for confirmation and then lifts human experience to a higher realm. W seeks life and growth with relish. Its desire is to get life completed and move on to new levels of existence. You avidly pursue life; very little can keep you in the doldrums for long. You push aside obstacles, following hunches in complete defiance of the natural odds. This quest brings you into every imaginable unique and bizarre experience. You are adaptable, with a pointed knack for taking old concepts and reworking them into updated ideas. You will find it hard to stay long in one place. This vibration is favorable for speaking and writing. You are able to dash up your presentations with a touch of real life drawn from your wide-ranging experiences.

As the first letter, W enhances the likelihood of service and working with diverse classes of people. As the last letter, there is an initial hesitation in dealing with people; however, this is generally overcome as you learn about yourself and others.

Progressed Chart

Fluctuation and instability; things work out well in the end; confusing emotional relationships; spiritual growth results from intensified life events; sudden changes; let go of the past and move ahead, travel emphasized; may bring legal settlements; be careful not to overdo and strain physical health.

X (24 or 6) L-Wl

The X forms an "as above, so below" meeting of the downward flow of light and an upward reach in consciousness. The two triangular motions meet on the mental-emotional level, where misunderstanding and false wisdom should be cancelled out and eliminated. When this letter appears, one is at a crossroad in consciousness—progression can occur or the temptation may bring on repetitive cycles. The need is to let go of personality so you may move more dedicatedly toward aspiration of the soul. Your life is best suited to one of service and improving the human condition. You may feel that the world demands too much from you, and you may seek recognition for your solution to others' problems. You possess a flair for theatrics and enjoy prestigious company.

As the first letter in your name, X very often brings you into public limelight. When X is the last letter, you hesitate to take on the responsibility of working to serve others.

Progressed Chart

Public attention and gains in finance; travel is accentuated; secret liaisons; various activities can place strain upon nerves; quick, decisive moves will be required; unusual family strains; may bring need of sacrifice for others; uplift thinking; time for purge and purification; seek soul guidance.

Y (25 or 7) Ws-Wl

The Y has a highly intuitive receptivity to higher insight. You are naturally psychic and intuitive and should learn to trust your strongest impressions. The Y gives a secretive tendency and inclination to probe deeply into the mysteries of humanity and the universe. You accumulate wisdom in great force until you are ready to make a decision or evaluation. This reserve makes you appear detached and unfeeling; yet your true feelings run deep. Do not underestimate your abilities. Now may be the time to let the world benefit from your abounding skills. You can become critical of circumstances where disorganization and confusion exist and seek solutions that clarify and establish order.

When Y is the first letter, your mental and intuitive acumen is pronounced. As the last letter, you will likely fail to take advantage of first impressions. You will derive much benefit from times in meditation and positive introspection.

Progressed Chart

Do not neglect physical realities in pursuit of knowledge; minor health problems may occur, a deeper sense of spiritual reality slowly emerges; may bring new circle of friends and professional compatriots; psychic occurrences; be cautious with intoxicants and stimulants; great insight now from self-examination, meditation and soul evaluation.

Z (26 or 8) Wl-Wl

The Z transfers information between levels like a bolt of lightning. The influence of Z is very potent, and its presence has a marked effect on consciousness. You have abundant self-confidence, drive and a great deal of energy. The Z is like pure energy and as such can be used constructively or with devious motive. When positively directed, it brings leadership, success with money and organizational efficiency. You should avoid exaggeration and excesses in personal habits. Misuse of material goods will chain the soul and bind growth. You have a magnetic influence over many and must guard how you use this influence.

As the first letter in your name, Z can bring prophetic abilities, enhance public recognition and often put you into unconventional professions. As the last letter, it warns of the pitfall associated with misuse of wealth and personal power. "Regeneration" is an important word for Z people.

Progressed Chart

Wise judgment can bring gains in wealth and/or prestige; overcome limitations, take tremendous strides, put universal law into practice; misguided emotions can be a strain on health; avoid schemes and earn your way honestly; brings unusual mate and friends; seek efficiency with occult and divine studies; stresses investigation and truth.

❀ ❀ ❀

When interpreting the significance of the letter symbolism in the progressed chart, you might want to consider the vibrational influence of each specific year the letter covers. For example, let us look at the letter G. The first year in the G's influence will have a slightly different shade than the second, third, fourth, fifth, sixth and seventh year of its periodicity. The accomplished student will eventually want to blend the numerical value of each year with the vibrational quality of the number.

For instance, in the fourth year of the G's influence, the individual will feel the need to discipline the self to best attune to accumulate wisdom within. In the fifth year, there will be expansion and more conscious expression of the innate capacities of mind and soul. By developing this awareness, you will add considerable subtlety and insight to your art of interpretation. With time and practice, you will be able to establish insights for more thorough personal evaluations.

12

Progressed Chart

The progressed chart provides a detailed outline of our life from birth to death. It is a road map created by the soul and offered to us as assistance on our journey of life. The progressed chart can be used to look back at the past to better understand the formation of our behavior; it can also be used to look ahead and become more aware of the potentials and possible pitfalls along the way. With greater awareness comes greater preparedness. With foresight we can more rapidly assimilate and integrate the experiences that come to us from life.

In *Numerology for the New Age*, I presented an entirely new format of constructing the progressed chart. The enthusiastic response from both professional numerologists and students has confirmed my earlier convictions: The new format offers a special tool for practitioners that enhances the art of interpretation. Since the publication of that earlier volume about numerology, I have improved the interpretive power of the progressed chart. The experienced practitioner who has been using the previous method will want to make special note of this latest development.

The experienced practitioner will know how to use the progressed chart and is encouraged to explore and test this new model. The beginning student may find the construction (and particularly the interpretation) of the progressed chart overwhelming. You can start by reading the appropriate personal year in Chapter 7. Then go to the symbolic meaning of the letters in the progressed chart from Chapter 11. Next, much can be learned from the introductory meanings to the numbers in Chapters 4 and 5. All of these combined will provide you with a good overview of the influencing factors.

One thing you can do to increase your learning curve is doing your own chart and the charts of people close to you. Because you know the years when certain events happened, you can begin to extrapolate what might have happened in the life of someone you do not know. Also, from the confidence of seeing what has happened in the past, you begin to have pretty high probability of seeing what may happen in the future. There is no substitute for experience, and improved interpretation comes only from practice, practice, practice.

For the trained professional therapist or counselor, the progressed chart during the formative years can be very helpful for recognizing likely moments of trauma and the cycle of subconscious patterns; intuitive and skilled numerologists can use this same doorway. However, one needs to be careful when opening the door into the shadow side. When you look at arrangements of the essence in adult years, you may find an exact or very similar arrangement in the early childhood period. If you go back to the underlying issues during the childhood years, you will usually find them being acted out similarly in the adult year.

Progressed Life Chart

Following is a sample chart for John Albert Jones to help you understand the construction of the progressed chart. Please note that this chart does not cover more than a few years; it is intended to demonstrate only the fundamentals of progressed chart construction. A lengthy example is provided in Appendix B to better illustrate a more complete arrangement.

Year	59	60	61	62	63	64	65	66	67	68	69	70	71	72	73	74	75	76	77
Age	0	1	2	3	4	5	6	7	8	9	10	11	12	13	14	15	16	17	18
Pers		J	H	H	H	H	H	H	H	H	N	N	N	N	N	L	L	L	
Soul		0	0	0	0	0	0	A	E	E	E	E	E	0	0	0	0	0	0
Ess		8	3	7	8	9	1	2	7	3	22(4)	2	3	22(4)	6	7	6	7	8
PY		2		4	5	6	7	8	9	1	2	3	4	5	6	7	8	9	1	2
OPT																			

Year and Age

These lines represent the calendar year and the age that person turns that year, respectively.

Pers

The personality line emphasizes external factors and the personality reaction to life events. Like with the personality number, this line is based on the consonants in the person's name. John Albert Jones's name starts with J, and the numerical value for J is 1 (see Chapter 6). Therefore, John Albert was influenced by J in his first year (see Chapter 11). The next consonant in John Albert's name is an H, which has the numerical value of 8, so the H influences John Albert for the next eight years of his life. This is followed by N (five years), L (three years) and so on. Once you have used all of the personality letters (consonants), you repeat them again in the same order, continuing to the desired age. (The same rule applies to the vowels.)

Soul

The soul line emphasizes the internal reaction of the individual to the events taking place. Like the soul number, this line is based on the vowels in the person's name. The first vowel in John Albert Jones's name is O, and the numerical value for O is 6 (see Chapter 6). Therefore, John Albert was influenced by O in his first six years (see Chapter 11). The next vowel in John Albert's name is an A, which has the numerical value of 1, so the A influences John Albert for the next year of his life. This is followed by E (five years), O (six years) and so on. Once you have used all of the soul letters (vowels), you repeat them again in the same order, continuing to the desired age.

Ess

The essence is the combined energies of the personality, the soul and the vibrational influence of the person's age. To calculate this number, add the person's age to the numerical values of the corresponding year's personality and soul letters.

Note: This factor of interpretation is introduced for the first time in this volume. The number of the age is rarely used in numerical evaluation, although there are a few practitioners who do factor it in as a meaningful indicator. The age vibration emphasizes the life factor impacting the individual during the specific year.

The combined number is a powerful indicator of the meaning for that particular year. It takes time and practice to develop a sense of integration of the essence. If you are a beginning student, you can use the following simple guidelines as a helpful start:

Essence Number	Lessons Relate to
1	Tests of will and individuality
2	Cooperation, criticism, social opinion
3	Creativity, self-expression, sexual issues
4	Work, discipline, determination
5	Sexual temptation, prejudice, change, variety
6	Responsibility, marriage (relationships), service
7	Withdrawal, introspection, arrogance, intuition

Essence Number	Lessons Relate to
8	Power, money, authority
9	Altruism, release, idealism, completion
11	Expanded intuition, increased public image, test of self-image
22	Deepening quest of life path, group participation, improved monetary situation
33	Healing crisis, service to others, expanded creative expression.
44	Increased leadership, universal money-making methods, inspired intuition
55	Existential lessons, overcoming deep prejudices, inspired innovation
66	Uncovering deep soul memories, inspired service, knowledge of universal archetypes
77	Investigating esoteric truths, application of inner law, higher life principles
88	Trusting higher authority, working the laws of manifestation, turning within
99	Inspired vision, death and transformation, archetypal artistry

PY

Personal year. This vibration has been heavily discussed in an earlier chapter. When the essence and personal year are the same, the lesson takes on even more intensity and significance.

The essence and its components are calculated from birthday to birthday, whereas the personal year is computed from calendar year to calendar year and changes with the first day of January. Therefore, the personal year is not combined with the others.

(I realize that this departure from the earlier interpretations can be confusing to someone who has been computing the essence by another system, particularly if you have been using the calculation presented in *Numerology for the New Age*. Like so many numerologists, I was influenced in my early years of practice by several different authors and teachers. I accepted their expertise and combined different techniques of interpretation where I felt the quality of interpretation was improved.

However, over the thirty-five plus years of my practice I have become uncomfortable on several occasions when some of the techniques I was using clashed with one another. So I looked for a more consistent and integrated methodology that I believed would further improve the art of interpretation. In particular, this new methodology for the progressed chart filled a missing link I had experienced while doing progressions. I believe that if experienced practitioners take the time to go back and compare this with earlier charts, many will find that this accuracy and depth present a wonderful contribution to their work.)

The slanted line is present in the first year of the chart to serve as a reminder that there is an overlap of the years. For example, in the chart of John Albert Jones, the progressed chart goes from June 26, 1959 to June 26, 1960.

OPT

Optional. You may want to use this line to include the changes in triune cycles, pinnacles and challenges. With time you may want to include some additional factor that you find adds to the strength of your interpretation.

Monthly Progressed Chart

The experienced practitioner might want to develop a more detailed portrait of the year by working with the monthly progressed chart. The monthly chart is constructed like the yearly chart but with some unique differences. The first month starts with the nth letter for the year of the progressed chart you have chosen. You then proceed through the remaining eleven months in order of progression in the name and in the yearly chart.

The other difference is that the essence number includes the vibration of the year of age plus the specific number of each month. In place of the personal year, the personal month is calculated.

Here is an example using the chart of John Albert Jones for his fifth year of age. Note that at the time John Albert is five years old, his personality line is in the fourth of eight Hs as indicated in the chart above. Therefore, the personality line in his monthly progressed chart shows five Hs, the fourth through the eighth H (H's numerical value is 8). Similarly, the soul line in John Albert Jones's monthly progressed chart starts with two Os, the fifth and the sixth (O's numerical value is 6).

Month	June	July	Aug.	Sept.	Oct.	Nov.	Dec.	Jan.	Feb.	Mar.	Apr.	May
Age + Month	11	12	13	14	15	16	17	6	7	8	9	10
Pers	H	H	H	H	H	N	N	N	N	N	L	L
Soul	O	O	A	E	E	E	E	E	O	O	O	O
Ess	7	8	22(4)	9	1	8	9	6	9	1	9	1
P Mn (7–8 PY)	3	4	5	6	7	8	9	8	9	1	2	3

Interpreting a monthly chart is similar to interpreting the yearly chart, but you modify a little to take into account that the amount of time is less and the impact is usually more moderate.

Daily Progressed Chart

For those who want to chart things at a very detailed level, there is the daily progressed chart. To set up the daily chart, start with the nth letter governing the year on the personality line. Then proceed continuously for each day, through the duration of the progressed year. Next, do the same with the soul line. To calculate the daily number, add the sequential value of each new day to the number of the age for that year. The essence is the sum of the numbers on the personality and soul lines and the accumulated day number. The last line indicates the personal day.

For an example, let us take the John Albert Jones chart for the 10th year. The letter on his personality line is the first of five Ns; the letter on his soul line is the third of five Es. To calculate the Ess, you add John Albert's age to the numerical values of N and E and the nth day of 365 days, starting with 1, the first day (the day of birth, not the first day of the calendar year). For the personal day (PD), add the month plus the day plus the personal year.

For his daily progressed chart, you would start on 6 (June) 26 and your chart would look like this:

	26	27	28	29	30	1	2	3	4	5
Age & Day	11	12	13	14	15	16	17	18	19	20
Pers	N	N	N	N	N	L	L	L	B	B
Soul	E	E	E	O	O	O	O	O	O	E
Ess	3	22(4)	5	7	8	7	8	9	9	9
PD	Month + day + personal year									
	8	9	1	2	3	1	11(2)	3	4	5

To interpret the personal day, you can use the information for the personal year and progressed meaning of the letters. Modify the interpretation by taking into account that a day is of small duration in relationship to the entire year; Modify the nuance of the interpretation to fit a daily cycle pattern.

The Regressed Chart

Throughout this book, I have made many references to uncovering the origin of unconscious tendencies and patterns of dysfunction, and more and more people are interested in methods of revealing these hidden components of their personality. The regressed chart is a form of interpretation that can be used by the layperson and the professional therapist alike. It is a numerical portal that can expose the sequestered secrets of the unconscious.

The regressed chart is like a reversed progressed chart. Using the date of birth of a child, you calculate back nine months in the combined charts of the parents. In the case of short-term pregnancies or premature births, the time of conception can be determined pretty closely once the length of the pregnancy is known. An analysis of the combined factors of the parents' charts provides a map of the numerical climate at the time of conception, and with this, the trained and intuitive practitioner can decipher possible unconscious factors surrounding the conception. This is a concept that can be confusing to the beginner and should be saved until one feels more comfortable working with the progressed chart and monthly chart.

You may wonder why I use the moment of conception. During my thirty-plus years as a therapist, I have conducted thousands of prenatal and past-life regressions, and the responses from my clients have made it clear that a child does have an awareness of its own at the moment of conception. Many metaphysical teachings indicate that the soul comes into contact with the aura of the parents at the moment of conception, and my clients have confirmed that awareness in almost all cases. The child's personality is a product of the exchange of energy between the father and mother on all levels, including the unconscious level. The hopes, fears, plans and anxieties of that moment leave an indelible imprint upon the soul and the unconsciousness.

The regressed chart can help to get a partial portrait of the issues taking place. To get this portrait, you can construct a composite chart of the interpersonal stress numbers of the parents at the time of conception. Obviously, you don't have to go all the way to the exact minute. If the parents know the exact day of conception of a child, a regressed chart could be done to the day. Since it is the month that is known in most cases, it is the month that is emphasized here.

Following is an example chart to give you a sense of what one might be able to derive with this interpretation. This is the chart of a child whose parents are known to me. The progressed personality letter of the mother was a D and her soul letter I. The progressed personality letter of the father was an H and his progressed soul letter was an O.

	Mother	Father
Age + Month	4	2
Pers	4	8
Soul	9	6
Ess	8	7
P Month	2	7

At the time of the child's conception, the mother was working in a job that no longer satisfied her. The father's work was unsteady, and the thought of a new child caused worry about having enough money to support the new mouth to feed. The child's soul number is a 4, which indicates that he/she has come to get some important work of the soul completed.

There can be resistance to finding that work because of sensitivity and probable guilt for creating a burden upon the parents' already tenuous work situations. Also, the father's work kept him away from home a lot. This could create resentment toward the father's work.

The 3 stress number between the soul numbers suggests emotional tension in the relationship. In fact, the father was seriously considering leaving the marriage just before the pregnancy. The 1 stress number between the essence numbers suggests tension of wills and different belief systems. The mother was materialistic and image oriented, whereas the father was deeply interested in spiritual and growth-oriented philosophies. The 5 stress number between the personal months suggests different social viewpoints and possible confinement. The parents shared very different social and ethnic backgrounds, and the father was feeling trapped in the ritual and superficiality of the mother's lifestyle.

The example here is but briefly examined. The trained professional can see that there is a lot of information here that can be very valuable in determining where the focus of therapy could be directed. The layperson can use this information to start the process of working through the layers of armor and denial that are so typical due to growing up in such a dysfunctional society.

Numerology and Male-Female Polarity

Throughout this volume, there has been repeated mention of the three primal forces translating into active (assertive), receptive (passive) and the equilibrium (balance). These are reflections of the original dynamics of the ring cosmos, ring chaos and ring pass-not. The oriental cultures refer to the yin, yang and tao, and in western culture, these have become feminine (yin), masculine (yang) and tao.

We see the dynamics of these forces everywhere in the universe and in the life process, and modern psychology reflects an understanding of them in the concept of anima-animus first presented by Carl Jung. It is the theory that within the male human is the anima, or his feminine side; within the female human is the animus, or her masculine side. The idea has been developed and refined over time, and it is now generally acknowledged within the psychological community that we have both a male and a female portion of self within.

One of the most desirable goals for individuals seeking well-being and resolution of the dysfunction within themselves is to establish a conscious and healthy connection with their inner female and inner male. This process requires resolving negative associations with the archetypes that are the result of growing up with toxic and dysfunctional parents. The distorted interaction with such parents causes major difficulties for the individual's connection to his or her real inner self.

We see external signs in society of the two opposite sexes trying to find a more harmonious and fulfilled way of life. Women are becoming more assertive and wanting equal pay and equal rights. They are speaking out against once-tolerated abuse. They seek more recognition in politics and the formation of social regulations and reforms.

At the same time, men have been given more permission to demonstrate feelings and emotions. They are wearing more demonstrative colors, growing their hair longer and talking of male-bonding support groups to nurture male needs. The growing acceptance of alternative lifestyles that include same-sex unions is another sign of society seeking to find a point of balance in identity. Working with numerology can help identify some of the ongoing struggles and act as a source of insight to shed light on these issues.

For purposes of definition, feminine energy is usually thought of as powerful, nurturing, wise and knowing. It possesses the potential and possibility of all that is to come. Masculine energy is active, linear and dynamic. The male energy takes the power and possibility of the feminine side, organizes it and does something with it. Feminine energy is the energy of being; masculine energy is the energy of doing.

Contrary to some popular thinking, men and women are not equal. They are complements to each other, and each needs the other to work through the balancing act upon this planet Earth. This struggle of duality reaching for a point of synthesis and integration is revealed in working with numerology. In the current social climate of our present western culture, the numbers 1, 4, 7 and 8 are more masculine in overt expression. The numbers 2, 3, 6 and 9 are more feminine. The number 5 is universal to all life and goes unequivocally both ways.

When you see many 1s, 4s, 7s or 8s in a woman's chart, you usually find a major struggle with father issues and negative animus issues. In an inordinately high (and, I am certain, statistically significant) number of cases I have seen a reoccurring pattern regarding the number 8. When 8 is the life number (or, similarly, the personality number), the woman was often the second or third daughter, and one or both of the parents had had a strong desire for a boy. Subsequently, on an unconsciousness level, the girl has tried to be that son in order to get Daddy's love and appreciation. Such an unconscious drive formed at conception often develops at the expense of the woman's own femininity, which can result in conflicts with men and sexual problems with her feminine anatomy.

Men with many 2s, 3s, 6s and 9s prominent in their charts often have strong maternal identification and creative, emotional temperaments. This often indicates underlying issues of conflict with Mother and the women in a man's life. Men are learning to be more open with their positive feminine attributes, which can be a real plus in social interaction.

Contrary to old role models, a man who is in touch with his feminine self does not lose his masculinity. In fact, he becomes more sensitive, complete and aware. The woman who is in touch with her masculine self does not become any less feminine. With the fullness that comes from a balanced polarity, she is more confident, assertive and accomplished. Ages and eons from now, as the search for integration continues, we will likely one day merge back into androgynous, angel-like beings of ethereal light.

14

Releasing Negative Patterns

T here is a lot of information in this volume related to dysfunction and the negative, dark side. The reason is that while practicing as a psychotherapist and providing intuitive counseling, I have come to realize that most of human behavior is more dysfunctional than healthy.

So I present these patterns in the hope that with recognition comes resolution. We live, to a large extent, unconsciously ignorant of so many hidden negative ego patterns. Eventually, though, events introduce us to someone or something that wakes us up and encourages us to make changes. That is one of several wishes I have in writing this book—that it might help awaken many people to their pattern of denial. If you have reached that point, you will find in this chapter some suggested guidelines to facilitate your transformation into conscious awareness.

Four Steps of Acknowledgment

1 The first major step has begun. Whatever casual interest you had when you opened the book certainly wasn't enough by itself to bring you to this page. Acknowledge to yourself that your life has been negatively impacted by a dysfunctional behavior pattern. You are a child of denial.

2 Commit to personal growth and change that will benefit and fulfill you. There are numerous avenues of growth available to the committed seeker. As a part of this step, you must also realize that you cannot do it all alone. We can benefit from others' insight so that we can recognize that which is

unconscious within us. You will benefit from a solid support group or, if you choose, a professional therapist/counselor.

3 Take the time and care to find a counselor/therapist who suits your needs. It would benefit you to choose someone who has a background of working with children of alcoholics or with issues of addiction and codependency. Most professionals specialize in counseling/therapy because their personal circumstances included being the child of dysfunction. It can be essential to work with someone who has faced his or her own personal "stuff." Once under way, you may benefit from group work or a pattern of sharing with trusted friends who are also dealing with their issues in a healthy way.

4 In this step, you will experience the stages of self-acceptance, recovery of self-esteem, forgiveness and reframing of values. Where guilt and doubt once ruled, positive action can take their place.

Nine Steps toward Recovery

The following stages of recognition and release are presented as a means to help you identify patterns of imbalance. After recognition comes the next step—that of choosing to either remain a victim of previous unconscious patterns or to become a conscious master of your life events and domain.

Because the topics of addiction and dysfunction are blessed with techniques for uncovering and recovering in other literature, the emphasis throughout this volume is on identifying the deeper spiritual and cosmological implications of disorder along with the traditional family concept. This information hopefully will enable you, the reader, to determine a course of personal action for your own growth.

1—Will

As the divine sparks became more immersed into bodies of matter, they lost their direct knowing. In this process, they began to substitute man-made theories and intellectual knowledge for the divine knowing of their innate nature. The rationalization was that they needed to establish order over their now chaotic existence. And we saw how they became angry with the will of the Father and rebelled in defiance. Humankind became arrogant and proud. The will in humans competed with God. In arrogance humans created kingdoms to emulate and to surpass God's creation. Through assertion of even more will, collective and individual, pride was rampant.

Today this excessive and misplaced pride is still an obvious factor in the separation of humans from their Source. Human ego works hard to help humans hold their chaotic lives together. In fact, ego never voluntarily lets go of the hold it established eons ago in the evolution of humankind. Having been such an intimate part of human existence, the ego may actually compete with the true self for control. Hence there is the development of another aspect of conflict of wills. The expression of divine will is one of the cosmic tides sweeping through creation. Think of will as the tide, or cycle, making itself apparent to initiate action and change. The effect on all levels of consciousness can be very subtle. As participants in creation, we can ignore the tide, defy it or deny it. We can also choose to cooperate and work in harmony with the higher will. In denial of divine will, we create a temporary illusion of our own omnipotence. Valuable experience is gained in the interim. Underneath the illusion, however, lingers the primal guilt of separation, which constantly reminds us of our illusion and encourages us to eventually return to our Source.

Alcoholics have denied the Source to live in an artificial belief system where ego is the God substitute (omnipotence). From the illusion of mental superiority, they are free to impose their will on everyone and everything in their universe: family, business, society and nature. By seduction, intimidation, charm, manipulation and other ploys, they struggle to maintain a facade of omnipotence. This temporary control feeds the ego's need for power.

The human ego has been attached to the power of will over eons of time and evolution—and you know well enough from personal experience that ego seldom surrenders its power willingly. The pride that arises from will and power continually justifies itself to keep control, and it also creates tremendous resistance to giving up will's domination.

Once the victim acknowledges that the payoffs and rewards of ego-centered will are false and illusory, the road to reconnection is open. Then comes the opportunity to release false pride, false ego and negative will. The path is open to realignment and harmony with the rhythm of divine will.

So many practitioners of self-help, spiritual aid and religion pay lip service, on a conscious level, to "Thy will be done." Too often they are using the doctrine as ego rationalization, justifying their own further control. A great many teachings speak of obliterating the human ego and will, but that creates a threat to the personal will and ego that it will be annihilated. The personality believes it will lose all identity—a part of the illusion. Your inner identity is timeless and centered within the spark, and once this becomes an experiential reality and not just an intellectual concept, the likelihood of performing the dance with divine will is increased.

Students of personal growth often exhibit a tendency to give away their will to please another person—a guru, lover, teacher, boss or parent. They believe that by surrendering their will, their lives and relationships can return to harmony. Not so! Examine any such tendency in yourself and you will see one curious feature: Your personal will seeks even more hidden and devious games to control your own life and manipulate the world you inhabit.

While this curtain of illusion continues, the eternal truth is that cooperation with higher will would add untold blessings to our lives. Power would expand. We could have unlimited access to joy, supply, power and creativity. And the choice is always in our hands.

2—Image

When the divine sparks first experienced the illusion of separation from their Source, the ego became manifest and created its own secondary image in order to survive in creation. Since that time, each of us has constructed false images to meet personal needs. Personal image serves us well in that we learn about self, thus developing self-consciousness. Today humans still cling to false images (even though their usefulness has passed) and fail to see their own divine image. Remember that one of the earliest commandments from the Bible was, "Thou shall have no other god [false identity or image] before me!" The process of returning to the Source includes releasing the images contrived by ego for its survival.

Children of dysfunction learn to take on many false images and roles to cover bad feelings and low self-esteem. Think of the roles of superman, social hero, clown, caretaker and superachiever. All of us use false roles and images to get along in the world. The downside is that the false images obscure the light of the spark, and so the most decent and profound God qualities are lost in the illusion. It is virtually impossible to discover all your own roles by yourself, since they are unconscious mechanisms created by the subconscious personality. Outside help will be important in the process of bringing them to light. Chemical dependency programs and self-growth groups offer a variety of therapies that can aid you by providing a support team. In a caring and supportive group environment, contributing individuals can spot the variety of images you project. This is also an environment for working through them together while enjoying the company of caring people. Also, one-on-one therapy/counseling can be most productive toward releasing the unnecessary masks of your persona.

3—Feelings

I have come to define feelings and emotions in a somewhat different way from the traditional psychological or therapeutic terminology. The origin of feelings goes back to the divine sparks and the relationship they shared with their Source. With immersion into matter, the sparks felt separated from their Source—and I use the term "felt," because the sparks knew only how to feel until that moment. At the moment of separation (the illusion) from the Source, the ego created a new self-image, and with that came the new attendant needs. Reaction to the needs of the false image constitutes the origin of emotions.

By definition, then, feelings are personal confirmations of intimations of awareness originating from the divine self. They yield internal clues about our relationship to our Source: Positive feelings relate to the harmony or move us closer to manifesting behavior consistent with the divine intent. Disquieting feelings are clues indicating we are discounting our divine self; at the very least, we are not behaving consistently with our highest inspirations. Emotions and feelings may periodically overlap.

Emotions are reactions to human needs and conditions of the personality and ego. Their spectrum can range from elation and euphoria to the depths of sadness and depression. Think of your emotions as forms of behavior resulting from expectations and needs. For example, we become angry when a lover doesn't behave in keeping with our expectation. The anger is a real feeling. The emotional reaction, however, may be inappropriate. Jealousy and envy, for example, are negative emotions that result from direct observation of other people's talents, relationships or possessions that we wish to have.

It makes sense that children of dysfunction learn to shut down feelings in order to avoid the overwhelming negative emotions from early childhood traumas. At that time, they lost full connection to feelings and became victims of emotion.

One very practical form of monitoring and processing both feelings and emotions is to keep a daily journal and log the events that trigger them. The journal can become a monitor of your true feelings and at the same time help you recognize negative emotions. As the truth of your emotional patterns emerges, you can follow deeper guidance from your heart and soul.

4—Discipline

You have probably experienced fluctuating between obsessive-compulsive orderliness and near chaos in handling life's situations. A useful clue for getting a peek at your internal state is to go check out your basement. No kidding! Its condition says much about your subconscious. Is it a mess, with things piled and dropped at random? Or is it so tidy you can find anything stored there without turning on the light? Now do the same exercise with your attic. It tells a similar story about your discipline patterns. Think of your basement as representing your subconscious and your attic as representing your relationship to the higher self. Now open the door to take an objective look into your closet. This reflects a part of you that is hidden from public view.

Discipline is far from being the same thing as compulsion. True discipline comes neither naturally nor easily to children of dysfunction. Unfortunately, this is true for all generations. As a reaction to their dysfunctional parents, your parents have probably also established rigid, nearly unyielding behavior patterns; it was discipline to a fault. Recall that we have already identified this as a fear-based reaction to an unsolved conflict within the self.

Discipline means establishing a behavior pattern that works consistently and well to connect you to your divine self. So what does that mean for you on a daily basis? It simply means learning and establishing ways of doing things that honor your individuality. For instance, if you know from sad experience that you don't function creatively before noon, don't push it. Arrange a lifestyle—and certainly a job schedule—that allows you to peak later in the day. Then you can give up complaining all the way to work at dawn!

The new discipline may include clearly defining and stating your needs, then mapping strategies leading directly to those needs. This will likely include consulting those who specialize in the desired behavior or area of expertise. It will surely require some very specific goal planning. You have been all too willing to accept what "fate" handed out, which is the biggest ploy of accomplished victims and martyrs. Know that you create your own destiny.

True discipline might include exercises to break up your rigidities. This can allow valid new patterns to form. For example, if you have been saying the same prayer at the same time each day without heart, it probably has turned into meaningless chanting. What is it good for without the participation of the heart? If you quite naturally offer a new prayer out of gratitude and sincerity any day, any time, the answer you get will match your sincerity and depth of feeling. Discipline is personal action that dances in harmony and rhythm with the divine self. Behavior may change from moment to moment, even under exactly the same circumstances, while remaining entirely consistent with divine order and will.

If you remain too rigid and compulsive, try this: With the objectivity of a casual observer, watch to see how you pull on your underpants in the morning. Can you see the extent of habit in even the smallest actions? Consciously switch to putting the other leg through first for ten consecutive days. Be aware of the disorientation, consternation and real effort it takes to alter even such a minor behavior. This little exercise provides quick insight into just how real rigidity and compulsion can be.

Know the cycles of life and be a master of them. There is an active (yang) force of doing, and there is also a receptive (yin) force of absorbing and nurturing. Know that there is a point of balance where everything at that moment is just right (tao)! These three basic attributes apply to every endeavor. Your spark within is attuned to the most fulfilling sojourn possible for you. Discipline is taking the steps necessary to align mind, emotions and body. In natural alignment, you will be able to honor the message of the high Source within you and move with universal cycles and rhythms of life to the fullest benefit of your human nature. Discipline is a simple dance. You can overdo it (too much), you can underdo it (too little) or you can do it just right (balance).

5—Play

Compulsion and rigidity either severely inhibit play or eradicate it entirely. Once true discipline is accomplished, one has considerably more real time for play. It is not easy for children of dysfunction to play; they do a lot of things to escape what you call play. You can put on the clown's face and act funny, but your innate sadness and distrust can't accept the possibility of pleasure and spontaneity in life. This might be a good time to attend a play seminar.

You might get a clue as to the nature of play from remembering your best moments as a preschooler. In your lightest, happiest hours, you would experience spontaneous moments of direct joy with your self, with nature, with humor, with paradox, with serendipity. Learning to play is partially giving the child in you permission to do the same. As you heal the wounded, battered and scarred child within, you can allow the healthy child to play once more in uninhibited splendor.

What do you truly enjoy and have fun doing? Give yourself permission to honor that activity. Commit to discovering those new activities that are genuinely fun and pleasurable to you. Consider yourself. Give enjoyment to yourself!

6—Responsibility

Your parents were either overly responsible, or they were irresponsible to the same extreme. You came to observe their widely varying responses with increasing suspicion. From the examples of both kinds of behavior, you received a faulty perspective on personal and social responsibility. If they were overly responsible, all your apparent needs were met, along with a myriad issues of no concern to you. They had to do "the right thing" as they saw it. They seldom, if ever, took the time to really listen to your concerns. They seldom heard your heart messages that simply requested their presence in your life, and you didn't know how to give particularly clear messages of need, because more often than not your real feelings were suppressed. As childhood wore on, you began feeling that as long as your needs weren't being anticipated, why bother to keep sending weak messages, if any at all? Ironically, the same basic reaction occurred within you if your parents were consistently irresponsible. From their irresponsibility, you got a consistent message that real needs and wants were outside their concern. Either way, the impact on you was neglect.

The later-generation child of dysfunction says with gusto, "By golly, I'm going to take care of me and get what I can in this life!" This attitude sounds harmless and is certainly well intended, but the results are usually disappointing. What you really need is not out in the world at large. It's not in your home, possessions, car or material rewards. Nor is it in your spouse, lover, social position or career status. It starts when and where you connect to your Source. It will become clear only when you are filled with your own being. From that awareness, "all things are added unto you." Children of dysfunction, all generations, are often insightful counselors simply because they have experienced the whole realm of emotional rubble. They can spot it in others even though they may not yet have fully worked out their own entanglements. A note of caution here: Such counselors are well intended; however, their counseling message is full of "You should . . ." and "You ought to . . ." because they are still unable to listen and really hear the inner feelings being expressed. The one giving the advice may not be in touch with his or her feelings. How then can this counselor fully connect honestly with another suffering soul?

Your first responsibility is to yourself. As you learn to hear your innermost guidance, you begin following the will and wisdom of your Source. The truth will be known, and you will be free. Newly freed from ego need, you can start to touch those who suffer in a heart-connected way. Then you become the attuned and appropriate counselor to other children of dysfunction; then you can approach others, not as a rescuer, but simply as a human being who is willing to share what you know. You can then be one who refuses to get hooked into codependency games.

7—Intuition

Intuition seems to be a link to the mother side of consciousness, our knowing. It acts as our link to the infinite universal mind of unlimited wisdom. The small voice of intuition has most likely been a quiet whisper for most of your life. Feelings of unworthiness and guilt have cut you off from trusting the "voice within." In your childhood, there were times when you responded to your inner voice. You also spoke out in truthful, childlike simplicity, and you were reprimanded or silenced for this truth: "Don't say things like that!" or "What's wrong with you?" Your parents could not handle the obvious, so they chastised you rather than admit to the truth you vocalized.

Now is a good time—appropriate because you have arrived this far in your thinking and awareness—to develop sensitivity in your intuition. Opportunity abounds in our society to explore and expand the psychic, intuitive channels to our Source. There are many systems, individual teachers and small groups suitable for enhancing intuitive awareness. Even academic and business communities now endorse the development of right-brain, creative thinking.

8—Authority and Power

For so long, child, you have feared your own power. Therefore, you gave over your domain and free choice to the rule of others. Why do you distrust it? Why do you deny its expression? There is only one ultimate Source of all power, and your individuality draws from that Source. Your power has always come from there; it does so now and it will continue to do so for all your life. Let us examine why you might feel unworthy to claim the power that is rightly yours.

Somewhere deep in the collective memory and in soul memory lingers knowledge of the consequences of separating from the Source. Egos grew in place of the divine being, fueled by negative emotions such as hurt, pain, pride and anger. The sparks' human behavior eventually degenerated into acts of the most vile, abusive and humiliating nature.

Many humans employed their power to intimidate, control, maim and tyrannize. Life during these epochs was like a living hell. The sparks, as humans, performed (by human judgment) unforgivable acts of cruelty upon their fellow humans. Isn't it amazing that so much of what we humans judge as unbelievably evil or utterly unthinkable has actually happened already? The sparks (humans) attempted to bury the memory of their heinous deeds by denial and escapism, but the memories are recorded in the genetic and soul memory. After eons of denying these experiences, unawakened humans created increasingly severe codes of control to compensate for the guilt and shame associated with such abusive behavior.

People who are hiding the most frantically from their repressed wrongs are frequently those who use their position of power and authority to create stringent and harsh controls over others and themselves. They quote bylaws, penal codes, scriptures, regulatory codes and on and on, in an endless attempt to stifle their fear of losing control.

This can manifest, for example, in the hanging-judge mentality previously mentioned in Chapter 4 or in the pious preacher who quotes scripture loudly on Sunday and is arrested for murder on Tuesday, with a hidden record of charges for child molestation.

Other examples of overbearing authority figures might be the unyielding parent; the tyrannical boss who neurotically follows company policies and must be obeyed explicitly; the acting director who imposes his/her own ego demands upon talented performers, preventing them from expressing their own creativity; the physician who is afraid to recognize alternative forms of healing (clinging to drugs and prescriptions) that could force him/her to uncover hidden issues of emotion and mind; even the security agent who goes beyond regulation in a morbid inspection of people's personal life and belongings. You can no doubt think of endless similar examples.

Shame-based individuals may attempt to erase deep-seated guilt and unacceptable fragments of experience by use of mood-altering chemicals. They remain disconnected from the Source as long as they continue to judge the self and deny the experience written in their soul journey. As long as individuals deny their shadow experiences, the "demons" will harass them and demand attention. By avoidance, they perpetuate the very hell they fear the most.

First- and second-generation dysfunctional children run from these demons just as their dysfunctional parents did. You have mixed emotions toward authority (power) figures. Trapped in this ambiguity, you alternate between hostility and fear on the one hand (something in you sees the shadow beneath the surface) and compliance and approval on the other hand. Perhaps this is in the hope that others will stop judging you and start accepting you. A balance of attitude can come only with reconnection to your power base—the spark within.

My personal suspicion is that God never judges us; we insist on doing that to ourselves. If so, then you are the one with the power to forgive, and it is up to you to exercise that option whenever you are ready.

9—Release

I was going to use the word "surrender" instead of "release" for this section, but I decided that surrender might sound too much like military defeat to the prideful children of dysfunction; it speaks of weakness and final failure. Of course, that is not the point I want to make here. Instead, think of release in terms of acceptance. Once you can simply accept yourself just as you are, you take charge of the issues. With the appropriate follow-up efforts on your part, many of the issues tend to almost take care of themselves.

Release in this context simply means the willingness to let go of negative patterns accumulated through eons of evolutionary growth. This objective purity of a higher and wider level of perception cannot be achieved all at once—the path of growth is a flowing, rhythmic process. But progress can be faster than people sometimes believe.

"Let go and let God," says the primer of Alcoholics Anonymous and other recovery or positive-thinking organizations. Let the spark in you reignite into a radiant light. Remember that light illuminates and dissolves the shadow. You will come to see yourself for all that you are, and then you can grow to become all that you can be.

The process of releasing can be made easier as we consciously grasp the reality of our identity in the expanded dimensions of our existence. At the personality level, we feel entrapped, victimized and limited, but as we start to reconnect to the soul awareness, we see our experience as an integral and wonderful drama of self-learning. We can start to accept the experience just as it is, and then we accelerate the process of integration.

As we more consciously accept our inner identity and reconnect to our spark (some call it higher self), we start to consciously recognize the universal drama unfolding and can then see our part more clearly. From that vantage point, we can reach even greater acceptance of self as well as of our brothers and sisters who are also on the evolutionary path. With deeper bonding to our core, or essence, we start to see the humor, paradox, irony and sublime intent in our life. An unmistakable new joy and enthusiasm starts to permeate our life, and from the very core of our being, we truly begin to radiate the ways of our Source.

You can learn to accept every single experience just as it is, and you will then come to appreciate that even the darkest steps were steppingstones on your path to awakening the knowledge of your true self. It is up to you to become a cocreator of the universe and contribute to the blessings and abundance of life in this world.

Does Love Heal All?

Love is a powerful remedy for the woes of life on our planet. Children with severe dysfunction often struggle more than the rest of society with the concept and fulfillment of love. Despite the multitude of spoken and written teachings on love, they struggle through life's issues in non-loving ways.

We each search a lifetime for love, constantly striving for an ideal. But in a cosmic sense, love just is. It is yin and yang reaching out to each other to find the way to the tao. Love is balance between the mother (feminine) and the father (masculine) forces. Love struggles not, searches not and suffers not, because love is. As divine sparks (child), we came from that cosmic moment of love (out of the union of Mother and Father God).

As the illusion of separation took place within the emerging sparks, they polarized and experienced duality. In our human form, this duality manifests in many ways: good/evil, night/day, birth/death, male/female and on and on. As humans we center our pursuit of love in the quest of reuniting man and woman within ourselves, and we act out this perennial search in our relationship with others.

A negative aftereffect of the separation was the polarization that later resulted in men and women finding themselves at odds with each other. They competed and warred for eons, creating tension and divisiveness. Evolutionary memory of this struggle is in the consciousness of the soul. Soul memory projects through our anima/animus to influence the ways we relate to both men and women.

The anima is our portal to the divine Mother. Feminine archetypes are stored and reflected through anima projection. Our personal anima is heavily biased by our perception of our mother and her expression of femininity during our formative years. The animus is our portal to the divine Father. Male archetypes are reflected through animus projection, and our personal animus is biased quite naturally by our perception of our father and his expression of masculinity.

A great deal of what we conceptualize as love is actually a long way from true loving. Romantic literature and music endlessly repeat the perils inher-

264 �># Forever Numerology

ent in romantic love. Start with the basic premise of romantic love as an archetype: Falling in love is largely the projection of anima/animus upon another person, the "loved one." He or she is seen as possessing qualities that mother or father was not able to offer during childhood. We expect and desire the loved one to make us happy, perhaps even to the point of being our salvation. So we project an ideal image of what we need from him or her, and in so doing, we fail to connect with that person as he or she really is. But no one can live up to the idealized expectations of anima/animus projection, nor should there be a price for love. So soon enough, the loved one is seen as imperfect, "not the person I thought you were," and the struggling child of dysfunction can go into the familiar game of anger, blame and resentment just like during the old times at home.

Anima/animus projection is also falling in love with something within another person that we cannot claim in ourselves. A man looks for his own femininity through the women in his life; a woman seeks her own maleness from relationships with men. But the completion of the balance cannot come from outside. Sure, that loved one may reflect something inside you, but it's up to you to claim it in yourself and not demand it from others. Get to know the male and the female in yourself, whatever your sex. Each part is a balanced segment of the divine essence and is individually unique. As we begin to integrate and nurture the man and woman within, fewer and less powerful ego demands are placed upon the partner. Consequently, we are better able to attract a partner who is compatible and a complement to our true nature.

I am convinced, at this moment of understanding (subject to change upon enlightenment), that love is not an emotion. It is much more than that. The ecstasy, euphoria and delight of being "in love" are artifacts of anima/animus projection. They are part of the excitement of anticipating becoming whole again. These three emotions accompany the illusion that wholeness can be reached through external sources. Love is not a feeling. It just is. We, in fact, go through a spectrum of wonderful feelings just having acted in a loving way or having received loving attention. Love just is. It is natural; it is obvious. It is. Love is also action. In loving you are committing yourself to an action that considers the loved one, which includes yourself.

Far too much of what we call "giving love" is merely exchanging, bartering to get what we need. True loving is not done out of neurotic ego need. A loving action is one that strengthens the loved one's will and security. The act facilitates the recognition and acceptance of the loved one's divine image; it allows true expression of feelings and intimacy; it accepts one's disciplines and allows play. True loving allows the loved one to take responsibility for self; it honors intuition and supports inner authority. A person truly loved is free from any obligation to the lover. A person in balance is free to love and be loved in all these features. Loving actions are possible for those people who love themselves, accepting themselves for what they are and allowing themselves to simply be.

If You're Not Ready to Love, Try Humor

So okay, you have read and digested the section on love, and you say, "All that sounds very possible and wonderful, but what if I'm still into self-pity or anger, or if I'm just plain ornery?" Well, the last door I offer in this book opens to the absurdity of life's travails: You might try laughing.

To repeat once more, this too is very difficult for children of dysfunction. We take life and ourselves too seriously. It's hard to laugh when you are holding so much hurt inside. One of the classic responses in a dysfunctional family is for one of the children to take on the role of mascot. He or she is stuck in the role of clown and is expected to use charm and levity to distract attention away from the real stress in the environment. This humor is tinged with sadness and a sarcastic edge as the child grows older. This is neither the type nor source of humor encouraged in this chapter.

I'm referring to a deeper and much healthier form of humor. As an illustration, let me relate a personal example. I remember one of the most healing therapy sessions I've ever experienced. The counselors had pushed pretty hard into my shadow space to uncover some painful issues of pride, shame, anger and self-deceit. We had tried acting out, gestalt techniques, forgiveness and numerous dialogues with self, but the ego stubbornly held on to my irresponsibility in the issues we'd uncovered.

Suddenly, within the frustration, confusion and self-judgment of the moment, I heard a tremor of laughter begin deep down near my solar plexus. As it came forth from my body, it seemed to somehow be beyond me or apart from my intention or control. The laughter felt simultaneously boundless, timeless and momentous. It seemed to be emanating from the depths of soul, as if a cosmic joke was being revealed to a part of me that could laugh even while my social self missed the point. I burst into prolonged, joyous spontaneous laughter. The total humanness of the moment was refreshing. The two counselors and I rolled around the room in tears of laughter as the revelation of absurdity, folly, irony and paradox merged into a loving and forgiving moment of healing and transformation. That was a major breakthrough in my consciousness.

In that moment, I glimpsed how our Source and the lesser deities must experience laughter in the observations and interactions with creation. The laughter of that day came as though it was a gift from the one Source of our universe. It was as if, in that moment of balance and love, an external perspective allowed me to joyously appreciate myself and all of creation just as it is. An entirely new door was opened for me in my expression of life.

When we find that point of balance and connection to our divine spark, it is possible to glimpse the silly, crazy, magical, perverse, sublime, ridiculous, wonderful and paradoxical nature of our humanness. The folly and absurdity of our human condition was seen not from judgment but from spontaneity and awareness of the sublime humor in the human condition. During that brief glimpse of infinite harmony, all the illusion of strife, sorrow, pain and anger disappeared. The separation from self was seen for the illusion it is. Love allows laughter, and the converse also holds true: Laughter can release the blocks that prevent us from loving.

The disarming and healing nature of humor is well documented. It lightens heartfelt burdens, removes false pretenses, releases tension, discharges conflict and promotes new self-awareness. It is one certain way to encourage healing and harmony. The nature of the divine spark in humans is to express itself through laughter, mirth, lightness and spontaneity. Give yourself permission to let your lightness shine forth. Be with people who give both themselves and you permission to have fun.

Humankind has been buried in the darkness and shadow side for eons of time. We stagger under the self-imposed burden of guilt and despair at having human foibles. Ah, there is the self-judgment again! We hide from our dark side. Through the ages, it has been big business for certain leaders to manipulate our guilt and denial. Through increased self-control, collective and individual, healing humor became rare and difficult to bring forth. Humor is discouraged in repressive societies, because it so frequently reveals the foibles of the ruling class.

Many religious, philosophical and therapeutic strategies are available for facing the shadow. In essence, it all boils down to the theory that we can love, confront or forgive our demons of darkness. Each has its merit, and in total awareness, all three are probably essential. Children of shame-based families must find the most appropriate path, and I firmly believe that a healthy sense of humor can facilitate any and all modern strategies.

A dear friend and spiritual teacher of mine tells the story of one encounter with her own shadow demons. During a meditative state, she experienced the presence of a huge, malevolent, hideous, monstrous entity within herself. She was momentarily overwhelmed by the horror in her vision, unable to face its awfulness with composure. She went into terror, weakness and doubt, all the while seeking an effective defensive posture. Moments passed without solution; she could neither dispel nor face this vision. It grew and came nearer. Just as it reached its largest size, too near now to avoid in any way, she found herself breaking into a childlike giggle. The presence seemed startled and simply shrank to a manageable size. In that moment of innocent laughter, she was able to accept the presence just for what it was, without fear and without judgment. Her life from that moment on was a quickened journey toward reintegration and reconnection to her Source.

Perhaps herein lies a major key to the process of reintegration with our Source: facing our demons of darkness with laughter. Not the laughter of arrogance, self-righteousness and conceit, but the laughter of merriment, innocence and acceptance from the child within. Remember, underneath every child of dysfunction is a child of God.

Appendix A

The Charts of Famous World Personalities

Below are the charts of many famous world personalities, including some of my most well-known clients. You can explore the examples to see if they shed more light upon the lives and personalities of these recognized individuals.

Note: Some public figures change the date of their birth and sometimes middle names in biographies are not complete. Although every effort has been made to present accurate dates and names, there is a slight chance of some inaccuracies below.

Social/Entertainment

Duchess of York

S	A	R	A	H		M	A	R	G	A	R	E	T		F	E	R	G	U	S	O	N				
1	1	9	1	8		4	1	9	7	1	9	5	2		6	5	9	7	3	1	6	5		= 100 = 1	IS
	1		1				1			1		5				5			3		6			= 23 = 5	S
1		9		8		4		9	7		9		2		6		9	7		1		5		= 77(5)	P

October (10) 15, 1959 = 31 = 4(22) LN

Princess Diana

D	I	A	N	A		F	R	A	N	C	E	S		S	P	E	N	C	E	R				
4	9	1	5	1		6	9	1	5	3	5	1		1	7	5	5	3	5	9		= 85 = 13 = 4	IS
	9	1		1				1			5					5			5			= 27 = 9	S
4			5			6	9		5	3		1		1	7		5	3		9		= 58 = 13 = 4	P

July (7) 1, 1961 = 25 = 7 LN

Oprah Winfrey

O	P	R	A	H		G	A	I	L		W	I	N	F	R	E	Y			
6	7	9	1	8		7	1	9	3		5	9	5	6	9	5	7		= 97 = 16 = 7	IS
6			1				1	9				9				5	7		= 38 = 11(2)	S
	7	9		8		7			3		5		5	6	9				= 59 = 14 = 5	P

January (1) 29, 1954 = 31 = 4(22) LN

Michael Jackson

```
M  I  C  H  A  E  L     J  O  S  E  P  H     J  A  C  K  S  O  N
4  9  3  8  1  5  3     1  6  1  5  7  8     1  1  3  2  1  6  5          = 80 = 8       IS
   9        1  5              6  5                 1              6        = 33(6)         S
4     3  8        3     1        1     7  8     1     3  2  1     5        = 47 = 11(2)    P
August (8) 29, 1958 = 42 = 6 LN
```

Stephen Sondheim

```
S  T  E  P  H  E  N     J  O  S  H  U  A     S  O  N  D  H  E  I  M
1  2  5  7  8  5  5     1  6  1  8  3  1     1  6  5  4  8  5  9  4       =95 = 14 = 5    IS
      5        5              6        3  1        6              5  9    = 40 = 4        S
1  2     7  8     5     1     1  8           1     5  4  8           4    = 55(1)         P
March (3) 22, 1930 = 20(11) = 2 LN
```

Steven Spielberg

```
S  T  E  V  E  N     A  L  L  A  N     S  P  I  E  L  B  E  R  G
1  2  5  4  5  5     1  3  3  1  5     1  7  9  5  3  2  5  9  7          = 83 = 11(2)    IS
      5     5              1        1              9  5           5       = 31 = 4        S
1  2     4     5           3  3     5     1  7           3  2     9  7    = 52 = 7        P
December (12) 18, 1947 = 33(6) LN
```

Martha Stewart

```
M  A  R  T  H  A        H  E  L  E  N        K  O  S  T  Y  R  A
4  1  9  2  8  1        8  5  3  5  5        2  6  1  2  7  9  1          = 79 = 16 = 7   IS
   1        1              5        5              6        7  1          = 26 = 8        S
4     9  2  8           8     3     5        2     1  2        9          = 53 = 8        P
August (8) 3, 1941 = 26 = 8 LN
```

Francis Ford Coppola

```
F  R  A  N  C  I  S        F  O  R  D        C  O  P  P  O  L  A
6  9  1  5  3  9  1        6  6  9  4        3  6  7  7  6  3  1          = 92 = 11(2)    IS
      1        9                 6                 6        6     1       = 29 = 11(2)    S
6  9     5  3     1        6        9  4     3        7  7        3        = 63 = 9        P
April (4) 7, 1939 = 33(6) LN
```

Tom Brokaw

```
T  H  O  M  A  S        J  O  H  N        B  R  O  K  A  W
2  8  6  4  1  1        1  6  8  5        2  9  6  2  1  5              = 67 = 13 = 4    IS
   6        1                 6                    6        1           = 20 = 2         S
2  8     4     1        1        8  5        2  9why     2     5          = 47 = 11(2)    P
February (2) 6, 1940 = 22(4) LN
```

Martin Luther King Jr.

```
M  A  R  T  I  N        L  U  T  H  E  R        K  I  N  G        J  U  N  I  O  R
4  1  9  2  9  5        3  3  2  8  5  9        2  9  5  7        1  3  5  9  6  9     = 116 = 8   IS
   1        9              3        5                 9                 3     9  6     = 45 = 9    S
4     9  2     5        3        2  8     9     2     5  7           1     5           9  = 71 = 8  P
January (1) 15, 1929, = 28 = 10 = 1 LN
```

Katie Couric

```
K  A  T  H  E  R  I  N  E        A  N  N  E        C  O  U  R  I  C
2  1  2  8  5  9  9  5  5        1  5  5  5        3  6  3  9  9  3          = 95 = 14 = 5   IS
   1        5     9     5        1           5              6  3        9    = 44(8)         S
2     2  8        9        5                 5  5           3           9  3  = 51 = 6       P
January (1) 7, 1957 = 30 = 3 LN
```

Barbara Walters

```
B  A  R  B  A  R  A     W  A  L  T  E  R  S
2  1  9  2  1  9  1     5  1  3  2  5  9  1                    = 51 = 6      IS
   1        1     1        1        5                          = 9 = 9        S
2     9  2     9        5     3  2     9  1                    = 42 = 6       P
September (9) 25, 1931 = 30 = 3 LN
```

The Amazing Randi

```
R  A  N  D  A  L  L    J  A  M  E  S    H  A  M  I  L  T  O  N    Z  W  I  N  G  E
9  1  5  4  3  3  3    1  1  4  5  1    8  1  4  9  3  2  6  5    8  5  9  5  7  5    = 117 = 9     IS
   1     3               5             1     9        6                    9     5    = 39 = 12 = 3  S
9     5  4     33      1     4     1    8     4     3  2     5    8  5        5  7    = 77(5)        P
August (8) 7, 1928 = 35 = 8 LN
```

Elton John

```
R  E  G  I  N  A  L  D    K  E  N  N  E  T  H    D  W  I  G  H  T
9  5  7  9  5  1  3  4    2  5  5  5  5  2  8    4  5  9  7  8  2    = 110 = 2      IS
   5        9     1          5        5                    9        = 34 = 7        S
9     7     5     3  4    2     5  5     2  8    4  5        7  8  2  = 76 = 13 = 4   P
March (3) 25, 1947 = 31 = 4(22) LN
```

Elvis Presley

```
E  L  V  I  S        A  R  O  N        P  R  E  S  L  E  Y
5  3  4  9  1        1  9  6  5        7  9  5  1  3  5  7        = 80 = 8       IS
5     9              1     6  5              5                    = 31 = 4        S
   3  4     1              9     5     7  9     1  3              = 42 = 6       P
January (1) 8, 1935 = 27 = 9 LN
```

John Lennon

```
J  O  H  N        W  I  N  S  T  O  N        L  E  N  N  O  N
1  6  8  5        5  9  5  1  2  6  5        3  5  5  5  6  5        = 82 = 10 = 1   IS
   6                    9              6              5        6        = 32 = 5        S
1     8  5              5     5  1  2        5        3     5  5     5  = 50 = 5       P
October (10) 9, 1940 = 24 = 6(33) LN
```

Paul McCartney

```
J  A  M  E  S        P  A  U  L        M  C  C  A  R  T  N  E  Y
1  1  4  5  1        7  1  3  3        4  3  3  1  9  2  5  5  7        = 65 = 11(2)   IS
   1  5                 1  3                       1              5  7    = 23 = 5       S
1     4     1        7        3        4  3  3     9  2  5              = 42 = 6       P
June (6) 18, 1942 = 31 = 4(22) LN
```

Larry King

```
L  A  W  R  E  N  C  E        H  A  R  V  E  Y        Z  E  I  G  E  R
3  1  5  9  5  5  3  5        8  1  9  4  5  7        8  5  9  7  5  9    = 113 = 5      IS
   1        5        5           1           5  7           5  9     5    = 43 = 7        S
3     5  9     5  3           8     9  4              8           7     9  = 70 = 7       P
November (11) 19, 1933 = 28 = 10 = 1 LN
```

Eminem

```
M  A  R  S  H  A  L  L        B  R  U  C  E        M  A  T  H  E  R  S    T  H  E    T  H  I  R  D
4  1  9  1  8  1  3  3        2  9  3  3  5        4  1  2  8  5  9  1    2  8  5    2  8  9  9  4    = 129 = 12 = 3   IS
   1        1                    3  5                 1        5              5           9          = 30 = 3         S
4     9  1  8     33          2  9     3           4     2  8     9  1    2  8       2  8     9  4    = 99(9)          P
October (10) 17, 1972 = 28 = 10 LN
```

Business/Industry

Bill Gates

```
W I L L I A M   H E N R Y   G A T E S   T H E   T H I R D
5 9 3 3 9 1 4   8 5 5 9 7   7 1 2 5 1   2 8 5   2 8 9 9 4        = 131 = 5      IS
    9       9 1       5       7       1 5           5       9    = 51 = 6       S
5   3 3       4   8   5 9       7   2   1 2 8     2 8     9 4    = 80 = 8       P
October (10) 28, 1955 = 31 = 4(22) LN
```

Ted Turner

```
R O B E R T   E D W A R D   T U R N E R   T H E   T H I R D
9 6 2 5 9 2   5 4 5 1 9 4   2 3 9 5 5 9   2 8 5   2 8 9 9 4      = 141 = 6      IS
  6   5       5     1         3       5           5       9      = 39 = 12 = 3  S
9   2   9 2     4 5     9 4   2   9 5   9 2 8     2 8   9 4      = 102 = 3      P
November (11) 19, 1938 = 33(6) LN
```

Sam Walton

```
S A M     M O O R E     W A L T O N
1 1 4     4 6 6 9 5     5 1 3 2 6 5                              = 58 = 13 = 4   IS
    1         6 6     5       1         6                        = 25 = 7        S
1   4     4       9       5     3 2     5                        = 33 = 33(6)    P
March (3) 29, 1918 = 33 = 33(6)  LN
```

Sebastian Spering Kresge

```
S E B A S T I A N     S P E R I N G     K R E S G E
1 5 2 1 1 2 9 1 5     1 7 5 9 9 5 7     2 9 5 1 7 5              = 99(9)        IS
    5   1       9 1           5   9               5       5      = 40 = 4       S
1   2     1 2       5     1 7       9       5 7   2 9     1 7    = 59 = 14 = 5  P
July (7) 31, 1867 = 33(6) LN
```

John Rockefeller

```
J O H N   D A V I S O N   R O C K E F E L L E R   T H E   T H I R D
1 6 8 5   4 1 4 9 1 6 5   9 6 3 2 5 6 5 3 3 5 9   2 8 5   1 8 9 9 4    = 153 = 9       IS
  6         1   9   6       6       5   5     5           5       9    = 57 = 12 = 3   S
1   8 5   4     1     5   9   3 2   6   3 3   9   2 8     1 8   9 4    = 96 = 15 = 6   P
March (3) 21, 1906 = 22(4) LN
```

Howard Hughes

```
H O W A R D   R O B A R D   H U G H E S   J U N I O R
8 6 5 1 9 4   9 6 2 1 9 4   8 3 7 8 5 1   1 3 5 9 6 9          = 129 = 12 = 3   IS
  6   1         6     1         3       5       3   9 6        = 40 = 4         S
8   5   9 4   9     2     9 4   8   7 8   1   1   5       9    = 89 = 17 = 8    P
September (9) 24, 1905 = 30 = 3 LN
```

Henry Ford

```
H E N R Y     F O R D
8 5 5 9 7     6 6 9 4                                          = 59 = 14 = 5   IS
  5     7         6                                            = 18 = 9        S
8   5 9       6       9 4                                      = 41 = 5        P
July (7) 30, 1863 = 28 = 10 = 1 LN
```

Actors and Singers

Marilyn Monroe

N O R M A	J E A N E	M O R T E N S O N		
5 6 9 4 1	1 5 1 5 5	4 6 9 2 5 5 1 6 5	= 85 = 13 = 4	IS
6	1 5 1 5	6 5 6	= 35 = 8	S
5 9 4	1 5 4	9 2 5 1 5	= 50 = 5	P

June (6) 1, 1926 = 25 = 7 LN

Mel Gibson

M E L	C O L U M C I L L E	G E R A R D	G I B S O N		
4 5 3	3 6 3 3 4 3 9 3 3 5	7 5 9 1 9 4	7 9 2 1 6 5	= 119 = 11(2)	IS
5	6 3 9 5	5 1	9 6	= 49 = 13 = 4	S
4 3 3	3 4 3 3 3	7 9 9 4	7 2 1 5	= 70 = 7	P

January (1) 3, 1956 = 25 = 7 LN

Madonna

M A D O N N A	L O U I S E	V E R O N I C A	C I C C O N E		
4 1 4 6 5 5 1	3 6 3 9 1 5	4 5 9 6 5 9 3 1	3 9 3 3 6 5 5	= 129 = 12 = 3	IS
1 6 1	6 3 9 5	5 6 9 1	9 6 5	=72 = 9	S
4 4 5 5	3 1	4 9 5 3	3 3 3 5	= 57 = 12 = 3	P

August (8) 16, 1958 = 38 = 11(2) LN

Jodie Foster

A L I C I A	C H R I S T I A N	F O S T E R		
1 3 9 3 9 1	3 8 9 9 1 2 9 1 5	6 6 1 2 5 9	= 102 = 3	IS
1 9 9 1	9 9 1	6 5	= 50 = 5	S
3 3	3 8 9 1 2	5 6 1 2 9	= 52 = 7	P

November (11) 19, 1962 = 30 LN

Denzel Washington

D E N Z E L	W A S H I N G T O N		
4 5 5 8 5 3	5 1 1 8 9 5 7 2 6 5	= 79 = 16 = 7	IS
5 5	1 9 6	= 26 = 8	S
4 5 8 3	5 1 8 5 7 2 5	= 53 = 8	P

December (12) 28, 1954 = 32 = 5 LN

Michael Douglas

M I C H A E L	K I R K	D O U G L A S		
4 9 3 8 1 5 3	2 9 9 2	4 6 3 7 3 1 1	= 80 = 8	IS
9 1 5	9	6 3 1	= 34 = 7	S
4 3 8	3 2 9 2	4 7 3 1	. = 46 = 10 = 1	P

September (9) 25, 1941 = 31 = 4(22) LN

Catherine Zeta Jones

C A T H E R I N E	Z E T A	J O N E S		
3 1 2 8 5 9 9 5 5	8 5 2 1	1 6 5 5 1	= 81 = 9	IS
1 5 9 5	5 1	6 5	= 37 = 10	S
3 2 8 9 5	8 2	1 5 1	= 44(8)	P

September (9) 25, 1969 = 41 = 5 LN

Ricky Martin

```
E N R I Q U E   J O S E   M A R T I N   M O R A L E S
5 5 9 9 7 3 5  1 6 1 5  4 1 9 2 9 5  4 6 9 1 3 5 1        =115= 7   IS
5     9 3 5      6   5      1     9      6 1   5          =55(1)     S
  5 9 7          1 1      4   9 2   5   4   9   3  1      =60 = 6    P
December (12) 24, 1971 = 27 = 9 LN
```

Tom Cruise

```
T H O M A S   C R U I S E   M A P O T H E R   T H E   F O U R T H
2 8 6 4 1 1  3 9 3 9 1 5  4 1 7 6 2 8 5 9  2 8 5  6 6 3 9 2 8      =143 = 8   IS
    6   1      3 9   5      1   6     5       5    6 3   2          = 52 =7    S
2 8   4   1  3 9       1  4   7   2 8   9  2 8    6     9   8       =91=10 =1  P
July (7) 3, 1962 = 28 = 10 = 1 LN
```

Nicole Kidman

```
N I C O L E   M A R Y   K I D M A N
5 9 3 6 3 5  4 1 9 7  2 9 4 4 1 5              = 77(5)      IS
    9   6 5      1   7      9     1            = 38 = 11(2) S
5   3   3    4   9    2   4 4   5              = 39 = 12 = 3 P
June (6) 20, 1967 = 31 = 4(22) LN
```

Dana Delany

```
D A N A   W E L L E S   D E L A N Y
4 1 5 1  5 5 3 3 5 1  4 5 3 1 5 7             = 58 = 13 = 4  IS
  1   1      5     5      5   1   7           = 25 = 7       S
4   5     5   3 3   1  4   3   5              = 33(6)        P
May (5) 13, 1956 = 30 = 3 LN
```

Cary Grant

```
A R C H I B A L D   A L E X A N D E R   L E A C H
1 9 3 8 9 2 1 3 4  1 3 5 6 1 5 4 5 9  3 5 1 3 8   = 99(9)      IS
1     9   1          1   5   1     5      5 1      = 29 = 11(2) S
  9 3 8   2   3 4    3   6   5 4   9    3    3 8   = 70 = 7     P
January (1) 18, 1904 = 24 = 6 LN
```

Julia Roberts

```
J U L I E   F I O N A   R O B E R T S
1 3 3 9 5  6 9 6 5 1  9 6 2 5 9 2 1           = 82 = 10 = 1  IS
  3   9 5      9 6   1      6   5             = 44(8)        S
1   3      6     5    9   2   9 2 1           = 38 = 11(2)   P
October (10) 28, 1967 = 34 = 7 LN
```

Steve Martin

```
S T E P H E N   G L E N N   M A R T I N
1 2 5 7 8 5 5  7 3 5 5 5  4 1 9 2 9 5         = 88(7)     IS
    5     5         5         1     9         = 25 = 7    S
1 2   7 8   5  7 3    5 5  4   9 2   5        = 63 = 9    P
August (8) 14, 1945 = 32 = 5 LN
```

Gillian Anderson

```
G I L L I A N   L E I G H   A N D E R S O N
7 9 3 3 9 1 5  3 5 9 7 8  1 5 4 5 9 1 6 5     = 105 = 6  IS
  9     9 1        5 9        1     5   6     = 45 = 9    S
7   3 3     5  3     7 8    5 4   9 1   5     = 60 = 6    P
August (8) 9, 1968 = 41 = 5 LN
```

David Duchovny

```
D  A  V  I  D       W  I  L  L  I  A  M       D  U  C  H  O  V  N  Y
4  1  4  9  4       5  9  3  3  9  1  4       4  3  3  8  6  4  5  7        = 96 = 15 = 6      IS
   1     9                 9        9  1              3           6        7    = 45 = 9          S
4     4     4       5        3  3           4        4     3  8     4  5        = 51 = 6          P
August (8) 6, 1960 = 30 = 3 LN
```

Britney Spears

```
B  R  I  T  N  E  Y       J  E  A  N       S  P  E  A  R  S
2  9  9  2  5  5  7       1  5  1  5       1  7  5  1  9  1              = 75 = 12 = 3      IS
         9        5  7          5  1                5  1                = 33(6)            S
2  9        2  5             1           5        1  7           9  1        = 42 = 6          P
December (12) 2, 1981 = 24 = 6 LN
```

Will Smith

```
W  I  L  L  A  R  D       C  H  R  I  S  T  O  P  H  E  R       S  M  I  T  H       J  U  N  I  O  R
5  9  3  3  1  9  4       3  8  9  9  1  2  6  7  8  5  9       1  4  9  2  8       1  3  5  9  6  9    = 158 = 14 = 5    IS
   9     1                       9        6        5                 9                    9  6         = 57 = 12 = 3    S
5     3  3     9  4       3  8  9        1  2     7  8     9       1  4     2  8     1     5        9    = 101 = 2        P
September (9) 25, 1968 = 40 = 4 LN
```

Helen Hunt

```
H  E  L  E  N       E  L  I  Z  A  B  E  T  H       H  U  N  T
8  5  3  5  5       5  3  9  8  1  2  5  2  8       8  3  5  2              = 87 = 15 = 6      IS
   5     5             5     9     1     5                 3                = 33(6)            S
8     3     5             3        8     2        2  8        8     5  2        = 54 = 9          P
June (6) 15, 1963 = 31 = 4(22) LN
```

Errol Flynn

```
E  R  R  O  L       L  E  S  L  I  E       T  H  O  M  S  O  N       F  L  Y  N  N
5  9  9  6  3       3  5  1  3  9  5       2  8  6  4  1  6  5       6  3  7  5  5    = 116 = 8        IS
5     6                 5           9  5              6        6                 7    = 49 = 13 = 4(22) S
   9  9        3        3     1  3              2  8        4  1        5       6  3        5  5    = 67 = 13 = 4(22) P
June (6) 20, 1909 = 27 = 9 LN
```

Clark Gable

```
W  I  L  L  I  A  M       C  L  A  R  K       G  A  B  L  E
5  9  3  3  9  1  4       3  3  1  9  2       7  1  2  3  5              = 70 = 7       IS
   9        9  1                 1                 1           5                = 26 = 8       S
5     3  3           4       3  3        9  2       7        2  3        = 44 = 44(8)      P
February (2) 1, 1901 = 14 = 5 LN
```

Meg Ryan

```
M  A  R  G  A  R  E  T       M  A  R  Y       E  M  I  L  Y       A  N  N  E       H  Y  R  A
4  1  9  7  1  9  5  2       4  1  9  7       5  4  9  3  7       1  5  5  5       8  7  9  1    = 128 = 11(2)    IS
   1        1     5                 1  7       5     9     7       1        5           7     1    = 50 = 5        S
4     9  7     9     2       4        9           4     3             5  5           8     9    = 78 = 15 = 6    P
November (11) 19, 1961 = 29 = 11(2) LN
```

Eddie Murphy

```
E  D  W  A  R  D     R  E  G  A  N     M  U  R  P  H  Y
5  4  5  1  9  4     9  5  7  1  5     4  3  9  7  8  7          = 93 = 12 = 3    IS
5        1              5     1           3              7       = 22 = 22(4)      S
   4  5     9  4     9        7     5     4        9  7  8        = 71 = 8         P
April (4) 3, 1961 = 24 = 6 LN
```

Whoopi Goldberg

```
C  A  R  Y  N     E  L  A  I  N  E     J  O  H  N  S  O  N
3  1  9  7  5     5  3  1  9  5  5     1  6  8  5  1  6  5        = 85 = 13 = 4    IS
   1     7        5     1  9     5        6              6        = 40 = 4         S
3     9     5     3           5        1     8  5  1        5     = 46 = 10 = 1    P
Novermber (11) 13, 1955 = 26 = 8 LN
```

Bing Crosby

```
H  A  R  R  Y     L  I  L  L  I  S     C  R  O  S  B  Y
8  1  9  9  7     3  9  3  3  9  1     3  9  6  1  2  7          = 90 = 9         IS
   1     7        9        9              6        7             = 39 = 12 = 3    S
8     9  9        3        3  3     1     3  9     1  2           = 51 = 6         P
May (5) 2, 1904 = 21 = 3 LN
```

Vivien Leigh

```
V  I  V  I  A  N     M  A  R  Y     H  A  R  T  L  E  Y
4  9  4  9  1  5     4  1  9  7     8  1  9  2  3  5  7          = 88(7)          IS
   9     9  1           1     7     1              5  7          = 40 = 4         S
4     4     5     4        9        8     9  2  3                = 48 = 12 = 3    P
November (11) 5, 1913 = 21 = 3 LN
```

Sophia Loren

```
S  O  F  I  A     V  I  L  L  A  N  I     S  C  I  C  O  L  O  N  E
1  6  6  9  1     4  9  3  3  1  5  9     1  3  9  3  6  3  6  5  5    = 98 = 17 = 8  IS
   6     9  1        9           1     9        9     6     6     5   = 61 = 7       S
1     6           4        3  3     5     1  3     3        3     5   = 37 = 10 = 1  P
September (9) 20, 1934 = 28 = 10 = 1 LN
```

Burt Reynolds

```
B  U  R  T  O  N     L  E  O  N     R  E  Y  N  O  L  D  S     J  U  N  I  O  R
2  3  9  2  6  5     3  5  6  5     9  5  7  6  6  3  4  1     1  3  5  9  6  9    = 120 = 3       IS
   3     6           5  6           5  7     6                 3     9  6          = 56 = 11(2)S   S
2     9  2     5     3        5     9        6     3  4  1     1     5        9     = 64 = 10 = 1   P
February (2) 11, 1936 = 23 = 5 LN
```

Clint Eastwood

```
C  L  I  N  T  O  N     E  A  S  T  W  O  O  D     J  U  N  I  O  R
3  3  9  5  2  6  5     5  1  1  2  5  6  6  4     1  3  5  9  6  9    = 96 = 15 = 6  IS
      9        6        5  1           6  6        3     9  6          = 51 = 6       S
3  3     5  2     5        1  2  5           4     1     5        9     = 45 = 9       P
May (5) 31, 1930 = 22(4) LN
```

Leaders/Presidents

George Washington

```
G E O R G E    W A S H I N G T O N
7 5 6 9 7 5    5 1 1 8 9 5 7 2 6 5              = 88(7)    IS
  5 6      5        1     9         6           = 32 = 5   S
7      9 7      5      1 8    5 7 2     5        = 56 = 11(2)  P
February (2) 22, 1732 = 19 = 10 = 1 LN
```

Abraham Lincoln

```
A B R A H A M    L I N C O L N
1 2 9 1 8 1 4    3 9 5 3 6 3 5                  = 60 = 6   IS
1    1   1          9       6                   = 18 = 9   S
  2 9      8     4    3   5 3     3 5           = 42 = 6   P
February (2) 12, 1809 = 23 = 5 LN
```

Franklin Roosevelt

```
F R A N K L I N    D E L A N O    R O O S E V E L T
6 9 1 5 2 3 9 5    4 5 3 1 5 6    9 6 6 1 5 4 5 3 2    = 105 = 6  IS
    1        9        5   1   6      6 6     5    5     = 44(8)    S
6 9    5 2 3     5     4    3   5     9       1    4   3 2  = 61 = 7  P
January (1) 30, 1882 = 23 = 5 LN
```

Harry Truman

```
H A R R Y    S    T R U M A N
8 1 9 9 7    1    2 9 3 4 1 5                   = 59 = 14 = 5 IS
  1     7         3   1                         = 12 = 3   S
8    9 9      1    2 9    4     5               = 47 = 11(2)  P
May (5) 8, 1884 = 34 = 7 LN
```

Dwight Eisenhower

```
D W I G H T    D A V I D    E I S E N H O W E R
4 5 9 7 8 2    4 1 4 9 4    5 9 1 5 5 8 6 5 5 9    = 115 = 7  IS
      9            1   9      5 9   5       6   5   = 49 = 13 = 4 S
4 5    7 8 2    4    4 · 4        1   5 8     5   9  = 66(3)    P
October (10) 14, 1890 = 24 = 6 LN
```

John F. Kennedy

```
J O H N    F I T Z G E R A L D    K E N N E D Y
1 6 8 5    6 9 2 8 7 5 9 1 3 4    2 5 5 5 5 4 7    = 107 = 8  IS
  6          9       5   1          5       5   7   = 38 = 11(2)  S
1    8 5      6    2 8 7     9    3 4    2    5 5     4  = 69 = 15 = 6 P
May (5) 29, 1917 = 34 = 7 LN
```

Lyndon Johnson

```
L Y N D O N    B A I N E S    J O H N S O N
3 7 5 4 6 5    2 1 9 5 5 1    1 6 5 8 1 6 5    = 85 = 13 = 4 IS
  7     6          1 9   5        6       6     = 40 = 4   S
3    5 4      5    2      5   1    1    5 8 1     5  = 45 = 9  P
August (8) 27, 1908 = 35 = 8 LN
```

Jimmy Carter

```
J A M E S     E A R L     C A R T E R     J U N I O R
1 1 4 5 1     5 1 9 3     3 1 9 2 5 9     1 3 5 9 6 9      = 92 = 11(2)   IS
  1   5       5 1           1       5         3   9 6      = 36 = 9       S
  1   4   1         9 3     3   9 2   9     1     5     9  = 56 = 11(2)   P
October (10) 1, 1924 = 18 = 9 LN
```

Ronald Reagan

```
R O N A L D     W I L S O N     R E A G A N
9 6 5 1 3 4     5 9 3 1 6 5     9 5 1 7 1 5      = 85 = 13 = 4   IS
  6   1           9       6       5 1   1        = 29 = 11(2)    S
9   5   3 4     5   3 1   5     9       7   5     = 56 = 11(2)   P
February (2) 6, 1911 = 20 = 2 LN
```

George Bush

```
G E O R G E     H E R B E R T     W A L K E R     B U S H
7 5 6 9 7 5     8 5 9 2 5 9 2     5 1 3 2 5 9     2 3 1 8      = 118 = 10 = 1   IS
  5 6           5   5   5             1     5         3        = 35 = 8         S
7     9 7       8   9 2   9 2   5   3 2   9     2   1 8        = 83 = 11(2)     P
June (6) 12, 1924 = 25 = 7 LN
```

Bill Clinton

```
W I L L I A M     J E F F E R S O N     B L Y T H E     T H E     F O U R T H
5 9 3 3 9 1 4     1 5 6 6 5 9 1 6 5     2 3 7 2 8 5     2 8 5     4 6 3 9 2 8      = 152 = 8     IS
  9     9 1           5       5     6           7   5         5     6 3          = 61 = 7      S
5   3 3   4     1     6 6   9 1     5   2 3     2 8         2 8     4     9 2 8  = 91 = 10 = 1  P
August (8) 19, 1946 = 38 = 11(2) LN
```

Hillary Clinton

```
H I L L A R Y     D I A N E     R O D H A M
8 9 3 3 1 9 7     4 9 1 5 5     9 6 4 8 1 4      = 96 = 15 = 6    IS
  9       1   7       9 1   5       6       1    = 39 = 12 = 3    S
8     3 3     9       4       5     9     4 8   4 = 57 = 12 = 3    P
October (10) 26, 1947 = 30 = 3 LN
```

Margaret Thatcher

```
M A R G A R E T     H I L D A     R O B E R T S
4 1 9 7 1 9 5 2     8 9 3 4 1     9 6 2 5 9 2 1      = 97 = 16 = 7    IS
  1       1   5         9       1     6   5          = 28 = 10 = 1    S
4   9 7   9   2     8   3 4       9     2   9 2 1    = 69 = 15 = 6    P
October (10) 13, 1925 = 22(4) LN
```

Condoleezza Rice

```
C O N D O L E E Z Z A     R I C E
3 6 5 4 6 3 5 5 8 8 1     9 9 3 5      = 80 = 8        IS
  6       6   5 5     1     9     5     = 37 = 10 = 1    S
3     5 4     3       8 8   9     3     = 43 = 7        P
November (11) 14, 1954 = 26 = 8 LN
```

Tony Blair

```
A N T H O N Y     C H A R L E S     L Y N T O N     B L A I R
1 5 2 8 6 5 7     3 8 1 9 3 5 1     3 7 5 2 6 5     2 3 1 9 9      = 116 = 8     IS
1       6   7             1     5         7     6         1 9      = 43 = 7      S
  5 2 8   5       3   8     9 3   1     3   5 2   5     2 3     9  = 73 = 10 = 1 P
May (5) 6, 1953 = 29 = 11(2) LN
```

Scientists

Albert Einstein

```
A   L   B   E   R   T       E   I   N   S   T   E   I   N
1   3   2   5   9   2       5   9   5   1   2   5   9   5              = 63 = 9          IS
1       5               5   9               5   9                      = 34 = 7          S
    3   2       9   2               5   1   2           5              = 29 = 11(2)      P
March (3) 14, 1879 = 33(6) LN
```

Charles Darwin

```
C   H   A   R   L   E   S       R   O   B   E   R   T       D   A   R   W   I   N
3   8   1   9   3   5   1       9   6   2   5   9   2       4   1   9   5   9   5        = 96 = 15 = 6      IS
        1       5                       6   5                       1           9        = 27 = 9          S
3   8       9   3       1       9       2       9   2       4       9   5       5        = 69 = 15 = 6      P
February (2) 12, 1809 = 23 = 5 LN
```

Luther Burbank

```
L   U   T   H   E   R       B   U   R   B   A   N   K
3   3   2   8   5   9       2   3   9   2   1   5   2                  = 54 = 9          IS
    3       5               3       1                                  = 12 = 3          S
3       2   8       9       2       9   2       5   2                  = 42 = 6          P
March (3) 7, 1849 = 32 = 5 LN
```

Michael Faraday

```
M   I   C   H   A   E   L       F   A   R   A   D   A   Y
4   9   3   8   1   5   3       6   1   9   1   4   1   7              = 62 = 8          IS
    9           1   5                   1       1       1   7          = 25 = 7          S
4       3   8           3       6       9       4                      = 37 = 10 = 1     P
September (9) 22, 1791 = 31 = 4 LN
```

Thomas Edison

```
T   H   O   M   A   S       A   L   V   A       E   D   I   S   O   N
2   8   6   4   1   1       1   3   4   1       5   4   9   1   6   5        = 61 = 7          IS
        6       1           1           1           5       9       6        = 29 = 11(2)      S
2   8       4       1           3   4               4       1       5        = 32 = 5          P
February (2) 11, 1847 = 24 = 6 LN
```

Sigmund Freud

```
S   I   G   M   U   N   D       F   R   E   U   D
1   9   7   4   3   5   4       6   9   5   3   4                      = 60 = 6          IS
    9           3                       5   3                          = 20 = 2          S
1       7   4       5   4       6   9           4                      = 40 = 4          P
May (5) 6, 1856 = 31 = 4(22) LN
```

Carl Jung

```
C   A   R   L       G   U   S   T   A   V       J   U   N   G
3   1   9   3       7   3   1   2   1   4       1   3   5   7          = 50 = 5          IS
    1               3           1               3                      = 8               S
3       9   3       7       1   2       4       1       5   7          = 42 = 6          P
July (7) 26, 1875 = 36 = 9 LN
```

Thomas Huxley

T	H	O	M	A	S		H	E	N	R	Y		H	U	X	L	E	Y			
2	8	6	4	1	1		8	5	5	9	7		8	3	6	3	5	7		= 88(7)	IS
		6		1				5			7			3			5	7		= 34 = 7	S
2	8		4		1		8		5	9			8		6	3				= 54 = 9	P

May (5) 4, 1825 = 25 = 7 = 8 LN

Carl Edward Sagan

C	A	R	L		E	D	W	A	R	D		S	A	G	A	N			
3	1	9	3		5	4	5	1	9	4		1	1	7	1	5		= 59 = 14 = 4	IS
	1					5		1					1		1			= 9	S
3		9	3			4	5		9	4		1		7		5		= 50 = 5	P

November (11) 9, 1934 = 28 = 10 = 1 LN

Rosalyn Yalow

R	O	S	A	L	Y	N		S	U	S	S	M	A	N			
9	6	1	1	3	7	5		1	3	1	1	4	1	5		= 48 = 12 = 3	IS
	6		1		7			3					1			= 18 = 9	S
9		1		3		5		1		1	1	4		5		= 30 = 3	P

July (7) 19, 1921 = 30 = 3 LN

Mae Jemison

M	A	E		C	A	R	O	L		J	E	M	I	S	O	N			
4	1	5		3	1	9	6	3		1	5	4	9	1	6	5		= 63 = 9	IS
	1	5			1		6				5		9		6			= 33(6)	S
4				3		9		3		1		4		1		5		= 30 = 3	P

October (10) 17, 1956 = 30 = 3 LN

Dorothy Crowfoot Hodgkin

D	O	R	O	T	H	Y		C	R	O	W	F	O	O	T		H	O	D	G	K	I	N		
4	6	9	6	2	8	7		3	9	6	5	6	6	6	2		8	6	4	7	2	9	5	= 126 = 9	IS
	6		6			7				6			6	6				6				9		= 52 = 7	S
4		9		2	8			3	9			5			2		8		4	7	2		5	= 74 = 11(2)	P

May (5) 12, 1910 = 19 = 10 = 1 LN

Annie Cannon

A	N	N	I	E		J	U	M	P		C	A	N	N	O	N			
1	5	5	9	5		1	3	4	7		3	1	5	5	6	5		= 65 = 11(2)	IS
1			9	5			3					1			6			= 25 = 7	S
	5	5				1		4	7		3		5	5		5		= 40 = 4	P

December (12) 11, 1863 = 23 = 5 LN

Sports

Christine Evert

C	H	R	I	S	T	I	N	E		M	A	R	I	E		E	V	E	R	T			
3	8	9	9	1	2	9	5	5		4	1	9	9	5		5	4	5	9	2		= 104 = 5	IS
		9				9		5			1		9	5		5		5				= 48 = 12 = 3	S
3	8	9		1	2		5			4		9					4		9	2		= 56 = 11(2)	P

December (12) 21, 1954 = 25 = 7 LN

Mary Lou Retton

```
M  A  R  Y      L  O  U      R  E  T  T  O  N
4  1  9  7      3  6  3      9  5  2  2  6  5                    = 62 = 18       IS
   1     7         6  3         5        6                      = 28 = 10 = 1    S
4     9        3            9     2  2     5                    = 34 = 7         P
January (1) 24, 1968 = 31 = 4(22) LN
```

Mia Hamm

```
M  A  R  I  E  L      M  A  R  G  A  R  E  T      H  A  M  M
4  1  9  9  5  3      4  1  9  7  1  9  5  2      8  1  4  4        = 86 = 14 = 5    IS
   1     9  5            1           1     5         1             = 23 = 5         S
4     9        3      4     9  7     9     2      8     4  4        = 63 = 9         P
March (3) 17, 1972 = 30 = 3 LN
```

Billie Jean King

```
B  I  L  L  I  E      J  E  A  N      M  O  F  F  I  T  T
2  9  3  3  9  5      1  5  1  5      4  6  6  6  9  2  2           = 78 = 15 = 6    IS
   9        9  5         5  1            6        9                = 44 (8)         S
2     3  3            1            5     4     6  6     2  2        = 34 = 7         P
November (11) 22, 1943 = 23 = 5 LN
```

Michael Jordan

```
M  I  C  H  A  E  L      J  E  F  F  R  E  Y      J  O  R  D  A  N
4  9  3  8  1  5  3      1  5  6  6  9  5  7      1  6  9  4  1  5     = 98 = 17 = 8    IS
   9        1  5            5           5  7         6        1       = 39 = 12 = 3    S
4     3  8        3      1     6  6               1     9  4     5    = 50 = 5         P
February (2) 17, 1963 = 29 = 11(2) LN
```

Hank Aaron

```
H  E  N  R  Y      L  O  U  I  S      A  A  R  O  N
8  5  5  9  7      3  6  3  9  1      1  1  9  6  5                  = 78 = 15 = 6    IS
   5why     7         6  3  9            1  1     6                 = 38 = 11(2)     S
8     5  9        3            1               9     5              = 40 = 4         P
February (2) 5, 1934 = 24 = 6 LN
```

Mickey Mantle

```
M  I  C  K  E  Y      C  H  A  R  L  E  S      M  A  N  T  L  E
4  9  3  2  5  7      3  8  1  9  3  5  1      4  1  5  2  3  5        = 80 = 8         IS
   9        5  7            1        5            1           5       = 33 (6)         S
4     3  2               3  8     9  3     1     4     5  2  3        = 47 = 11(2)     P
October (10) 20, 1931 = 17 = 8 LN
```

Muhammad Ali

```
C  A  S  S  I  U  S      M  A  R  C  E  L  L  U  S      C  L  A  Y      J  U  N  I  O  R
3  1  1  1  9  3  1      4  1  9  3  5  3  3  3  1      3  3  1  7      1  3  5  9  6  9     = 98 = 17 = 8    IS
   1        9  3            1           5        3            1            3     9  6       = 41 = 5         S
3     1  1            1      4     9  3     3  3        1     3  3     7     1     5        9 = 57 = 12 = 3    P
January (1) 17, 1942 = 25 = 7 LN
```

Larry Bird

```
L  A  R  R  Y      J  O  E      B  I  R  D
3  1  9  9  7      1  6  5      2  9  9  4                         = 65 = 11(2)     IS
   1     7            6  5         9                               = 28 = 10 = 1    S
3     9  9         1            2     9  4                         = 37 = 10 = 1    P
December (12) 7, 1956 = 31 = 4(22) LN
```

OJ Simpson

```
O R E N T H A L     J A M E S     S I M P S O N
6 9 5 5 2 8 1 3     1 1 4 5 1     1 9 4 7 1 6 5          = 84 = 12 = 3   IS
6   5       1       1   5         9       6              = 33 (6)        S
  9   5 2 8   3     1   4   1     1   4 7 1       5      = 51 = 6        P
July (7) 9, 1947 = 37 = 10 = 1 LN
```

Joe Montana

```
J O S E P H   C     M O N T A N A     J U N I O R
1 6 1 5 7 8   3     4 6 5 2 1 5 1     1 3 5 9 6 9        = 88 (7)        IS
  6   5             6     1   1       3     9 6          = 37 = 10 = 1   S
1 1   7 8   3     4   5 2   5       1   5         9      = 51 = 6        P
June (6) 11, 1956 = 29 = 11(2) LN
```

Authors

Jules Verne

```
J U L E S     G A B R I E L     V E R N E     E
1 3 3 5 1     7 1 2 9 9 5 3     4 5 9 5 5     5         = 77 (5)        IS
  3   5       1       9 5           5         5         = 33 (6)        S
1   3   1     7   2 9       3     4   9 5               = 44 (8)        P
February (2) 28, 1828 = 29 = 11(2) LN
```

Tom Clancy

```
T H O M A S     L E O     C L A N C Y     J U N I O R
2 8 6 4 1 1     3 5 6     3 3 1 5 3 7     1 3 5 9 6 9   = 91 = 10 = 1   IS
    6   1       5 6           1     7     3     9 6     = 39 = 12 = 3   S
2 8   4   1     3         3 3   5 3       1   5     9   = 52 = 7        P
April (4) 12, 1947 = 28 = 10 = 1 LN
```

Stephen King

```
S T E P H E N     E D W I N     K I N G
1 2 5 7 8 5 5     5 4 5 9 5     2 9 5 7                 = 84 = 12 = 3   IS
    5   5   5         9           9                     = 33 (6)        S
1 2   7 8   5     4 5   5       2   5 7                 = 51 = 6        P
September (9) 21, 1947 = 33(6) LN
```

Jane Austen

```
J A N E     A U S T E N
1 1 5 5     1 3 1 2 5 5                                 = 29 = 11(2)    IS
  1   5     1 3     5                                   = 15 = 6        S
1   5       1 2   5                                     = 14 = 5        P
December (12) 16, 1775 = 30 = 3 LN
```

Maya Angelou

```
M A R G U E R I T E     A N N I E     J O H N S O N
4 1 9 7 3 5 9 9 2 5     1 5 5 9 5     1 6 8 5 1 6 5     = 111 = 3       IS
  1     3 5   9   5     1     9 5     6         6       = 50 = 5        S
4   9 7       9   2           5 5     1   8 5 1   5     = 61 = 7        P
April (4) 4, 1928 = 28 = 10 = 1 LN
```

Barbara Cartland

```
M  A  R  Y      B  A  R  B  A  R  A      H  A  M  I  L  T  O  N
4  1  9  7      2  1  9  2  1  9  1      8  1  4  9  3  2  6  5           = 84 = 12 = 3   IS
   1     7         1        1     1            1     9        6           = 27 = 9        S
4     9         2     9  2        9         8     4     3  2     5        = 57 = 12 = 3   P
July (7) 9, 1901 = 27 = 9 LN
```

JA Jance

```
J  U  D  I  T  H      A  N  N      J  A  N  C  E
1  3  4  9  2  8      1  5  5      1  1  5  3  5                          = 53 = 8        IS
      3     9            1            1        5                         = 19 = 10 = 1   S
1     4     2  8               5  5      1     5  3                       = 34 = 7        P
October (10) 27, 1944 = 28 = 10 = 1 LN
```

Military

Robert E. Lee

```
R  O  B  E  R  T      E  D  W  A  R  D      L  E  E
9  6  2  5  9  2      5  4  5  1  9  4      3  5  5                       = 74 = 11(2)    IS
      6     5            5        1                  5  5                 = 27 = 9        S
9     2     9  2         4  5        9  4   3                             = 47 = 11(2)    P
January (1) 19, 1807 = 27 = 9 LN
```

Ulysses S. Grant

```
U  L  Y  S  S  E  S      S  I  M  P  S  O  N      G  R  A  N  T
3  3  7  1  1  5  1      1  9  4  7  1  6  5      7  9  1  5  2           = 78 = 15 = 6   IS
3     7     5            9              6            1                   = 31 = 4        S
   3     1  1     1      1     4  7  1        5      7  9     5  2        = 47 = 11(2)    P
April (4) 27, 1822 = 26 = 8 LN
```

George McClellen

```
G  E  O  R  G  E      B  R  I  N  T  O  N      M  C  C  L  E  L  L  E  N
7  5  6  9  7  2      2  9  9  5  2  6  5      4  3  3  3  5  3  3  5  5  = 108 = 9       IS
   5  6        2            9        6                     5        5    = 38 = 11(2)    S
7        9  7         2  9        5  2     5   4  3  3  3         3  3  5 = 70 = 7        P
December (12) 3, 1826 = 23 = 5 LN
```

Douglas MacArthur

```
D  O  U  G  L  A  S      M  A  C  A  R  T  H  U  R
4  6  3  7  3  1  1      4  1  3  1  9  2  8  3  9                       = 65 = 11(2)    IS
      6  3        1            1        1        3                       = 15 = 6        S
4           7  3     1   4        3        9  2  8     9                 = 50 = 5        P
January (1) 26, 1880 = 26 = 8 LN
```

William Frederick Jr.

```
W  I  L  L  I  A  M      F  R  E  D  E  R  I  C  K      H  A  L  S  E  Y      J  U  N  I  O  R
5  9  3  3  9  1  4      6  9  5  4  5  9  9  3  2      8  1  3  1  5  7      1  3  5  9  6  9  = 144 = 9       IS
   9        9  1            5     5     9              1           5  7         3        9  6  = 69 = 15 = 6   S
5     3  3         4      6  9     4        9  3  2     8     3  1            1     5        9  = 75 = 12 = 3   P
October (10) 30, 1882 = 23 = 5 LN
```

Chester Nimitz

```
C H E S T E R     W I L L I A M     N I M I T Z
3 8 5 1 2 5 9     5 9 3 3 9 1 4     5 9 4 9 2 8          = 104 = 5      IS
    5       5         9       9 1           9   9        = 69 = 15 = 6   S
3 8   1 2   9         5       3 3           4   5   4   2 8   = 75 = 12 = 3   P
February (2) 24, 1885 = 30 = 3 LN
```

George S. Patton Jr.

```
G E O R G E     S M I T H     P A T T O N     J U N I O R
7 5 6 9 7 5     1 4 9 2 8     7 1 2 2 6 5     1 3 5 9 6 9       = 119 = 11(2)   IS
    5 6       5         9             1       6     3   9 6     = 50 = 5        S
7     9 7       1 4     2 8     7     2 2   5     1   5       9   = 69 = 15 = 6   P
November (11) 11, 1885 = 26 = 8 LN
```

Erwin Rommel

```
E R W I N     J O H A N N E S     E U G E N     R O M M E L
5 9 5 9 5     1 6 8 1 5 5 5 1     5 3 7 5 5     9 6 4 4 5 3      = 121 = 4      IS
5       9         6   1       5     5 3   5         6       5    = 50 = 5       S
    9 5   5       1   8   5 5     1       7   5     9   4 4   3   = 71 = 8       P
November (11) 15, 1891 = 27 = 9 LN
```

Appendix B

Preparation of the Chart

In the pages that follow are two charts to help you with the process of setting up the complete personal chart. The first example is the completed personal chart for Harvey Peter Doright, to give you an expanded example of a progressed chart. The second chart is a blank personal chart for your use.

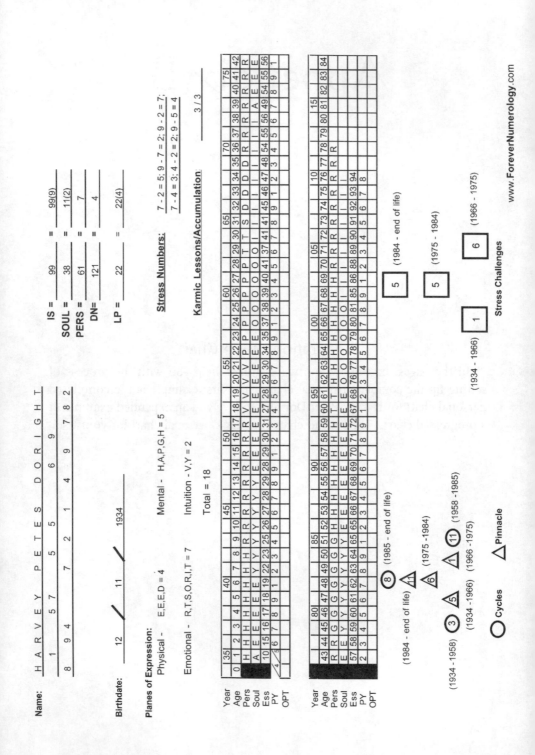

Name:

H	A	R	V	E	Y		P	E	T	E	S		D	O	R	I	G	H	T
1		5	7	5	5		6		9				4		9		7	8	2
8	9	4		7	2		1		4				9				7	8	2

Birthdate: 12 / 11 / 1934

Planes of Expression:

Physical - E,E,E,D = 4   Mental - H,A,P,G,H = 5

Emotional - R,T,S,O,R,I,T = 7   Intuition - V,Y = 2

Total = 18

IS = 99 = 99(9)
SOUL = 38 = 11(2)
PERS = 61 = 7
DN = 121 = 4

LP = 22 = 22(4)

Stress Numbers:
7 - 2 = 5; 9 - 7 = 2; 9 - 2 = 7;
7 - 4 = 3; 4 - 2 = 2; 9 - 5 = 4

Karmic Lessons/Accumulation: 3 / 3

Year					35				40					45					50					55					60					65					70					75	
Age	0	1	2	3	4	5	6	7	8	9	10	11	12	13	14	15	16	17	18	19	20	21	22	23	24	25	26	27	28	29	30	31	32	33	34	35	36	37	38	39	40	41	42
Pers		H	H	H	H	H	H	H	H	R	R	R	R	R	R	R	R	R	V	V	V	V	P	P	P	P	P	P	P	O	O	O	O	O	I	I	I	I	I	I	A	A	A
Soul	A	E	E	E	E	E	E	E	E	Y	Y	Y	Y	Y	Y	E	E	E	E	E	E	V	V	V	P	P	P	P	T	T	S	D	D	D	D	R	R	R	R	R	E	E	E	E
Ess	10	15	16	17	18	19	22	23	25	26	27	28	29	30	31	27	28	29	30	34	35	37	38	39	40	41	37	41	45	46	47	48	54	55	56	49	54	55	56
PY	4	5	6	7	8	9	1	2	3	4	5	6	7	8	9	1	2	3	4	5	6	7	8	9	1	2	3	4	5	6	7	8	9	1	2	3	4	5	6	7	8	9	1
OPT																																											

Year					80				85					90					95					00					05					10					15			
Age	43	44	45	46	47	48	49	50	51	52	53	54	55	56	57	58	59	60	61	62	63	64	65	66	67	68	69	70	71	72	73	74	75	76	77	78	79	80	81	82	83	84
Pers	R	R	G	G	G	G	Y	Y	Y	Y	Y	H	H	H	H	H	H	T	T	H	H	H	H	R	R	R	R	R	R	R	R	R	R	R	R	R	R	R	R	R	R	R
Soul	E	E	Y	Y	Y	Y	Y	G	G	H	H	H	H	H	H	H	H	T	H	H	H	O	O	I	I	I	H	H	R	R	R	R	R	R	R							
Ess	57	58	59	60	61	62	63	64	65	66	67	68	69	70	71	72	67	68	76	77	78	79	80	81	85	86	88	89	90	91	92	93	94									
PY	2	3	4	5	6	7	8	9	1	2	3	4	5	6	7	8	9	1	2	3	4	5	6	7	8	9	1	2	3	4	5	6	7	8								
OPT																																										

Cycles

⑧ (1985 - end of life)

③ (1934 -1958)   ⑤ (1934 - 1966)

⑥ (1966 -1975)

Pinnacle

⑪ (1975 -1984)   ⑪ (1958 -1985)

① (1966 -1975)

Stress Challenges

5 (1984 - end of life)

5 (1975 - 1984)

6 (1966 - 1975)

1 (1934 - 1966)

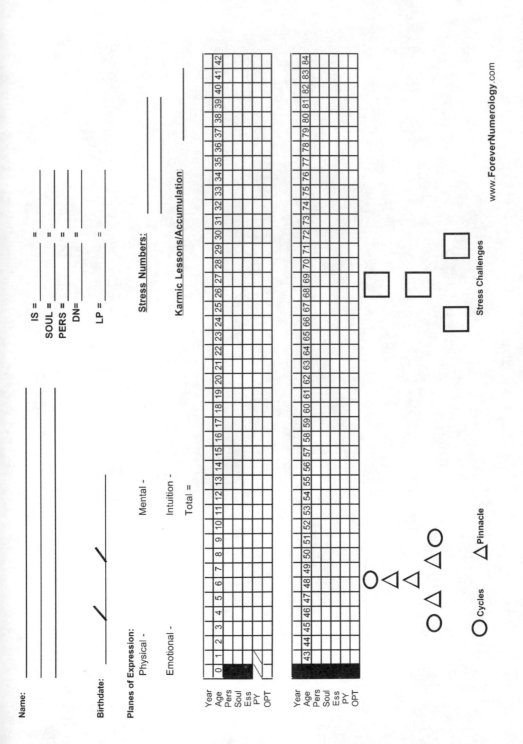

About the Author

Lynn Buess, MA, EdS has been active in the self-awareness movement for nearly forty years. Since the publication of *The Tarot and Transformation* in 1973, he has become an international speaker, practitioner and author. He has written seven books on a range of metaphysical topics. *Numerology for the New Age*, for years a best-selling numerology text, was his second graduate thesis paper written on an esoteric subject. It was translated into several foreign languages and launched Buess into international recognition.

Since 1980 he has practiced world over as a speaker, healer, psychotherapist and intuitive consultant. His list of clientele would make an impressive who's who of international personalities. Buess's introduction to so many cultures has added to the depth and perspective of his insights. He has worked with the issues of the adult children of alcoholism, abuse, codependency and addiction, along with transpersonal topics and personal growth. In his previous work, *Numerology: Nuances in Relationships*, he sheds numerological light upon the age-old issue of interaction between couples. His combination of academic skills and intuitive wisdom has caused many students and professionals around the globe to consider him the world's foremost spokesman on the relationship between numbers and human behavior. With the presentation of *Forever Numerology*, Buess gives us considerable reason why so many agree. In this new volume, he again takes a gigantic leap for numerology with extraordinary new insights and methods of interpretation. It is a book that will define new standards for years to come.

LYNN BUESS

Lynn Buess has come into national prominence since the success of his first book, The Tarot and Transformation. *His popularity as a speaker and instructor has taken him across the country many times to universities, churches, professional organizations and New Age centers of light.*

Although his work with tarot and numerology causes most people to associate him with symbolic studies, Lynn spends most of his time today working with various alternative metaphysical healing methods. Since his gift of healing awakened years ago, he has demonstrated and taught numerous techniques of psychospiritual healing. He is also the author of Synergy Session©, which teaches an entirely new system of multiple-level wholistic counseling/healing.

Along with his national tours, he has taught courses on parapsychology, healing, tarot, meditation and self-awareness at several colleges and one university within the university system of Georgia. As a tireless worker, Lynn is dedicated to bringing sincere seekers into a deeper awareness of the light within.

NUMEROLOGY FOR THE NEW AGE

Our own vibrations or cyclical patterns are numerologically determined by our date of birth and given name. By understanding these cycles, we can learn to more effectively express our potential, human and divine. This volume concentrates more upon the experiential value of numerology than the historical. If you are interested in the details of the history of numerology, other authors have given more attention to developments and personalities in the field. The focus throughout this volume is on using numbers to benefit your life right now.

As humankind approaches the awakening of the Aquarian Age consciousness, with its revelation of our divine origin and relation to the cosmos, it becomes increasingly important for teachers of the symbolical sciences to emphasize humankind's relationship to Creator and to the divine laws of manifestation. This book first presents the cosmology of numbers, followed by the descent and ascent of the divine self as portrayed through the symbolism of numbers. Finally, it examines the application of numerical guidance for your current lifetime on this physical plane of material existence.

11^{00} SOFTCOVER 262 P.
ISBN 0-929385-31-4

Chapter Titles:

- Condensed History
- The Cosmology of Numerology
- The Vibrational Aspects of One to Nine
- What You Choose to Receive from Life
- The Wisdom in Your Name
- Dealing with Karma

- Recognizing the Stress Numbers
- Symbology of the Letters
- A New and Revised Progressed Chart
- Changes in Your Name
- Yin-Yang, Sexuality, Male-Female Polarity
- Setting Up a Chart

NUMEROLOGY: NUANCES IN RELATIONSHIPS
LYNN BUESS

Welcome to a new and meaningful application of numbers in your life. You have probably done some exploration and utilization of numbers to better understand yourself and your own behavior. Now you find that you would like to know more about your relationship with that significant other in your life.

Perhaps the significant other is your spouse, live-in partner, lover, parent, child, boss, coworker, friend and/or social acquaintance. Wherever we interact with someone else, it is a relationship. The relationships we value the most are the ones in which we invest the most and from which we desire to receive the greatest joy, gratification, growth and fulfillment. As we individually become more comfortable and harmonious within ourselves, there is an increasing desire to experience greater harmony and contentment in our external relationships.

This volume is intended to assist you in your quest to better understand yourself in relation to other people. You will discover many new insights and avenues toward more mature and compatible interaction with others.

13^{75} SOFTCOVER 309 P.
ISBN 0-929385-23-3

Chapter Titles:
- **The Search for Healthier Relationships**
- **Fundamentals of Chart Comparison**
- **Clues on Compatibility**
- **Getting Acquainted with the Format**
  - **Dynamics of the Relationship**
  - **The Lessons and Potential**
  - **Stress Factors in the Relationship**
  - **When Things Become Dysfunctional**
  - **Strategies to Encourage Growth**
- **Combination Comparisons**

CHILDREN OF LIGHT CHILDREN OF DENIAL

LYNN BUESS

There is a rapid and expansive awakening within the self-awareness movement that integration of self includes a harmonious dance between the light (conscious) and dark (unconscious) aspect of human nature.

In an attempt to "live in the light," many New Age followers in fact deny access to their own shadow self—from which comes the most significant and powerful creative manifestations.

Lynn Buess addresses the cycle of denial that leads to so much dysfunction in our time. He opens the door to establishing a more dynamic and conscious interaction with the potential within our shadow side.

With this fourth volume, Buess introduces new insights and deeply penetrative perspectives upon the issues of abuse, alcoholism, codependency and the shame-based dysfunctional behaviors in today's society. Hopefully, this volume will contribute to the demise of the deep and destructive behavior that occurs when people individually and collectively insist upon ignoring the shadow side of being human.

$8 95   SOFTCOVER 124 P.
ISBN 0-929385-15-2

Chapter Titles:

- Defining Denial and Dysfunction
- Some Characteristics of Dysfunction
- The Darker Side of Repression and Denial in Children of Light
- The Evolution and Struggle of Children of Light
- Looking at the Dark Side Lightly: Examining the Shadow Self
- Acknowledging Anger, Self-Pity and Guilt
- Alcoholism, Gambling and Self-Abuse: A Concept of Origin
- Nine Stages toward Releasing Old Patterns
- Does Love Heal It All?
- If You Aren't Ready to Love, Try Humor

CHARLES KLOTSCHE

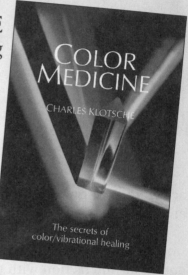

COLOR MEDICINE
The Secrets of Color Vibrational Healing

A new dimension in holistic healing, *Color Medicine* provides a powerful technique for treating specific imbalances and strengthening the immune system. By combining aura-attuned chromatherapy with harmonious sounds, tissue salts and hydrochromatherapy, the forty-ninth vibrational technique was developed. A breakthrough, yet as old as recorded medicine, it utilizes subtle energy vibrations similar to those found in the visible spectrum. A textbook and how-to handbook, this book encompasses an encyclopedia of fascinating information, charts, diagrams and tables as well as methods of treatment and technical advice. Whether you are a holistic practitioner or merely curious, this book marks a new frontier in the world of alternative healing.

$11⁹⁵ SOFTCOVER 114 P.
ISBN 0-929385-27-6

Chapter Titles:

- Does Color Medicine Really Heal?
- Color Physics: The Scientific Explanation of Color Medicine, or Vibrational Therapy
- Color Energetics: How Color Medicine Works with the Subtle Energy Fields of the Body
- Color Harmonics: The Twelve Healing Colors and Their Use
- Color Practice: Materials and Practical Techniques for Applying Color Medicine
- Color Schedule Application: Determining the Appropriate Color(s) for Relieving/Healing the 123 Major Illnesses
- Color Medicine Schedules for 123 Specific Human Disorders
- Quick-Reference Checklist for Color Tonation
- Suggested Readings

JONATHAN GOLDMAN AND SHAMAEL, ANGEL OF SOUND

Jonathan Goldman is an internationally acknowledged teacher, musician and pioneer in Sound Healing. He is the author of Healing Sounds, *president of Spirit Music and director of the Sound Healers Association.*

Shamael is the Angel of Sound. An extraordinary being of light and love, he is an aspect of the Metatronic energy of Kether.

SHIFTING FREQUENCIES
How Sound Can Change Your Life

Now, for the first time, Healing Sounds pioneer Jonathan Goldman tells us about shifting frequencies—how to use sound and other modalities to change vibrational patterns for both personal and planetary healing and transformation. Through his consciousness connection to Shamael, Angel of Sound, Jonathan shares his extraordinary scientific and spiritual knowledge and insights, providing information, instructions and techniques on using sound, light, color, visualization and sacred geometry to experience shifting frequencies. The material in this book is both timely and vital for health and spiritual evolution.

In this book, you will:

- Explore the use of sound in ways you never imagined for healing and transformation.
- Discover harmonics as a key to opening to higher levels of consciousness.
- Learn about the angel chakra and what sounds may be used to activate this new energy center.
- Find out how to transmute imbalanced vibrations using your own sounds.
- Experience the secrets of crystal singing.
- Understand the importance of compassion in achieving ascension.

$14^{95} **SOFTCOVER 147 P.**
ISBN 1-891824-04-X

Chapter Titles:

- Sound Currents: Frequency and Intent
- Vibratory Resonance
- Vocalization, Visualization and a Tonal Language
- The Harmonics of Sound
- Vocal Harmonics and Listening
- Harmonics and the Brain
- Energy Fields
- Creating Sacred Space
- Compassion through Sound
- Sacred Geometry and Sound
- Merkabahs

- Sound, Color and Light
- Sound and Crystals
- Crystal Singing
- Breath
- The Waveform Experience
- Harmony
- Healing
- The Language of Light, Part I
- The Language of Light, Part II
- The Angel Chakra

THE ANCIENT SECRET
OF THE FLOWER OF LIFE
VOLUME 1

Once, all life in the universe knew the Flower of Life as the creation pattern—the geometrical design leading us into and out of physical existence. Then, from a very high state of consciousness, we fell into darkness, the secret hidden for thousands of years, encoded in the cells of all life.

Now we are rising from the darkness and a new dawn is streaming through the windows of perception. This book is one of those windows. Drunvalo Melchizedek presents in text and graphics the Flower of Life Workshop, illuminating the mysteries of how we came to be.

Sacred Geometry is the form beneath our being and points to a divine order in our reality. We can follow that order from the invisible atom to the infinite stars, finding ourselves at each step. The information here is one path, but between the lines and drawings lie the feminine gems of intuitive understanding. You might see them sparkle around some of these provocative ideas:

- Remembering Our Ancient Past
- The Secret of the Flower Unfolds
- The Darker Side of Our Present and Past
- The Geometries of the Human Body
- When Evolution Crashed, and the Christ Grid Arose
- Egypt's Role in the Evolution of Consciousness
- The Significance of Shape and Structure

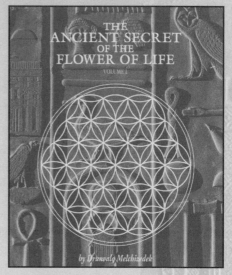

25^{00} Softcover 228 P.
ISBN 1-891824-17-1

Available from your favorite bookstore or:

LIGHT TECHNOLOGY PUBLISHING
PO Box 3540 • Flagstaff, AZ 86003
928-526-1345 • 800-950-0985 • FAX 928-714-1132
Or use our online bookstore: www.lighttechnology.com

Drunvalo Melchizedek's life experience reads like an encyclopedia of breakthroughs in human endeavor. He studied physics and art at the University of California at Berkeley, but he feels that his most important education came after college. In the past 25 years, he has studied with over 70 teachers from all belief systems and religious understandings.

For some time now, he has been bringing his vision to the world through the Flower of Life program and the Mer-Ka-Ba meditation. This teaching encompasses every area of human understanding, explores the development of humankind from ancient civilizations to the present time and offers clarity regarding the world's state of consciousness and what is needed for a smooth and easy transition into the 21st century.

THE ANCIENT SECRET
OF THE FLOWER OF LIFE
VOLUME 2

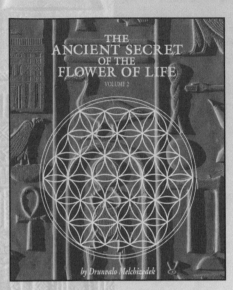

$25⁰⁰ Softcover 252 P.
ISBN 1-891824-21-X

The Unfolding of the Third Informational System

Whispers from Our Ancient Heritage

Unveiling the Mer-ka-ba Meditation

Using your Mer-ka-ba

Connecting to the Levels of Self

Two Cosmic Experiments

What We May Expect in the Forthcoming
Dimensional Shift

*Available
from your
favorite
bookstore or:*

LIGHT TECHNOLOGY PUBLISHING
PO Box 3540 • Flagstaff, AZ 86003
928-526-1345 • 800-450-0985 • FAX 928-714-1132
Or use our online bookstore: www.lighttechnology.com

The sacred Flower of Life pattern, the primary geometric generator of all physical form, is explored in even more depth in this volume, the second half of the famed Flower of Life workshop. The proportions of the human body, the nuances of human consciousness, the sizes and distances of the stars, planets and moons, even the creations of humankind, are all shown to reflect their origins in this beautiful and divine image. Through an intricate and detailed geometrical mapping, Drunvalo Melchizedek shows how the seemingly simple design of the Flower of Life contains the genesis of our entire third-dimensional existence.

From the pyramids and mysteries of Egypt to the new race of Indigo children, Drunvalo presents the sacred geometries of the Reality and the subtle energies that shape our world. We are led through a divinely inspired labyrinth of science and stories, logic and coincidence, on a path of remembering where we come from and the wonder and magic of who we are.

Finally, for the first time in print, Drunvalo shares the instructions for the Mer-Ka-Ba meditation, step-by-step techniques for the re-creation of the energy field of the evolved human, which is the key to ascension and the next dimensional world. If done from love, this ancient process of breathing prana opens up for us a world of tantalizing possibility in this dimension, from protective powers to the healing of oneself, of others and even of the planet.

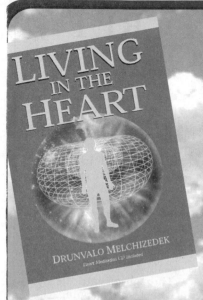

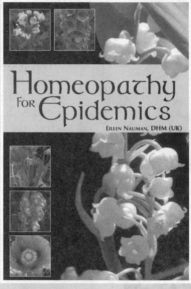

SHAMANIC SECRETS for PHYSICAL MASTERY

The purpose of this book is to allow you to understand the sacred nature of your own physical body and some of the magnificent gifts it offers you. When you work with your physical body in these new ways, you will discover not only its sacredness, but how it is compatible with Mother Earth, the animals, the plants, even the nearby planets, all of which you now recognize as being sacred in nature.

It is important to feel the value of yourself physically before you can have any lasting physical impact on the world. The less you think of yourself physically, the less likely your physical impact on the world will be sustained by Mother Earth. If a physical energy does not feel good about itself, it will usually be resolved; other physical or spiritual energies will dissolve it because it is unnatural. The better you feel about your physical self when you do the work in the previous book as well as in this one and the one to follow, the greater and more lasting will be the benevolent effect on your life, on the lives of those around you and ultimately on your planet and universe.

25^{00} SOFTCOVER 544 P.
ISBN 1-891824-29-5

Chapter Titles:

- Cellular Clearing of Traumas and Unresolved Events
- Feeling is Our Body's First and Primary Language
- The Resolution of Fear, Trauma and Hate
- Dealing with Fear, Pain and Addiction
- Shame, Arrogance, Safety and the Inability to Trust
- The Role of Trauma in Human Life
- Letting Go of Old Attitudes and Inviting New Energy
- The Waning of Individuality
- Clearing the Physical Body
- Using the Gestures to Protect, Clear and Charge
- The Flow of Energy
- Connecting with the Earth
- Communication of the Heart

- More Supportive Gestures
- Sleeping and Dreamtime
- Responsibility and Living prayer
- Communicating with the Natural World
- Life Lessons and the Vital Life Force
- The Sacrament of Food
- Working with the Elements
- Communication with Those Who Would Follow
- Elemental Connections
- Taking Responsibility
- Creating Personal Relationships